McHENRY COUNTY JEWISH CONGREGATION
8617 RIDGEFIELD ROAD
RIDGEFIELD, ILLINOIS 60014

NORTH SUBURBAN SYNAGOGUE BETH EL
1175 SHERIDAN ROAD
HIGHLAND PARK, ILL. 60035

UNDER-
STANDING
ISRAEL

UNDER-STANDING STANDING ISRAEL:

a social studies approach

AMOS ELON

educational materials prepared by
MORRIS J. SUGARMAN

 BEHRMAN HOUSE, INC. PUBLISHERS new york, new york

design: Miriam Woods
       Marsha Picker
picture editor: Dennis Backer

Frontispiece: *The Pillars of King Solomon.*

Library of Congress Cataloging in Publication Data

Elon, Amos.
    Understanding Israel: a social studies approach.

    Includes index.
    SUMMARY: A history of the founding of the state
of Israel which asks the reader pertinent questions
regarding Judaic issues and values.
    1. Israel—History—Juvenile literature.
2. Zionism—History—Juvenile literature. 3. Jewish religious education—Text-books for young people.
[1. Israel—History. 2. Zionism—History.
3. Jewish religious education] I. Title.
DS126.5.E4196   956.94   76-18282
ISBN 0-87441-234-X

10 9 8 7 6 5 4 3 2
83 82 81 80 79 78 77

Published by Behrman House, Inc., 1261 Broadway, New York, N.Y. 10001
Manufactured in the United States of America

TABLE OF CONTENTS

toward an understanding

zionism and the first aliyah 1881-1905

from dream to reality 1905-1948

the state of israel

israel and the israeli: environment and personality

the israeli way of life

understanding the jewish state

TOWARD AN UNDER-STANDING

perspective

Israel is a sovereign state in the family of nations, but in many ways it is unique. In its relationship with world Jewry there is both mutual concern and commitment. Israel's history is a complex blending of national and religious traditions. The fact and manner of Israel's rebirth as a Jewish state, after 1900 years of dispersion, is utterly without precedent. And the danger that Israel has lived with for over 25 years is extraordinary too. The long-standing conflict is not over territory, natural resources, sea rights, national honor, or any of the conventional causes of war. Rather, the conflict centers on Israel's right to exist as a sovereign state.

All countries differ from one another in their culture, traditions, laws, language, political order, or economic system. But Israel seems especially unlike the others. Its uniqueness is a blend of various elements, some happy, others tragic. All have had a profound effect, especially upon Israel's view of itself.

A UNIQUE REBIRTH

First of all, there is the unusual way Israel was born of a collective memory that lay dormant but not dead for almost 2000 years. An ancient people—dispersed all over the world, forced to speak a hundred tongues—gathered once more in their ancestral homeland, the land from which their forefathers had been expelled.

In the course of history, other peoples were expelled from their homelands but subsequently forgot them. The Jews are probably the only expelled people who remembered their homeland. When they finally reassembled in their own land, after centuries of exile and dispersion, their return was so different from other national revivals as to be regarded by many as a "miracle."

TOWARD
UNDER-
STANDING

PERSECUTION AND SURVIVAL

Second, there is the people of Israel's background of persecution and massacre. There is something unique about that, too. Other peoples have also been persecuted and massacred, for one reason or another. But the Jews are the only people in known history who were condemned to die as a people and were exterminated like vermin—not because of their faith, or because of what they were doing or not doing, but simply because they were alive.

ISRAEL'S ISOLATION

Third, there is something unique in Israel's isolated position in the world. Israel is isolated culturally, as a nation which speaks a language that is used by no other; religiously, as a nation which professes a faith to which no other people on earth adhere; and politically, as a nation which does not border on a single friendly country and is surrounded by bitter enemies.

Perhaps because its experiences, past and present, have been so unique, Israel has often found it difficult to secure the understanding of others. Perhaps this is why there are as many stereotypes, good and bad, about Israel today as there were nasty clichés about "Jews" in the past.

ISRAEL TODAY

Today Israel is in a process of dramatic change. One of the hardest things to remember is that all this changing has taken place in such a short time. A country which has been through so many wars and terrorist attacks, which has built so dramatically and achieved so much, which has absorbed so many poor and downtrodden peoples and given so many former outcasts a new sense of dignity—such a country has had enough experiences to last for hundreds of years. And yet the State of Israel was established only in this century, after World War II, in 1948.

A particular celebration, some years ago, dramatized this condensation of time. In 1968, Israel was celebrating its 20th anniversary as an independent state. Merely 51 years had passed since Britain formally recognized Palestine in the Balfour Declaration as a "national home" for the Jews, and not yet a century since the first modern Zionist pioneers had settled on the desolate malaria-ridden swamps some 10 miles from the Mediterranean Sea.

So much drama had unfolded in so little time that many of those watching the anniversary celebrations of 1968 had been among the prime movers and shapers of modern Israel. It was as though George Washington and Thomas Jefferson had been present at the parades following America's great victory in World War II.

For the old leaders, the twentieth anniversary celebration was an achievement such as is given to few people in public life. The entire government was there, headed by the president and flanked by scores of 70- and 80-year-old settlers, the last survivors of the first wave of Jewish immigration to Palestine in the early part of the century. Their record was probably unparalleled in modern history, for these old veterans in the grandstand had not only revolutionized their society but also largely created it. Israel had come into being, contrary to the usual rules of statecraft, in the course of their own lifetimes, through a modern folk-migration of Jewish outcasts and idealists. Such things had happened before, of course, but never so quickly, and never within the life span of a generation of founding fathers. Other immigrant communities that were established overseas, on new territories, had enjoyed the powerful military and political support of a mother country. The Zionist settlers had accomplished their task alone, aided only by the financial support of their fellow Jews overseas.

ISRAEL'S PIONEERS

Let us pause here for a moment and look closely at these proud men and women as they perch upon wooden planks, perspiring uneasily in the sun. Their stormy lives reflect much of the drama and grandeur as well as the irony and tragedy of the moment. From the circumstances of their lives, their achievements, their pious dreams and illusions, there emerges a saga not merely political but human and dramatic.

With few exceptions, the veterans were now in their 70's and 80's, their skins parched, their taut faces lined by deep furrows, their heads snow white or bald. Remnants of a small group of Eastern European romantics, they now saw the efforts of their long lives rewarded in a way and form which few had ever imagined.

Nearly all had come to the country before 1914, or immediately after World War I, as young men and women. Most had left behind relatively well-to-do, middle-class homes. Perhaps their fathers and mothers had wanted them to become great scholars or business people. Instead, the children had settled on the land as farm laborers. Dressed in rags, they frequently went hungry, were regularly struck down by attacks of typhoid and malaria. Often they were forced to defend their farms against armed Arab neighbors.

Founding a new settlement in the Galilee.

In the late 1920's the future leaders gradually went into trade union work, journalism, and politics. Their lives were totally dedicated to a cause. Some directed the financial affairs of their settlements, managed workers' sick funds, or purchased land for resettlement. They colonized hard, arid, seemingly impossible desert and mountain regions. Some worked as organizers of an underground defense force; some ran an underground route for illegal immigrants in defiance of British immigration regulations. Others tirelessly toured Jewish communities abroad to collect the huge funds necessary to finance it all. The men had little time for their families; their wives were often engaged in similar work. Few had hobbies; hardly anyone pursued a sport. They pursued and served only the idea of reviving Zion. When elected to public office, they lived on ridiculously low salaries. They were paid according to the number of dependents, and not according to status or position.

But when it came to the cause—a *kibbutz,* a school, a political party, a land reclamation agency, a community center—their capacity to raise (and occasionally squander) large sums of money was boundless. They were fabulous fund raisers. Jews have always responded generously to appeals for help. But the skill of these people in putting that tradition to work has probably never been equaled.

IN ONE SHORT LIFETIME

There were moments now when it was difficult for them to believe what they had done. In one short lifetime, a modern welfare state had grown up in what had been a backward, partly barren, thinly populated region. In one short lifetime, a spirited nation had developed out of a horde of frightened refugees, the outcasts of Europe, survivors of concentration camps, joining the primitive, half-literate masses from the shoddy marketplaces of the Middle East and North Africa. A common language, painfully resurrected from the dead, had emerged from a babel of tongues. In one short lifetime, big cities, theaters, orchestras, and ballet troupes had sprouted in numbers rarely seen in much larger nations. Zoos, ports, airfields, industries, superhighways, traffic jams, great universities—all these exceeded the founders' dreams.

Many of the marching soldiers were sons of Oriental immigrants, dark-skinned young men of Moroccan or Iraqi origin and as ignorant of the Zionist dream of the first Eastern European settlers as Sicilian or Polish immigrants to America must have been of the dreams of the Pilgrims who landed at Plymouth Rock. The young marchers of European origin were also a new breed. The founding group was already losing touch with them, for the new generation spoke a language that in both form and content sounded strange to these old people. Israel, in 1968, was on the verge of change.

related themes

Judaism's Continuing Vitality   The uniqueness—and special strength —of the Jewish people stems, in part, from the fact that Judaism is not just a religion or a nation; it is both. In his essay "Toward an Explanation of our Ideology," the religious Zionist thinker Solomon Landau sees in this continuity of Judaism a key reason for its continuing vitality and for the establishment of a new Jewish state after 1900 years of exile.

This "Torah," the heritage of Israel, has two basic meanings: the first refers to the Torah as a code of Law . . . which every single Jew must obey; the second connotes the Torah . . . as the national spirit, the source of its culture and life. . . . The Torah, interpreted in this [second] sense, fulfills the process of national rebirth . . . which is inconceivable without the national spirit. For our people is not a people except through its Torah, and the spirit of our people cannot express itself unless there be a national revival in our own land. . . .

Israel and the Family of Nations   In an article called "Israel Must Live," the longshoreman-turned-philosopher Eric Hoffer discusses some of the ways in which Israel is "unique."

The Jews are a peculiar people. Things permitted to other nations are forbidden to the Jews. . . . Other nations drive out thousands, even millions of people and there is no refugee problem. Russia did it; Poland and Czechoslovakia did it; Turkey drove out a million Greeks; and Algeria a million Frenchmen; Indonesia threw out heaven knows how many Chinese and no one says a word about refugees.

But in the case of Israel, the displaced Arabs have become eternal refugees. . . . [The historian] Arnold Toynbee calls the displacement of the Arabs an atrocity greater than any committed by the Nazis. Other nations when victorious on the battlefield dictate peace terms. But when Israel is victorious it must sue for peace. Every one expects the Jews to be the only real Christians in this world. Other nations when they are defeated survive and recover. But should Israel be defeated it would be destroyed. Had Nasser triumphed in June, 1967, he would have wiped Israel off the map, and no one would have lifted a finger to save the Jews. . . .

The Jews are alone in the world. If Israel survives it will be solely because of Jewish efforts. And Jewish resources. . . .

I have a premonition that will not leave me: as it goes with Israel, so it will go with all of us. Should Israel perish, the Holocaust will be upon us.

Israel must live!

issues and values

To Be a Jew   Jewish tradition stresses ethical and compassionate relationships between human beings. In his autobiography *In Search*, the American author Meyer Levin focuses upon these values as he speaks of his personal definition of Jewish identity:

Once in Paris, Marek Szwarc asked me "What do you want? What do you want to be?" And the definition that slipped out was a bit startling to me, for I blurted "a good Jew."

I didn't say a great writer or a happy man or a good person or a good American though I want to be all of those, too. The first response, which I must regard as the true response from within me . . . was "a good Jew."

And what is that?

When we think of "a good American" we think in patriotic terms. When we think of "a good Christian" we think in moral terms. I suppose a good Jew is more of a moral than a patriotic concept, but there is an overtone of folk approval sought. And amongst the Jews themselves what was good? It was not piety, for then one said "a pious Jew." It was close to "just" and it included a sense of responsibility and usefulness to the community. . . . These are ways in which we are unique, and in our souls we know and are proud of this uniqueness. . . .

What is your definition of "a good Jew"? What in your opinion are the most essential elements of Jewish identity?

Jews Are Different   Both the anti-Semite and the committed Jew find themselves in agreement on one point: the Jewish people are "different." The anti-Semite implies that this differentness is somehow unwholesome, immoral, or even vaguely sinister. The committed Jew believes that remaining apart is essential to the integrity of the Jewish tradition and the creative survival of the Jewish community. To the Jew, the greatest dangers confronting the Jewish state are that they may lose their unique identity and purpose by becoming "a nation like all other nations," or by yielding to the temptation of assimilation. Much of American Jewish education today is devoted to instilling in young Jews a sense of being distinctively and proudly different. Do you feel that you are "different" from your non-Jewish friends? If so, how? Is Jewish "differentness" a quality that you cherish and wish to cultivate, or is it a source of trouble and embarrassment?

JERUSALEM

Photo Essay Jerusalem has been the capital of Israel since 1948. In a setting of incomparable beauty, high in the barren hills 700–800 meters above sea level (between 2100 and 2800 feet), the city sits astride a watershed. On the eastern side lies the stony desert of Judea; toward the west, the green slopes overlook the lush Mediterranean coastal plain.

The Talmud says, "Ten measures of beauty came down [from Heaven]; nine measures were taken by Jerusalem, and one by the rest of the world." Jerusalem has been identified with holiness and divine revelation for at least 3000 years. It is sacred to Jews, Christians, and Muslims alike. The Muslims call it *el Kuds* (the Holy), and all three religions associate the idea of Jerusalem with the idea of redemption. But only the Jews have regarded Jerusalem as their spiritual center and national capital.

Numerically, Jews have been a majority in Jerusalem since the middle of the nineteenth century. The city has many names: Jerusalem of Gold, *The* City, God's City, the Holy City, City of Justice, City of

Jerusalem: The Holy City.

For centuries, Jews have hidden prayers
in the niches of the Western Wall.

Building Talpiot: A new section of Jerusalem.

Eternity, Faithful City, City of Beauty, and
most meaningfully, City of Peace.

The earthly Jerusalem, however, has
had little peace. Not just in our own days
but even in ancient times, as when the
prophet Isaiah lamented that Jerusalem
had been punished by the Lord "doubly,
for all her sins."

Jerusalem is mentioned only once in
the Pentateuch, and then only inciden-
tally. It first achieved its unique status
under David, as the royal city of Israel
("thrones for judgment were set, the
thrones of the House of David"—Psalms
122:5) and as the City of the Temple ("a
place for Thee to dwell forever"—I Kings
8:13).

To the Psalmist, Jerusalem was the
symbol of divine righteousness and justice. In the Song of Songs it is the sacred
symbol that stands also for worldly love.
After the destruction of Jerusalem, the
Book of Lamentations mourns its ruins
and its loveliness: "how has she become

a widow," this city which once was full of people, a princess among all the cities of the earth. This lament was destined to occupy a central place in the Jewish sensibility for centuries to come. By the rivers of Babylon the Jewish exiles sat weeping as they remembered Jerusalem. "If I forget thee, O Jerusalem," vowed the Psalmist, "let my right hand lose her cunning" (Psalms 137:5).

Throughout their wanderings and tribulations, the Jews never forgot Jerusalem. In the Jewish daily prayer, Jerusalem, or Zion, is synonymous with Eretz Israel as a whole. In the daily *Amidah* (the "Standing" Prayers), we beseech God "and to Jerusalem Thy city, return . . . rebuild it soon in our days. . . . Blessed art Thou, *Adonai,* who builds Jerusalem." There is in all probability no other city on earth that has played as important a role in the imagination or memory of its people, even centuries after they were exiled from it.

Windmill in Yemin Moshe.

A street in the New City.

Many years before Israel was established, Chaim Weizmann, the first president of Israel, was asked by a British Inquiry Commission by what right the Jews of Poland or Canada were claiming Jerusalem as their own. Weizmann answered, "Memory is right." Other peoples had been expelled from their lands and then forgotten them. Weizmann's point was that the Jews had always remembered theirs: "Next year in Jerusalem."

Dome of the Rock: A Moslem mosque built in the center of the ancient temple area.

The Church of the Holy Sepulchre: A sacred Christian shrine.

perspective

The generation of settlers who came to Palestine during the first two decades of this century are known to most Israelis as the *vatikim* (the veteran pioneers, the old-timers). These idealists dreamed of a Jewish homeland and have spent their lives making it a reality. The feud between David Ben-Gurion and Levi Eshkol, referred to in this chapter, suggests that relations between the vatikim have sometimes been stormy—marked by clashes of personality and quarrels over principles and ideas. And yet, as the accounts of their youth unfold, it becomes clear that the issues that may have divided these aging pioneers are not nearly so compelling as the forces that have drawn them together.

ZALMAN SHAZAR

The president reviewed the troops from a small wooden stage, upon which a few armchairs had been placed. At 79, President Zalman Shazar was a small, noble, white-haired, kindly old gentlemen of great personal charm. He was now a political figurehead; in past decades he had played a considerable role, first as a Zionist agitator, later as Israel's first minister of education. He was a prolific writer and poet in Hebrew, Russian, and Yiddish. A public speaker of great fervor and effectiveness, his speeches sometimes lasted up to ten hours. Once, in Tel Aviv in the 1930's, he was so carried away by an argument in favor of social democracy that he stepped over the edge of the stage and fell 3 feet into the orchestra pit.

Shazar was born in 1889 in Mir, a little Russian hamlet near Minsk. When it burned down a few years later, his family moved to the nearby town of Stoibitz. There the small Jewish community was coming into ever-increasing contact with its Russian neighbors.

The distinguished Hassidic family from which Shazar came was

VIEW
FROM THE
GRANDSTAND

13

just beginning to trade its orthodox Judaism for European culture. Families like this were producing in almost equal numbers leading Zionist pioneers and Socialist revolutionaries. Not infrequently, as with Shazar, the two movements overlapped. His underground work in Russia ended in a czarist jail. After serving his sentence, he went to Palestine in 1911, working briefly as a farm laborer in Galilee. He returned to Russia to do military service but was discharged on medical grounds. Russian universities at that time were closed to most Jewish young men, so Shazar went to Germany to study. He returned to Palestine and settled there permanently in 1924.

ESHKOL AND DAYAN—TWO KINDS OF LEADERS

Flanking President Shazar on the main grandstand were Premier Levi Eshkol and his defense minister Moshe Dayan. Eshkol, already sickly (he was to die within a year), was a man of considerable political skill. He had succeeded the fiery David Ben-Gurion as premier in 1963. Dayan, a former general, had been the architect of Israel's victories in the wars of 1956 and 1967. It would be hard to imagine two more different men.

Eshkol, at 72, was a man of the old, passing order of wider Jewish loyalties. Dayan represented a new, locally bred, locally oriented generation of younger men, self-reliant, asking no one for sympathy and having little sympathy of their own to give. Tough and competent at 53, Dayan had been in four wars and in frequent border skirmishes between. He often said he feared he might have to go to war again. His oval head was balding. His face was smooth and sunburned, and his cheekbones high. His thin lips sarcastically drooped to one side, cutting a diagonal line across his boyish face.

Eshkol was a sociable, rather friendly, marvelously witty, experienced party politician; he was widely liked but not much respected. Dayan, a lone wolf in politics, was much admired for his war record but feared for alleged dictatorial tendencies. Eshkol, a typical committee man, was much given to compromise, for which he had earned a not undeserved reputation for indecision in a crisis. He was the butt of innumerable political jokes. According to one of the better known stories, when he was asked by a waiter in a cafe whether he would like coffee or tea, he stammered awhile, then finally blurted: "You know what, make it *hetzi-hetzi* [half and half]."

Dayan, scornful of committee work and "unnecessary blabber," was a believer in lone decisions, for which he was prepared to shoulder all responsibility. Eshkol was a political tactician; he owed his position as head of the current national coalition to his colleagues' fear of stronger men and to his own talent for reconciling opposites in a cabinet containing rightists and leftists, religious people and secularists, hawks and doves.

Eshkol had spent most of his public life as a trade union man; as head of the Settlement Department of the Jewish Agency, he initiated and directed vast irrigation schemes. He was Ben-Gurion's minister of finance. His life was bound up with the ever-growing construction efforts during the previous 50 years. Dayan had been in the military from his earliest manhood; his life had been forged by war. Eshkol was an early immigrant, while Dayan was native-born, a *sabra,* the second child born in the country's first kibbutz, Degania, on the shore of the Lake of Galilee. Eshkol had lost his father in a Russian pogrom; he remembered huddling in a tightly shuttered home as a child, hiding from the rampaging Cossacks. He carried in his heart the gloom and sad humor, the lack of certainty fostered by the Diaspora.

Dayan had lost his left eye in one war and his only brother in another. He grew up in a hard frontier atmosphere, where men did not hide behind shutters but often kept their lives because they fought for them. An Australian officer, who was present when Dayan lost his eye while fighting in the British army in 1941, later wrote: "What a pity

Reviewing Stand: Twentieth-Anniversary Independence Day parade.

that this courageous lad—who used to cast one eye down to the plow while the other was on guard—will now possess only one eye. Will that eye be turned to Mars?" *

GOLDA MEIR

Other survivors of the fast-shrinking group of pioneers were sitting nearby, on another stand reserved for VIPs. There was Golda Meir, at 70 the Grand Old Lady of the ruling Labor Party, Israel's first ambassador to Moscow, and a former foreign minister (later to be Israel's first woman premier). She had arrived in the country in 1921 from the United States, where she had been a schoolteacher in Milwaukee. But as a native of czarist Russia, she too had childhood memories of the sound of hammers boarding up doors and windows against marauding Russian peasants, and of the clatter of the horses the Cossacks rode through Jewish streets in Kiev as they put houses to the torch. "If there is any logical explanation necessary to the direction which my life has taken," she once said, "maybe this is the explanation: the desire and determination to save Jewish children, four or five years old, from a similar scene, from a similar experience."

A little farther down the grandstand there were more survivors of the founding generation. The "quiet little great," they had stayed out of public life to remain on the land, where they watched their children and grandchildren work the fields they themselves had cleared of boulders and drained of swamps in the first decades of the century.

RACHEL BEN-ZVI

In the front row, on a padded chair placed especially for her comfort, Rachel Yanait Ben-Zvi watched the parade go by. A frail, thin old lady of 81, she was the widow of Israel's second president, Yitzhak Ben-Zvi. Rachel Ben-Zvi was a pioneer and a political figure in her own right. She too had been a veteran of underground socialist and Zionist work in czarist Russia. At the age of 17 she had been arrested by Russian police for participating in a secret socialist meeting. At her release from prison more than a year later, her worried father had assured the director of the prison: "I promise you, sir, that she will stay out of trouble from now on. We will keep her at home." But the young girl had broken in: "No, I will not!" She had then gone on to tell the warden, "But don't worry, I have no use for this Russia of yours. I don't need it. We have our own country—the land of Israel."

* Mars—the Roman god of war.

DAVID BEN-GURION

On a stand far away from the other celebrities, sharing the benches reserved for paying foreign tourists but known nevertheless by all around him, sat one of the main heroes of the drama, the old man of Israel politics, David Ben-Gurion. He had spent the last five years in semi-retirement at his desert retreat, a little wooden hut on the edge of Kibbutz Sdeh Boker. He was still pursuing a bitter argument with his successor, Levi Eshkol.

David Ben-Gurion had run the affairs of the new state from its beginning in 1948. Before 1948, with a terrible simplicity of vision and single-mindedness of purpose, he had led the community of Jewish pioneers and urban settlers on the road to self-determination and independence. He was now 82 years old. Aging but very much alert, Ben-Gurion was still taking his daily 5-mile walk.

Born David Grien in 1886, Ben-Gurion was a native of Plonsk, a small town some 40 miles northwest of Warsaw in czarist-ruled Poland. He was the sixth child of Sheindle and Avigdor Grien. In 1906, seized by an irresistible urge, the young David Grien left his father's house. Three weeks later he arrived at the port of Jaffa. He was 20 at the time, and already caught up in the dream that would not leave him his entire life.

The Promised Land, as it appeared to him that day, was a small dusty town of 15,000 Arabs and 3000 Jews engaged in petty business. Ben-Gurion did not like Jaffa; he found it filthy and depressing. He did not even stop overnight when he came off the ship after his long journey. He continued on foot across barren and swampy sand dunes (these would later become the traffic-choked metropolitan area of greater Tel Aviv) to the nearby colony of Petaḥ Tikvah.

Petaḥ Tikvah, today a city of more than 100,000 and an important industrial center, at that time was a small village of a few hundred souls. A muddy path led through its single street. He spent his first night in a workers' hostel, a wooden shack with straw mats. He could not sleep. In a poetic mood he wrote:

I did not sleep. The rich smell of corn rose about me. I heard the braying of donkeys and the rustling of leaves in the orchards. Above were the massed clusters of stars clear against the deep blue firmament. My heart overflowed with happiness as if I had entered the realm of joy. . . . A dream was celebrating its victory. I was in Eretz Israel, in a Hebrew village in Eretz Israel, in a Hebrew village called *Petaḥ Tikvah* ("Gate of Hope").

He hired himself out as a field worker to the Palestinian Jewish farmers who had settled in Petaḥ Tikvah some 20 to 25 years earlier. Economically the settlement was still a shaky enterprise. The farmers' deficits were covered by generous donations from Baron Edmond de Rothschild of Paris, but there were no economic subsidies for the hired laborers and their lives were especially harsh. Malaria was a frequent visitor, as was hunger. In a letter to his father, Ben-Gurion wrote a short time after his arrival: "But who is to complain, to sigh, to despair? In twenty-five years our country will be one of the most blooming, most beautiful and happiest; an old-new nation will flourish in an ancient-new land. Then we shall relate how we fevered and worked, hungered and dreamed." His vision was to take much longer to achieve.

related themes

The Significance of Israel   The description of David Ben-Gurion as a young man who "left his father's house" to settle in "the Promised Land" calls to mind the story of Abraham, who was commanded by God to "go out of your land and from your father's house unto the land which I will show you; And I will make of you a great nation . . ." (Genesis 12:1–2). The land of Israel has played a crucial role in Jewish history and tradition from earliest recorded memory until today. It is expressed, for example, in the story of the Exodus from Egypt; in the return to their homeland of the Jewish exiles from Babylon under Ezra and Nehemiah; in the fact that living in the Land of Israel, according to tradition, represents God's ultimate reward to His people, while exile represents the ultimate penalty that He visits on them; in the words *Leshanah Haba'ah Bi–rushalayim* ("Next Year in Jerusalem")— the last declaration made on Yom Kippur; and, finally, in the immigration of the Zionist pioneers to Palestine to reclaim their ancient homeland and in the rebirth of the State of Israel.

Dreams and Longings   The first four *Aliyot* (waves of immigration *) came mainly from the lands of Eastern Europe, where anti-Semitism and persecution were rampant. The attachment that they held for the land of Israel was deeply embedded. In 1903, following the disastrous Kishinev pogroms in Russia, Theodor Herzl put forward what he described as an "emergency measure." The British government had offered to Herzl and the Jewish people the land of Uganda as a Jewish

* The word *Aliyot* comes from the singular *Aliyah* and literally means "going up" or "ascending"; it has come to mean the act of "ascending" to Israel through immigration.

homeland. And in this moment of dire need, it seemed a blessing to Herzl. "Not as a replacement," he said, but ". . . to prevent the loss of those detached fragments of our people." But to Herzl's astonishment, the Russian delegates to the World Zionist Congress flatly rejected any alternative to Palestine. "These people have a rope around their necks, and still they refuse!" declared Herzl (who soon after abandoned the Uganda plan). Chaim Weizmann, the Russian Zionist leader later to become Israel's first president, placed the action of the Russian Jews in perspective, saying that ". . . with all their suffering, the Jews of Russia were incapable of transferring their dreams and longing from the land of their forefathers to any other territory."

issues and values

Anti-Semitism One of the main reasons the vatikim pulled up roots and went to Palestine was that the world around them had grown so dismal and hopeless. Anti-Semitism was an ever-present fact of life and seemed likely to remain so for a long time to come. Hatred of the Jew was encouraged by church and government; it did not seem that improvement would come through better social and economic conditions or even through religious enlightenment. In the introduction to his classic work *The Jewish State*, Theodor Herzl observed ". . . old prejudices against us are deeply ingrained . . . he who would have proof of this need only listen to people when they speak candidly and artlessly; folk wisdom and folklore are both anti-Semitic." Have you as an American Jew ever been confronted by anti-Semitism? Have you come across anti-Semitism in the form of jokes, stories, or personal opinions?

A Creative Jewish Life A second factor that helped bring the vatikim to Palestine was their desire to be themselves—that is, to express themselves fully and creatively in terms of their identity and their heritage. This, they felt, could only be achieved in their own homeland. Rabbi Abraham Isaac Kook, the chief rabbi of Palestine (1921–1935), summed up their thoughts in his essay "The Land of Israel": "Jewish original creativity, whether in the realm of ideas or in the arena of daily life, is impossible except in the Land of Israel. . . . A Jew cannot be true to his own ideas, sentiments, and imagination in the Diaspora." What does Rabbi Kook mean by original Jewish creativity? Do you feel that you live an active and satisfying Jewish life?

3/ ZIONISM AS A REVOLUTION

perspective

The Zionist movement sought to establish a homeland for the Jews, a place where Jews would no longer be a minority dependent on the goodwill of others for safety and well-being. And yet the Jewish state has been in danger of destruction since the day of its creation. The early Zionist pioneers tried to fashion a just society; the fact that some Palestinian Arabs have been living in refugee camps since the first Arab-Israeli war in 1948 continues to gnaw at the national conscience, regardless of who is to blame. Finally, Zionism believed that a basic cause of anti-Semitism would be removed by "normalizing the Jew"—that is, by making the Jew a citizen of his own country— yet the very existence of Israel has given rise to a deep-rooted Arab anti-Zionism.

It is not customary to speak of Zionism as a revolution. Yet it has been one of the deepest, truest revolutions of the past hundred years. It taught a persecuted people to help themselves. It took a great many people out of near serfdom and offered them the dignity of free life in a rebuilt country and the equal opportunities of a modern, socially conscious state. In the kibbutz it created a society which still expresses some of the noblest aspirations of mankind.

It also gave people a new language and, in many ways, an entirely new culture. It changed not only their socioeconomic structure but also their climate, diet, and geography.

But the Zionist revolution failed in one of its major aims. It did not automatically protect Jews from attack. Still, a people who for centuries had been helpless victims of recurring massacres by religious and political bigots were now at least in a position to undertake their own defense.

TOWARD
UNDER-
STANDING

BETWEEN ARAB AND JEW

20

Every revolution has its price, of course, and the Zionist revolution was no exception. By a brutal twist of fate, unexpected, undesired, even unconsidered by the early pioneers, this price was partly paid by the Arab inhabitants of Palestine who became refugees, to be used and victimized by their own fanatical leaders.

This is not how the Zionist pioneers had intended it. Quite the contrary. They had hoped that two nations, Jews and Arabs, could live together peacefully and amicably for the benefit of both. To the centuries-old Jewish conflict with Christianity, a conflict with Islam was now added. This was the second great price of Zionism, and the conflict is likely to continue and even deepen. It may last for generations.

Muslim-Jewish relations, of course, were not exactly rosy even before Zionism. Islamic societies were seldom as tolerant of Jewish minorities as is often claimed. Jews, like Christians, were always second-class citizens in the Muslim world. In countries such as Yemen, Iraq, and Morocco, they were subjected to severe and special hardships.

But in the Middle East there had almost never been a pogrom of Jews. Nor was Islamic hatred of Jews based on purely racial grounds, as in Europe. In this sense, the Arabs, being Semites themselves, had never been "anti-Semitic." But they were now becoming anti-Zionist. The Arab-Israeli conflict was producing a new form of Arab hostility to Jews, making it almost impossible for Jewish communities to continue to live in Arab countries.

BETWEEN DREAM AND REALITY

The Zionists had come to Palestine to cultivate the swampland and desert. It seemed empty to them, except for a few backward peasants who would also benefit from their advanced social ideas. They could not foresee that one day the Arabs would develop their own nationalism which would not accept a Jewish presence in Palestine.

After the Israeli victory of 1967 it was hoped that some agreement might be reached. But Arab leaders soon announced that another war was "inevitable," and the chance for concessions on all sides was again lost. Even after the hard-fought battles of the Yom Kippur War of 1973, the two sides could not find enough common ground for broad peace negotiations. Only slowly and with great effort could a few piecemeal advances be made.

related themes

Rootless Victims   When the Arab-Israeli War of 1948 began, Azam

The great shift of population: Thousands of Jewish refugees being brought to the new State of Israel from Arab lands.

Pasha, secretary-general of the Arab League, called it "a war of extermination and a momentous massacre which will be spoken of as the Mongolian massacres and the Crusades." The Israelis asked their Arab neighbors to stay and promised that no harm would come to them. Those who remained (about 140,000) have become full citizens of Israel, but those who left (about 587,000) became refugees. The Arab governments, with the exception of Jordan, have refused to grant citizenship to the Palestinians (or even to contribute substantially to their support), on the grounds that the United Nations was responsible for Israel's creation and should therefore bear the cost of all the damages involved. In 1954, Ralph Galloway, then a United Nations Work and Relief Agency employee, explained the situation this way: "The Arab states don't want to solve the refugee problem, they want to keep it an open sore as an affront to the UN and a weapon against Israel. . . ."

Contradictions Hatred of the Jew is not logical. It has often been based on reasons that directly contradict one another. For example, the Jew has been accused at one and the same time of being both a capitalist ("the Jews have all the money") and a communist (conspiring to overthrow those who have all the money); as an unwelcome intruder into Gentile society ("the Jews are so pushy!") and as a snob who wants nothing to do with Gentile society ("the Jews always stick together"). Since the creation of the State of Israel, a new contradiction has been added. The old anti-Semitic idea that Jews were cowards always looking for other people to fight their battles for them has now been joined to the new image of Israeli Jews as military-minded citizens of an "expansionist state."

issues and values

"A People Like No Other" In his essay "Hebrew Humanism," the Jewish philosopher Martin Buber stated that "Israel is not a nation like other nations . . . [but] a people like no other, for it is the only people in the world which, from its earliest beginnings, has been both a nation and a religious community." So the establishment of a homeland for the Jews, as important as that is, should not be the only goal of the Zionist revolution. Zionism should also try to create a society that expresses, in Buber's words, "the values of Israel." How has the State of Israel proved to be "not a nation like other nations"? (Consider, for example, its relations with world Jewry.) Can you point to Israeli attitudes and values that are specifically Jewish? How do these same values play an active role in your life?

Prisoners in Spirit The early Zionists wished to create a homeland in which the Jew would be free spiritually as well as politically. They thought of Jews who lived in a free and democratic society of Gentiles as prisoners in spirit—that is, people who worried constantly about what the Gentiles might say. Indeed, in free countries, some Jews converted to Christianity because they viewed baptism as "a ticket of admission." Others remained Jewish but tried to negate their ties to the land of Israel. Thus, the French-Jewish financier and communal leader Abraham Fortado declared at the beginning of the nineteenth century: "We are no longer a nation within a nation. France is our country, Jews. Your obligations [to France] are outlined; your happiness is waiting." What Fortado considered happiness, the early Zionists considered a kind of imprisonment. Do you feel that you are a prisoner in spirit in any sense? Have you ever found yourself, or other Jewish people you know, worrying about what the Gentiles will say?

THE DREYFUS TRIAL

Photo Essay The Dreyfus Affair of 1894–1906 was a landmark in both Jewish and French history. It almost brought the Republic of France to civil war. It triggered a sudden crisis of conscience and of identity in the heart and mind of a 35-year-old Viennese journalist named Theodor Herzl, who was destined to become the founder of modern Zionism.

Until 1895, Herzl had been a playwright and the Paris correspondent of the *Neue Freie Presse* (considered the New York *Times* of Austria), one of the most important journals of opinion in Europe. Herzl was himself an assimilated Jew. He had not even bothered to have his son circumcised. But the Dreyfus Affair convinced him that there was no future and

Alfred Dreyfus: 1859–1935.

Theodor Herzl: 1860–1904.

no security for Jews in Europe. It convinced him that there must be another exodus and the establishment of a Jewish state somewhere.

Alfred Dreyfus was the scion of a wealthy Jewish family. He was a professional officer in the French army. Loyal to a fault, he was taken completely by surprise. In the fall of 1894, French counterespionage agents discovered that important military secrets had been betrayed to the Germans. Captain Dreyfus was arrested, and on the basis of charges trumped up by anti-Semitic fellow officers, who were eager to exonerate Gentiles and save the honor of the army, he was convicted in secret court hearings of high treason.

Dreyfus was degraded at a public ceremony attended by Herzl, who was acting as a reporter for the Viennese newspaper.

Degradation of Captain Dreyfus: An engraving.

It was also attended by a huge crowd of Parisians, who screamed "Death to the Jews!" Dreyfus was stripped of his rank, put into chains, and deported to a prison on Devil's Island. Throughout his trial, Dreyfus had proclaimed his innocence; now, as the crowd spat upon him and screamed "Traitor!" and "Dirty Jew!" he again proclaimed his innocence, saying, "I forbid you to insult me!" and calling out, "Vive la France!" Herzl watched closely, absorbing all that was happening.

Within a year after the conviction, a French intelligence officer uncovered evidence which cast doubt on the testimony produced at the Dreyfus trial. The new evidence strongly suggested that Dreyfus had served as a scapegoat; the treason had actually been committed by others. But when this came to no avail liberal journalists took up the cause. France quickly divided into two camps, the so-called Dreyfusards and anti-Dreyfusards. The Dreyfusards were mostly liberals, democrats, and republicans anxious to uphold the principles proclaimed by the French Revolution in the Declaration of the Rights of Man. Their opponents, the anti-Dreyfusards, were mostly conservatives, monarchists, militarists, militant Catholics who opposed the separation of church and state, and supporters of a new "science," racism. Contrary to what most people believe today, racism was invented by Frenchmen a few decades before it was adopted by German writers.

In the end—but only after a decade—the Dreyfusards were victorious. Dreyfus was eventually exonerated and restored to his former rank. But meanwhile, the national debate on Dreyfus' guilt or innocence had revealed the depths and violence of anti-Semitic prejudice in France. The revelation came as a great shock. 25

If the Dreyfus Affair had occurred in a traditionally anti-Semitic, pogrom-ridden countries such as czarist Russia or Rumania, it would not have surprised anyone. But France was the supposed home of liberty. Herzl was shaken by the affair precisely because it was taking place, as he put it, in "modern republican France, only a century after the *Declaration of the Rights of Man.*" If such things could happen in the most civilized country of the West, what could be expected in the East? Surely disaster would follow.

As the Dreyfus Affair lingered on, Herzl's view of the Jewish condition sharpened; clearer than any of his contemporaries, Herzl saw the dangers looming on the horizon. He could not foresee a Hitler, of course, for Hitler's bestiality went beyond all limits of the imagination. But better and more sharply than any of his contemporaries, Herzl realized that the days of European Jewry were numbered.

Moreover, Herzl saw a bitter irony in the fact that throughout the affair, Captain Dreyfus refused to believe that anti-Semitism had played a role in his conviction. Dreyfus held onto a naïve theory that he was the victim of a "juridical error"; he remained loyal to the morals and mores of the military caste within which he had tried, and would try again, to make a career. Anatole France, the great French novelist, said of Dreyfus that he was "the same type as the officers who condemned him. In their shoes he would have condemned himself."

In Herzl's view, Dreyfus represented the whole tragedy of emancipated Jewry, trapped in a gilded ghetto, robbed of inner freedom. Dreyfus was to Herzl the symbol of the Jew in modern society, who conformed to its ways, spoke its language, thought its thoughts, and sewed its insignia onto his shoulders, only to have it violently torn off early on a gray morning as the mob screamed "Death to the Jews!"

Dreyfus in disgrace.

PREUVES ÉCRASANTES de la TRAHISON

Appel à tous les Français. — Mort aux Traîtres !

L'HONNEUR DE L'ARMÉE — L'INDIGNATION DE NOS SOLDATS

INFAMES MACHINATIONS

Le Syndicat Dreyfus — A bas les juifs! — D'où vient l'argent

LES RÉVÉLATIONS DE LA FEMME VOILÉE

Un Complot de faussaires. — A Mazas ! — Les aveux du traître

Défense impossible
Témoignages irrécusables
Les vols
au ministère de la guerre
Les aveux du traître
Campagne de reptiles juifs
Juste condamnation

Tous les jours de nouveaux témoignages abondent, écrasants pour le traître de l'Île du Diable et pour ceux qui osent encore le défendre.

SCHEURER-KESTNER
INDUSTRIEL ALLEMAND

Il suffisait cependant de savoir que le misérable avait livré, entre autres documents de la plus haute importance : le plan de concentration des troupes de première ligne à la frontière de l'Est, le plan des forts de la Savoie et celui du camp retranché de Nice — ces derniers pour le compte de l'Italie.

Il suffisait qu'un conseil de guerre l'eût prouvé — de la plus irréfutable façon — que Dreyfus avait bien livré ces pièces et que pas un des membres du conseil ne pourrait démentir ces faits.

N'y avait-il pas aussi les propres aveux du traître au capitaine Lebrun-Renault, de la garde républicaine à cheval : J'ai livré des documents à l'Allemagne dans l'espoir d'en obtenir sur l'armée allemande.

Eh bien, non, tout cela n'a fait que susciter le syndicat Dreyfus, et les amis du gredin ont engagé, pour prouver que tout cela était non seulement insuffisant, mais faux, la campagne de calomnies, de mensonges et de diffamations que l'on sait.

Campagne admirablement conduite, disent les dilettantes, en applaudissant M. Bernard Lazare, le chef des reptiles. Pardieu ! Avec l'or des juifs, quel forban de lettres n'en eût fait autant, à condition d'être intelligent mais dépourvu de conscience et de préjugés ?

---

rer-Kestner, les Mathieu Dreyfus, tous les avocats, tous les journalistes payés par la caisse du syndicat n'avaient pu prévoir, c'est que cette campagne se retournerait contre eux.

En effet, de tout ce bruit, de toute cette boue remuée, la culpabilité de Dreyfus ressort plus claire que jamais, et nous avons eu ça plaisir d'apprendre que le misérable n'est pas le seul à avoir commis le crime de trahison, ce dont on ne doutait bien un peu, hélas !

Oui, comme l'a dit l'honorable M. Bailie, il y a des choses qu'on ne commet pas seul. Mais en quoi cela pourrait-il blanchir Dreyfus ?

Que ses semblables soient comme lui jugés et frappés, la France entière applaudira. Mais que l'on n'essaye point, en détournant les responsabilités, et de faire aller à ce misérable l'opinion publique en faveur de la foule. Celle-ci, d'ailleurs, ne se trompait pas à ce jeu d'un nouveau massacre d'innocents... peut-être. Ce qu'il lui faut, c'est que justice soit rendue, pour les uns comme pour les autres.

Tentatives de déshonorer
l'armée
Le patriotisme
du commandant Pauffin
de Saint-Morel
Les sympathies
du
commandant Forzinetti
Un général de carabiniers

Au milieu de toute cette fange, se débattent des noms estimés jusqu'ici, traîne l'honneur d'officiers français, et le ministre de la guerre, et le gouvernement, tous ceux sur lesquels on a le droit de compter pour savoir la vérité — quelque épouvantable qu'elle soit — tous ceux-là se taisent.

Le général de Boisdeffre ayant fait dire dans un journal que l'on avait, au ministère de la guerre, des preuves irrécusables de la culpabilité de Dreyfus, le commandant Pauffin de Saint-Morel est frappé de trente jours d'arrêts de rigueur, et, pour essayer de public un peu comprendre pas rien à ce conflit entre le chef de l'état-major de l'armée française et le ministre de la guerre, le général Billot relève de ses fonctions le commandant Forzinetti, directeur de la prison du Cherche-Midi, dont les sympathies pour Dreyfus, son ancien prisonnier, sont connues de tous. Cette juste se...

LA VICTIME DES JUIFS
Le Commandant ESTERHAZY

PAUFFIN DE SAINT-MOREL
Victime du Syndicat Dreyfus
DÉFENSEUR DE L'ARMÉE FRANÇAISE

Le gâchis et la honte
Le but
du syndicat Dreyfus
Chute
du ministère possible
La femme voilée
Un Panama militaire

Comment pourrait-on s'empêcher dans tout ce gâchis d'en infâmes et de hontes ? De ce côté, certes, le but du syndicat Dreyfus est atteint : le scandale est complet, et nous ne serions pas surpris qu'il en résultât à brève...

---

vérité du général Billot a, de plus, le tort de venir un peu tard... ce que l'on n'admet que d'un général de carabiniers.

A cette tragédie, la partie comique ne pouvait manquer. C'est la fameuse femme voilée.

nant à la police française et ayant eu des relations avec un membre de la famille Dreyfus.

Il y a, à n'en pas douter, sous tous ces racontars inexplicables, on ne sait quoi de louche, d'invraisemblable, qui étreint péniblement le pays. Et, ce qui l'alarme davantage encore, c'est toutes ces réticences, ces ménagements, cette répugnance du pouvoir à tirer les choses au clair.

On sait ce qu'il en a coûté de n'avoir pas eu le courage de dire la vérité lors du Panama. Qu'on se mêle. Une pareille attitude aujourd'hui aurait des résultats encore plus terribles, plus irréparables.

L'avachissement
Les lâchetés et les souffrets
L'armée
Les Sans-Patrie
Les juifs
La suspicion partout
Campagne
d'infâmes calomnies
Inertie
du gouvernement
Qu'on les tue ! ...

Est-il donc entendu que les pleutres qui nous gouvernent — aussi peu soucieux de l'honneur national que de leur propre dignité — nous feront boire jusqu'à la dernière lie le calice de toutes les amertumes, de toutes les hontes, sans qu'un cri de révolte — voire même simplement d'indignation — jaillisse enfin de la poitrine de ce peuple, jadis si fier de ses nobles traditions, aujourd'hui avachi, dégradé par une puante indifférence, veule et mol au point de recevoir chaque jour sans broncher le coup de botte au cul de ce gendarme imbécile qu'est le POUVOIR ?

En ces dernières années, tous les affronts nous furent infligés. Cependant, malgré toutes nos lâchetés, quoique l'échine toujours tendue aux coups, il est vrai et le visage prêt aux crachats des gouvernants quels qu'ils soient, une chose chez nous était restée encore pure, grande, respectée : l'Armée — arche sainte de la Patrie.

Eh bien, voilà que la meute des sans-patrie qui se sont rués sur ce pauvre pays, qu'ils couvrent aujourd'hui comme des poux le corps d'un vagabond, voilà que les juifs, nuées de sauterelles venues du désert, tentent de mordre, de ronger...

---

nier membre encore sain de ce vieux sol gaulois.

Les magistrats du conseil de guerre sont accusés par les uns d'injustice, par les autres d'imbécillité, par ceux-ci d'iniquité, par ceux-là d'inconscience. C'est la suspicion jetée sur de vaillants et loyaux soldats. C'est M. de Rougemont, c'est M. Esterhazy, demain un autre, dont les noms sont jetés tout vifs en pâture à la foule des bandits d'Israël.

LE TRAITRE

Et le gouvernement ne fait rien pour arrêter cette campagne infâme du syndicat Dreyfus ! Les arlequins ministériels se croisent les bras devant ce torrent d'infamies. La vieille fripouille qu'est Scheurer-Kestner reste toujours muette après avoir promis de tout dire, et le pachyderme Billot ne défend même pas l'honneur de l'armée dont il a la garde, honneur outragé dans la personne d'un de ses officiers !...

Ah ! si nous avions encore du sang de nos aïeux dans les veines, s'il nous restait une lueur de leur énergie, une étincelle de leur probité civique, quelle belle charrette nous conduirions un de ces matins à la guillotine de la Révolution !

Le malheureux commandant Esterhazy, dans l'explosion de sa douleur, a laissé échapper le seul mot vrai de la situation. Il s'est écrié :

— Les misérables !... Que me reste-t-il à faire ? Les tuer !

Eh bien oui, les tuer !... Ou sont les juges qui condamneraient les justiciers qui feraient place nette de toutes ces crapules du syndicat Dreyfus, les Monod, les Bernard Lazare et tutti quanti ? Quel tribunal oserait blâmer, devant le peuple enfin attenti, l'honnête homme qui aurait demandé qu'à sa conscience et son bras le soin de châtier comme il le méritait l'infâme dénonciateur, le frère...

Contemporary newspaper account identifies Dreyfus as "Le Traitre."

perspective

The Six Day War—Israel's third full-scale conflict with its Arab neighbors in 19 years —was so named because it began on the morning of June 5, 1967 and lasted until the final cease-fire went into effect on the evening of June 10. Brief as it was, this period marked a major turning point in Israel's history. In six days the Israelis had fought the combined armies of Egypt, Syria, and Jordan, and had won—decisively. Israel's northern, southern, and eastern frontiers were suddenly secure—or so it seemed. And Jerusalem was now a united city, fully in Jewish hands for the first time in 1900 years. Israelis no longer talked of the survival of their state in terms of a question; they had come to view it finally as an irreversible fact.

In the Six Day War of 1967, the Israeli people came of age. It was their third war. The 1948 War of Independence had been harder to win. It had taken place before the arrival of mass immigration, but at a unique moment of grace: during their first war with the Arabs the Israelis had been able to rely on the support of both the United States and the Soviet Union. In the 1956 Suez war they had fought together with England and France. But in 1967 they stood alone and shaped their own future.

The 1967 war was a military triumph; the psychological effect was even greater. They won a great victory, at no small cost to themselves in human life, and in what is often dearer than property—nerves. The war came after a long period of tense waiting. For Israelis it marked the transition from adolescence to maturity.

The war changed not only Israel's position in the Near East but, even more, the Israelis' self-image. As the army of hastily drafted civilians rolled up to the Suez Canal, the men in the tanks and armored trucks knew it was the end of an era.

For most Israelis, the almost century-old debate over the rightness or wrongness of Zionism reduced itself to a purely academic matter. Must there be a Jewish state? If so, where? Or should the Jews remain dispersed among the nations? For all practical purposes, such questions became irrelevant and obsolete. There was now a state. Israel was a nation, resourceful and united, whatever the argument over Zionism. For Israelis it was no longer a discussion of theory but a matter of survival. For Israelis there was no other place to go.

KIND CONQUERORS

As conquerors the Israelis remained civilized. There were few outrages, few cases of pillaging and wanton destruction. The enormous territorial gains of the fighting were unexpected. Most Israelis were conquerors against their will. The military interfered as little as possible in the internal affairs of the occupied territories. In a goodwill gesture rare in the history of countries at war, Israel took a calculated risk and permitted free travel between the occupied west bank of the Jordan River and the adjacent Arab countries. The risk proved worthwhile; calm and prosperity were the benefits. The shocking acts of Arab sabotage or terrorism were not initiated locally but came from abroad.

The war added self-assurance. There was little bragging, and much compassion for the loser. In his victory address, General Yitzhak Rabin, chief of the armed forces during the war, spoke of the fighting soldiers' "incomplete joy." They had seen with their own eyes not only the glories of victory but also the price. After the war, some soldiers told reporters that when they saw the frightened Arab refugees fleeing

Israelis distribute bread to Arab refugees.

their homes—women, children, and old men, thirsty and hungry, dragging only a bundle of clothes behind them—they felt sick. One said, "I could not help thinking of the Jew in the Diaspora."

Some Israelis in years past had dreamed of a binational Arab-Jewish state. This was still a possibility, but only in theory. Jewish supporters of binationalism had never met with cooperation from any Arab party. Now the Israelis were hardened by strife, disillusioned and embittered by the growing awareness of Arab hatred. Few were now prepared to risk a binational state. The Israeli-Arab writer Attalah Mansour, borrowing an Oriental image, described the plight of the Israelis in these words: "Instead of stepping on the snake that threatened them, they swallowed it. Now they have to live with it, or die from it."

related themes

A Different Kind of War   Israel's military victory in the Six Day War was not the beginning of a time of peace, nor even of a period of quiet. In Khartoum in August 1967, an Arab summit conference resulted in three *no*'s: *no* recognition, *no* negotiation, *no* peace. Armed with new Soviet weaponry, Egypt launched a war of attrition against Israel, which lasted from November 1968 until August 1970. The war of attrition was a different kind of conflict. It was limited to massive artillery bombardments of Israeli positions across the Suez Canal, and was designed to wear down Israel's will to keep the territories acquired in the Six Day War (which Israel planned to use in bargaining for peace). The war of attrition did not succeed, but before the U.S.-negotiated cease-fire went into effect, more than 600 Israeli soldiers had lost their lives—nearly as many as were killed during the Six Day War.

An Unfounded Lie   One of the most bizarre aspects of the Six Day War was the fact that it was set into motion by a lie. The sequence of events leading up to the war was logical enough—the convergence of 90,000 Egyptian soldiers and 900 tanks on Israel's southern border; the removal, at Egypt's request, of the United Nations Emergency Force, which had patrolled the Egyptian-Israeli border for more than ten years; Egypt's closing of the Straits of Tiran to all ships bound for Israel; the conclusion of a war pact against Israel by the Arab states, followed by the concentration of Jordanian, Syrian, and Iraqi troops along Israel's borders; the inability of the UN to persuade the Arabs to change course. But the reason for these Arab moves, a Soviet intelligence report that Israel had massed troops along the Syrian border and was preparing to attack, was totally mistaken. UN observers agreed that no such concentration existed, but their testimony was ignored by the Arab leaders. Prime Minister Levi Eshkol even invited the Soviet ambassador to Israel to travel to the Syrian border to see for himself; the invitation was refused. And so, after three weeks of mounting tension, the Middle East was again at war.

issues and values

The Human Aspects of War " . . . The terrible price our enemies paid touched the hearts of many of our men," said Yitzḥak Rabin in his victory speech. The Arab soldiers had to be defeated at all costs; yet they were people as well, whose suffering stirred the Israelis. The Palestinian refugees are also a people who have suffered greatly; they have paid perhaps the greatest price for Israel's creation. Ironically, they are sometimes called "the Jews of the Middle East"—homeless, dispersed, in a state of continuous exile. Do you feel that Israel has a moral responsibility to help the Palestinians? What do you think should be done? Does the plight of the refugees trouble or embarrass you in any way?

Is It Good for Israel? The Arab-Israeli conflict confronts Jews in the United States with a troubling question: Should an American Jew vote for a political candidate just because that candidate supports the State of Israel? What if the candidate stands opposed to a number of things the voter believes in but happens to be a good friend of Israel? Or what if the opposing candidate shares the voter's social and political philosophy but is, at best, lukewarm to the Jewish state and supports policies that might weaken Israel's defense position? What should the American Jewish voter do? What would you do? Where does the consideration of "Is it good for Israel? (or for the Jews in general?)" stand on your scale of political priorities?

Fifty years after their arrival in the land of Israel, the heroes and heroines of the First Aliyah pose for a reunion photograph.

ZIONISM & THE FIRST ALIYAH 1881-1905

perspective

The Pale of Settlement in the latter half of the nineteenth century was a world of poverty, political corruption, and social unrest; there was a smell of revolution in the air. Under Czar Alexander II, the Russian Jews had hoped for reforms and better times, but when the czar was assassinated in 1881, the Jews were singled out as special victims both by the masses and by those in power.

A traveler to European Russia in the 1870's saw a gray, desperately backward, sorely depressing, and monotonous land. Its most outstanding features were poverty, a primitive life-style, and a low level of social welfare. While the fortunate few lived sheltered lives in fabulous homes, most Russians nearly starved in pitifully squalid homes.

There were few cities. The countryside was teeming with wretchedly poor, illiterate peasants who lived under the crushing double yoke of superstitious religion and autocratic government. The czarist regime was barbaric and untrustworthy. The government was one of the most corrupt in Europe.

JEWS IN RUSSIA

Here, against this dreary, bleak background, 7 million Jews eked out a miserable existence. They were wedged in as aliens between Poles and Lithuanians, White Russians and Little Russians (as the Ukrainians were called), Letts, Rumanians, Magyars, Germans, Slovaks, and Carpathians, a multitude of diverse people whose separate backgrounds, beliefs, and hopes were, as a rule, mutually and savagely hostile. But on one subject they all agreed. They hated and suspected the Jews and subjected them to violence and oppression.

The Jews were not newcomers to the region. Some of their ancestors had lived in those areas since Roman times, others since the seventh century. But the majority were descendants of Jews who had wandered

ZIONISM AND
THE FIRST
ALIYAH
1881-1905

east from the twelfth century on, in order to escape the slaughter and pillage of the Rhine and Danube valleys during the Crusades.

They were an extremely proud and stubborn people. With a single gesture—conversion—they might have saved themselves from banishment and death. But they chose to move on, as Jews. They had their own languages and folkways, a "tradition on wheels" (as Isaiah Berlin said) which they had preserved almost intact and would continue to preserve through the centuries. Over the generations they became a middle class of tradesmen, artisans, and stewards. Despite their wretched poverty, they constituted a major civilizing force in an area still largely on the fringes of European culture.

THE PALE OF SETTLEMENT

Deliberate government anti-Semitism required most Russian Jews to live within a clearly defined area, known as the Pale of Settlement. The area originally comprised much of northwestern Russia, but it was subsequently made smaller, despite the growing Jewish population. At first, Jews were simply forbidden to live outside the Pale. Later the main cities within the Pale were also declared out of bounds. Here, and in the adjacent territories of Austrian Galicia and Rumania, lived the great Jewish population of Eastern Europe; it has since disappeared through emigration, assimilation, or the Nazi death camps of Treblinka, Auschwitz, and Sobibor. But in 1897, Russian Jewry still numbered more than 7 million people.

Inside this Pale of Settlement the Jews lived in tight clusters containing anywhere from a few hundred to a few thousand souls, a people within peoples, clinging tenaciously to their own traditions, their own Yiddish language, their own diet, even their own dress.

Though touched by the winds of change, as were all who lived in Eastern Europe at that time, the Jews of the Pale lived the traditional, orthodox, closely knit life of their forebears. Life revolved around the family, synagogue, house of study, small workshop, weekly market day, poorhouse, ritual bath, old-age home, communal burial society, and cemetery.

LIFE IN THE SHTETL

The stronghold of Russian Jewry was the *shtetl*, or small town. The inhabitants dwelt not in Russia but in their dreams; or as the historian of the *shtetl*, Maurice Samuel, has written, they lived "in the holy land," either in the distant past or in the messianic future.

Their festivals were tied to Israel's climate and the ancient Hebrew calendar. Though physically in the middle of Russia or Poland, in their hearts they were residents of an imaginary Jerusalem. Daily they repeated the words of Maimonides: "I believe with all my heart in the coming of the Messiah; and even though he delays, nevertheless I expect him every day."

In the last half of the nineteenth century, however, the *shtetl* and its culture were rapidly decaying. For Jews and Gentiles alike, the still medieval world of Eastern Europe was coming to an end. Also, beginning in the 1880's, a series of government-inspired pogroms (in which local peasants were incited to attack a Jewish community), began to take its toll. The czar's closest adviser, Pobedonostsev, who sponsored these pogroms, was a fanatical anti-Semite and put forward his own solution to the Jewish problem. "One-third emigration, one-third conversion, one-third death."

THE SAVAGE YEARS: 1881–1903

Czarist repression and discrimination created tremendous economic problems for Jews of the Pale. In midcentury, the average Jew had been somewhat better off financially than the average Russian peasant; by 1887 a government commission of inquiry stated that "90 percent of the Jews are of such poverty and destitution as is otherwise impossible to see in Russia." Almost 40 percent of Russian Jews were living on charity.

Following a particularly savage outburst of persecution, tolerated by the government, a committee of privileged Jews visited the czar. They hoped for an imperial statement deploring the riots. The czar replied that the riots were the fault of the Jews themselves, since they insisted on continuing to "exploit the Russians."

When the pogroms which swept Russia between 1881 and 1903 were not government-inspired, they were government-ignored. Because army and police either stood idly by or showed up too late, hundreds were killed, maimed, raped, robbed, or made homeless. The wave of horror swept from Warsaw to Odessa, through hundreds of villages and small towns, with a violence not seen since the Crusades.

related themes

Creative Responses The history of European Jewry sometimes seems only a history of persecution after persecution. But the Jewish people responded to these persecutions in positive and creative ways. The last two centuries included the following developments: the rise of the Hassidic movement; the *Haskalah* (the Jewish Enlightenment); the development of Yiddish literature; the rebirth of Hebrew as a living language and the beginnings of modern Hebrew literature; Reform Judaism; the Jewish *Bund* (Socialist) Movement; the establishment of a strong American Jewish community; modern Zionism; the kibbutz; and, finally, the creation of the State of Israel.

"Der Haim" For many years after they arrived in the United States, Eastern European Jews referred to their native towns and villages as *der haim* (Yiddish for "the home"). It wasn't that they longed to go back—they had had their fill of anti-Semitic officials and of drunken peasants going out to "break a few Jewish heads." The attachment of these immigrants to the "old country" stemmed from memories of a way of life that they deeply cherished and which, they feared, could not be recreated in *der goldene medine* ("the golden land"—the United States). In his story "The Little Shoemakers," the Yiddish writer Isaac Bashevis Singer portrays the yearning of Eastern European Jews for permanent roots, for der haim. His main character is Abba Shuster, a simple shoemaker whose life revolved around his house, his shop, his synagogue, and above all, the town of Frampol where his family had lived for generations. "It seemed to him that his little town was the navel of the universe, and that his own house stood at the very center. He often thought that when the Messiah came to lead the Jews to the Land of Israel, he, Abba, would stay behind in Frampol in his own house, on his own hill. Only on the Sabbath and on holy days would he step on a cloud and let himself be flown to Jerusalem."

Typical shtetl marketplace in the Pale of Settlement.

37

issues and values

The Concept of Kehillah   Jewish life in the shtetl (the small Eastern European Jewish community) has often been called an "island of culture." This expresses the idea of *kehillah*—a close-knit and actively caring community—which has always been of major importance in Jewish tradition. For instance, Jews are instructed to pray in groups of ten or more (the *minyan*), and on Yom Kippur we ask forgiveness as a collective unit (in prayers such as *Al Het Shehatanu*—"for the sins that *we* have committed"). Jewish life is most often described in communal terms, whether on the level of a small town or an entire country. And Israel's unique kibbutz society ("kibbutz" literally means "a gathering together") is an intensive community, held together by shared beliefs, a common purpose, and a sense of commitment to one another. Do you feel part of a Jewish kehillah? Does it add anything to your life? What do you think that such a community should be doing?

The Meaning of Jewish Identity   If a time machine were to transport a nineteenth-century Eastern European Jew to our American Jewish community today, our visitor might wrinkle his brow and exclaim: "All this talk about the meaning of Jewish identity. I just don't understand. Where I come from we don't discuss it, we live it. Everything that we do is Jewish. It's that simple." He would have a point. In the shtetl, Jewish identity was defined by looks, language, culture, cookery, lifestyle, daily rituals, and physical separation from the non-Jewish community. Today, few if any of these elements remain for most of us. And so we find ourselves constantly searching for new means of self-definition and affirmation as Jews. What does Jewish identity mean to you? What is there about the way you live, the things that you do and think about, that is especially Jewish? How would you go about building a solid Jewish identity for your children?

ZIONISM AND
THE FIRST
ALIYAH
1881-1905

perspective

The situation of Russian Jewry was desperate as the nineteenth century came to a close. Some Jews set about the task of reforming Eastern European societies by joining radical political groups seeking social revolution. Others emigrated to the West—by far the majority of them to America—hoping to transplant themselves into cultures that would be more open and humane. But a small percentage of Jews turned to Zionism. As long as the Jewish people remained a dispersed minority, the Zionists claimed, there would be a "Jewish problem." They held four beliefs: (1) that anti-Semitism was, in Pinsker's words, "an incurable disease"; (2) that the Diaspora Jew would always be a stranger in his chosen country; (3) that the Jewish people needed an independent political homeland; (4) that because of tradition and heritage, this homeland should be in the land of Israel.

This, then, was Eastern Europe at the turn of the century. Lenin called Russia the great "prison of nations." The Jews, like others, were trying to break out. To czarist authorities, freedom was a disease that could lead the people only to misfortune. To liberals, freedom meant social justice and civil rights. To the Jews it was first and foremost a chance to escape discrimination, looting, rape, arson, and murder.

The more the Jews of Russia were oppressed, the more they clung to their distinct ways; the more they were thrown together into areas of forced residence of ever-diminishing size, the more they sought refuge in the narrow confines of orthodox religion, in messianic dreams, or in radical avenues of escape.

AVENUES OF ESCAPE

Basically, there were three such avenues. By far the most popular was emigration to the West. America was an obvious choice. New York was the *Goldene Land,* the "promised city," a new Jerusalem beyond the seas. Within less than 40 years, almost one-third of all Eastern European Jews went forth in search of a new life in Western Europe and in the Americas.

Politics was a second avenue of escape. Its ultimate end was revolution. Radical politics would have come naturally to many Eastern European Jews even if, as Jews, they had not been singled out for persecution. As outsiders they had fewer prejudices and emotional restraints, more enthusiasm for daring concepts of change. The prophetic dream of justice on earth was an integral part of their religious heritage and led to political radicalism for many young people. Rebel and rabbi were more closely related to one another than they seemed at the time.

Jewish nationalism was the third avenue of escape. It was closely related to social revolution. Zionism became intertwined with Russian radicalism. A large part of the Jewish national revival actually occurred within the inner circle of the Russian revolutionary parties, particularly within the Bund of Jewish Workers. The Bund was a labor movement of Yiddish-speaking Jews affiliated with Lenin's Russian Social Democratic Workers' Party. The men and women of the Bund strongly affirmed Jewish nationhood; they favored a form of cultural and, to some degree, political autonomy for Jews within a socialist Russia.

The point of division between the Bundists and the Zionists was geographical. The Bund wanted national control within Russia. Plekhanov, the Revolutionary Social Democratic Party philosopher, called them "Zionists afraid of a sea voyage." The Zionists, on the other hand, were committed to a solution beyond the borders of Russia. They shared with the Bundists, socialists, and anarchists a deep faith in social revolution. But the Zionists held that this would be meaningful for Jews only in Palestine. There, within a socialist framework, all of Jewry's social and national problems would be solved.

By temperament, motivation, or upbringing, the young socialist Zionists who met in secret clubs throughout Russia were hardly distinguishable from other radicals. Jewish families were often split by socialists of the "pure" (Bund) and the "Zionist" variety. The same people often moved back and forth from one group to another, despite the bitter antagonism between them. "Zionist" and "international" socialists debated each other ferociously, especially at universities outside Russia. At one such meeting, the speaker for the "internationalists" was Parvus-Helphand, a Russian Jew who, to emphasize how international the world had become, pointed to his jacket and exclaimed: "The wool in this jacket comes from Angoran sheep; it was spun in England and woven in Lodz. The buttons come from Germany, the thread from Austria!" As he spoke, Parvus-Helphand raised his arm and the seam of his sleeve suddenly burst. A Zionist student immediately jumped up: "And the tear on your sleeve comes from the pogrom of Kishinev!"

THE "LOVERS OF ZION"

In 1882 a group of young men, mostly students, gathered in Kharkov and formed the "Lovers of Zion," or Bilu, a Hebrew acronym taken from the phrase "House of Jacob, come and let us go." It was the beginning of an organization that was to be instrumental in launching the first wave of emigrants to Palestine.

Imagine, then, small groups of passionate young Jews, living uncomfortably under an alien regime which not only did little to prevent riots but often actively encouraged them; young men and women in their late teens and early 20's, embittered by their exclusion from the universities and high schools, strongly influenced by the radical fervor of their immediate intellectual environment.

Women immigrants learning to till the soil.

Many of these young people were later destined to take a leading role in Israeli affairs. Several cabinet ministers in the early years of Israel's existence, as well as the country's first three presidents—Chaim Weizmann, Yitzḥak Ben-Zvi, and Zalman Shazar—began their political careers in a Zionist club in Russia or Galicia at the turn of the century.

This was the political school which educated them; its blind spots and ideals, its hopes and dreams, its passions and prejudices were to pursue them throughout their lives. Some of its qualities became the heritage of the first generation of native-born Israelis.

In October 1905 the first, ill-fated Russian revolution began. Its failure, and the persecutions of Russian Jewry which followed it, helped to launch a major wave of migration to Eretz Israel. It came to be known as the *Second Aliyah,* and would be the most decisive force in the development of the Jewish presence in Palestine.

related themes

Central Values   In 1878, about three years before the young people of the First Aliyah set out for the Holy Land, the American social thinker, Henry George; summed up what he felt to be the central value of Jewish tradition:

> The Hebrew commonwealth was based upon the individual—a commonwealth whose ideal it was that every man should sit under his own vine and fig-tree, with none to vex him or make him afraid; a commonwealth in which none should be condemned to ceaseless toil; in which for even the beast of burden there should be rest. It is not the protection of property, but the protection of humanity, that is the aim of the Mosaic code. Its Sabbath day and Sabbath year secure, even to the lowliest, rest and leisure. With the blast of the jubilee trumpets the slave goes free, a redivision of the land secures again to the poorest his fair share in the bounty of the common Creator. The reaper must leave something for the gleaner; even the ox cannot be muzzled as he treadeth out the corn. Everywhere, in everything, the dominant idea is that of our homely phrase—"Live and let live."

Ugly Underside   Many young Jews saw Zionism as too narrow, too parochial, too Jewish because it did not consider the needs of all mankind. This view may have grown out of the Jewish "messianic dream of justice on earth," but there was an ugly underside to this call for universalism. Those who preached and believed in this dream often were looking for a particularly attractive excuse to escape Judaism by becoming a part of something larger, a universal cause. When this chosen cause happened to be on a collision course with Jewishness, the result may well have fitted the description offered by the Zionist thinker Berl Katznelson, who spoke of "those Jews who . . . even distributed proclamations calling for pogroms in the name of the revolution. . . ." Or, for a more modern example, there are Jewish young people today who call for the dismantling of the State of Israel in the name of the Palestinian Arabs.

issues and values

The Price of Success Jewish immigrants to the United States used to say that in America a Jew could be safe and free; but in the old country, for all its cruelties, a Jew could more easily remain a Jew. To many Jews, the price of success in this country seems to have been the weakening of one's ties to Jewish tradition. Sometimes the reasons are economic. In his novel *Journey to the Dawn*, Charles Angoff tells of the agonizing decision of one of his main characters to work on the Sabbath. It was a shattering move, made out of economic necessity, but it signified the first of many steps away from the old life.

In *The Americanization of Shadrach Cohen*, Bruno Lessing reveals a different motivation: the desire to be a "real" American. Shadrach's sons had come to America five years before he did, and when Shadrach arrived they all looked at each other in dismay. "Come father," they said, "let us go to a barber who will trim your head and make you look more like an American." Later, after they had eaten, Shadrach "donned his praying cap and began to recite the grace after meals. . . . When it came to the response Shadrach looked inquiringly at his sons. It was Abel who explained the matter: 'We have grown out of, that is, done away with, sort of fallen into the habit, of leaving out the prayer at meals. It's not quite American!'"

Do you think there are areas of conflict between being an American and being a Jew? Are there also areas of conflict between being an Israeli and being a Jew?

The Role of Jewish Youth The Lovers of Zion movement was made up primarily of young students and marked the crucial role which youth was to play in the Zionist revolution. The first three waves of immigration (Aliyot) to Palestine were made up principally of young people barely out of their teens. They were the dreamers and the builders. Young people have often been at the center of revolution and change in society. They sometimes feel that they can change the world, either single-handedly or through collective action. And every once in a while, they do—for better or worse. Why do you think young people are more open to change? Are there specific changes in society that you would like to make? What would you be willing to sacrifice to see these changes made? Home? Family? Money? Pleasure? Friendships?

perspective

The pogroms convinced many Jewish intellectuals that anti-Semitism was an enduring reality. It could not be wished away, reasoned away, or even legislated away. Many came to the realization that, try as they might, Jews would never win full acceptance in a Gentile society—Jews would always be in danger. Pinsker, Lilienblum, and Bialik, some of the finest minds of their generation, turned their efforts to getting across a new message to their people: the real alternative for the Jews was a homeland of their own in Palestine.

MOSES LEIB LILIENBLUM

During the Odessa pogrom of 1881, Moses Leib Lilienblum, a former teacher at an orthodox religious seminary, hid from the rioters in the cellar of his barred house. A few years earlier he had turned his back on orthodox religion; now, at the age of 37, he was attending a Russian school in order to acquire a general, secular education.

"I am glad I have suffered," he wrote in his diary on May 7, one day after the riots. He described what happened as the rioters approached his house:

> The women shrieked and wailed, hugging their children to their breasts, and did not know where to turn. The men stood by dumbfounded. . . . At least once in my life I have had the opportunity to feel what my ancestors felt every day of their lives. Their lives were one long terror, why should I experience nothing of that fright? . . . I am their son, their suffering is dear to me and I am exalted by their glory.

It was not the first pogrom Lilienblum had heard of, but it was the first he had personally witnessed. What shocked him in particular was the fact that "cultured" Russians, university students, and high school

ZIONISM AND
THE FIRST
ALIYAH
1881-1905

boys participated in the bloody riots. The experience changed his entire outlook and set him firmly on the course of Jewish nationalism. He quit his studies at the Russian school. "It was not a lack of high culture that was the cause of our tragedy," he wrote, "for aliens we are and aliens we shall remain, even if we become full to the brim with [Russian and secular] culture."

Lilienblum became the first prominent thinker among the Jewish nationalists in Russia. He inspired the first pioneers who left Russia in 1882 to settle in Palestine. "Why should we be aliens in foreign lands," he wrote, "when the land of our forefathers is not yet forgotten on the face of the earth, is still desolate and capable . . . of receiving our people. We must purchase much land and innumerable estates and slowly settle them."

LEO PINSKER

Leo Pinsker was a distinguished physician in Odessa. In 1881 he was already 60 years of age. His youth had coincided with the years of repression under Czar Nicholas I (1825–1855). But Pinsker's father had somehow managed to escape the restrictions of ghetto life. Pinsker was one of the lucky few who attended a Russian high school and then received a medical degree from the University of Moscow. Moreover, he had been decorated by the czar for his loyal service in the Crimean War. Most of his adult life he had believed that Russia would gradually become a constitutional monarchy with social progress and equality for all.

For Pinsker, as for Lilienblum, the pogroms of 1881 were a turning point. He too was horrified by the participation in the riots of "cultured" elements and left-wing intellectuals, and by the role played by leading newspapers in whipping up the mob. Deeply shocked, Pinsker decided that Jews, even if they wanted to assimilate, would never be allowed to. Anti-Semitism, he concluded, was an incurable disease, its main cause the homelessness of the modern Jew. Jews must therefore once more become a nation and possess their own territory. He did not much care where that territory was. Palestine was one possibility, but not the only one.

Soon after, Pinsker wrote a pamphlet entitled *Auto-Emancipation— An Appeal to His People by a Russian Jew*. He took the pamphlet with him on a tour through Western Europe, where he tried to impress his ideas on those he met. Not everybody was impressed. A typical view was that of Rabbi Adolf Jellinek, the chief rabbi of Vienna. Jellinek advised Pinsker that he must be in a state of shock and should see a

Leo Pinsker: 1821–1891.   Moses Leib Lilienblum: 1843–1910.

doctor. Pinsker's plan was a "joke," said the rabbi. It could not be carried out. More realistic ways must be found to alleviate Jewish suffering.

PINSKER AND THE LOVERS OF ZION

Pinsker's pamphlet appeared in 1882. The Lovers of Zion held their first national convention in 1884, in the small town of Katowitz across the German border, out of the reach of the Russian police. The Lovers of Zion were enthusiastic Pinskerites. And Pinsker, who attended the meeting, was slowly converted by them to the idea that the separate territory for Jews could not be just anywhere, but had to be in Palestine, since this was the "instinctive" wish of the people.

During this period, too, a new kind of Zionist literature developed, reflecting the nationalist impulse. In this sense, Zionism developed in much the same way as modern nationalism in Europe. In Ireland, Italy, Germany, Poland, and Greece, national liberators always stood, as it were, on the shoulders of poets. Hebrew poets served a similar role. The new Hebrew literature not only summarized people's feelings but was itself an active agent of change.

CHAIM NACHMAN BIALIK

Chaim Nachman Bialik was the greatest of the new Hebrew writers.

ZIONISM AND
THE FIRST
ALIYAH
1881-1905

46

None before Bialik had expressed the Jewish will to live in words and rhymes of such beauty and poetic force; he is rightly known today as *the* national poet of Israel. Within the Pale of Settlement, Bialik's poems passed from hand to hand, as printed copies were scarce. Some poems were duplicated by hectograph, a system still used in Russia 60 years later for the distribution of underground literature. Bialik's *Poems of Wrath*, written immediately after the Kishinev pogrom of 1903, left a tremendous impression upon young Jews. "If there be any justice, let it shine now!" Bialik exhorted the young in one of his most celebrated poems, "City of Slaughter."

Bialik and his fellow poets of the Hebrew literary revival wrote passionate verse glorifying the land of Israel. The poems were filled with longing for the ancient homeland. The poets had never seen Palestine nor, in all probability, any reliable pictures. And yet, they clearly envisioned a land of glorious rivers and mountains, flowers and birds, and they poured this image into their poetry. Under the iron sky of the north they sang of sunny Galilee; in the vast flatlands of the Ukraine they dreamed of the craggy mountains of Judea.

It has been said that young Russians at the turn of the century were extremely sensitive to literary influences; young people would suddenly change their entire way of life after reading a single poem or pamphlet. "Two books set me on my present course," a Zionist pioneer wrote in his diary in 1907, "the Communist Manifesto, and a slim volume of poems by Chaim Nachman Bialik. I shall never forget the first day I read Bialik's 'Rise, wanderer in the desert, get out of the wilderness. The road is still long, the battle still great!' I knew then and there what I had to do."

related themes

The Will to Live   The Zionist idea is an expression of the Jewish will to live—as a people, as a nation, as part of a culture and tradition. This will to live is one of Judaism's cherished values. A classic Jewish toast is *L'Hayyim*, which means "To Life!" The phrase *Pikuah Nefesh*, which means "saving a life," remains the highest obligation in Jewish law: almost any law may be broken in order to save the life of a human being. When the Yom Kippur War broke out, rabbis in Israel instructed the young men in the synagogues to go home and eat before reporting to their units. What applies to the individual is true of the nation as well. It is common to hear the expression *Am Yisrael Hai*, "The People of Israel Lives."

The expression of this Jewish will to live and commitment to the future has come in many forms throughout the ages. God promised Abraham that a great and mighty nation would be born of Abraham's children. One Talmudic legend tells of a rabbi who saw an old man planting a date tree which would take many years to bear its first edible fruit. "Why do you plant this tree?" the rabbi asked. "Surely you do not expect to live long enough to eat its fruit?" The old man replied, "My ancestors planted trees for me that I might enjoy both shade and fruit. I am doing the same for those who will come after me."

Yiddish Humor   While Bialik's poetry spoke of suffering and of longing for a homeland, Yiddish humor responded to the oppressiveness of the ghetto in a different way. It projected no visions of hope or rebirth, but it made daily life more bearable. The basic ingredients of shtetl humor were poverty, a sense of uncertainty, a lack of pretense, and a certain intimacy with trouble. People did not really laugh at a shtetl joke, they answered it with a sad, knowing smile. Here are a few samples of shtetl humor:

A man should live, if only to satisfy his own curiosity.

"For dust thou art and unto dust thou shalt return"—betwixt and between, a drink comes in handy.

The *shlemiel* lands on his back and bruises his nose.

God loves the poor, but He helps the rich.

Shrouds are made without pockets.

One father supports ten children, but ten children do not support one father.

So many Hamans, but one Purim.

issues and values

The Jew As Alien   Lilienblum's remark that "aliens we are and aliens we shall remain" raises a question which has often been asked here in the United States. Is the United States different? Is it the one place in the world, outside of Israel, where the Jew is truly not an alien? Those who say that the United States is different point to its democratic institutions, its variety of social and economic possibilities, and above all, to the fact that it is a nation of immigrants in which Jews are but one of many minority groups. Those who say "no" point out that Jews remain a minority of 6 million among a Christian majority of more than 200 million; that anti-Semitism has more than once appeared in American life; and that Jews themselves still feel insecure and apart. On which side of the question do you place yourself? Do you feel in any way an alien in America?

The Responsibility of Jewish Writers   As Israel's national poet, Bialik (and his writings) came to be an inspirational source for many Jews. But here in the United States, a number of Jewish writers have portrayed the Jew in ways which have often been criticized for their negative effect. For example, in his novel *What Makes Sammy Run?*, Budd Schulberg tells of a ruthless, greedy Jew named Sammy Glick who steps over everyone in his path to achieve success in Hollywood. In a short story, "Defender of the Faith," Philip Roth deals with a young Jewish wheeler-dealer who has been inducted into the army during the last year of World War II. The wheeler-dealer tries to play on the sympathy of his Jewish sergeant to wheedle special favors, and ultimately to get his name scratched from the list of those to be sent to combat overseas. More recently, certain films have been bitterly criticized for portraying Jewish pushiness and vulgarity. On the one hand, one could argue that artists should be permitted to portray life as they see it without apologies; that is what freedom of expression is all about. The argument against this kind of portrayal is that it draws a misleading stereotype of Jews in general, contributes to prejudice, and weakens the position of the Jew in the community at large. On which side of the argument do you stand? Why?

perspective

Palestine in the early 1880's was a land of stagnation and decay. Jaffa, its major port of entry, teemed with sickness, poverty, and official corruption. Newcomers, especially the first Zionist pioneers, were greeted with suspicion and hostility by the small Jewish community already living in the land. These settled Jews were all ultra-orthodox. They looked upon the newcomers as nonbelievers, trying to tamper with God's judgment and design. After all, they said, God would decide when and how the Jewish people would be allowed to return to their ancient homeland. The young Zionists soon realized that it was not vision and dreams which would be required of them in their newly chosen home, but endurance—a willingness to bear the day-by-day drudgery and the constant dangers in order to achieve their distant goal.

THE LAND OF PALESTINE—A FIRST DESCRIPTION

Jaffa, as the first Jewish colonists saw it in the 1880's, was a small cluster of houses, built of mud and porous sandstone, perched unevenly on low mounds of ruins, the accumulated debris of innumerable previous civilizations. The site is one of the oldest continuously inhabited places in the world.

Today Jaffa is little more than a run-down section of Tel Aviv. But in the 1880's it was a far more important place. It was the main seaport and trade center of Palestine, the pilgrim's gate to Jerusalem.

The harbor and its facilities were very primitive. Steamers moored at some distance from the shore; passengers and cargoes were ferried to shore by rowboat between dark jutting rocks (believed to be the spot where Andromeda of Greek mythology was chained and rescued from the dragon by Perseus). With a population of about 8000 Arabs and 2000 Jews, Jaffa was the largest city along the entire Mediterranean coastline between Beirut in Lebanon and Port Said in Egypt.

Many early pioneers, as they disembarked at Jaffa, were shocked at

ZIONISM AND
THE FIRST
ALIYAH
1881-1905

50

the Oriental confusion, the filthy bazaars, the thoroughly corrupt Turkish government, the swarms of unhealthy children, by the money changers, peddlers, beggars, and lepers, and by the wild-looking porters who haggled with pilgrims and tourists over the price of a mule ride up the hills to Jerusalem. "The stench drove me sick," a colonist arriving in 1882 remarked. When Ben-Gurion landed at Jaffa 24 years later, his reaction was similar: "I left Jaffa as soon as I could, a few hours after I arrived. This was not my idea of a new life. It was worse than the Plonsk I had come from."

A few foreign settlements, mostly founded by Christian pilgrims, dotted the landscape around Jaffa. Beyond this, "civilization," as the early colonists understood the word, was largely nonexistent. Here was the swampy coastal plain, a silent, mournful expanse, ravaged by centuries of warfare, piracy, and neglect, and bearing the pockmarks of a tragic history. This was the ancient land of the Philistines. Its freshwater rivers and ancient waterways had turned into large stagnant swamps infested by malaria mosquitoes. The sandy soil was overgrown with weeds; its ancient towns, which in antiquity had held over a million inhabitants, lay in ruins, buried under sand dunes.

In the hills farther east, the scene was much more inviting. There were almond and olive trees, shepherds with flocks of sheep, and small Muslim villages perched on stony hilltops and bearing famous biblical names. The local way of life, food, dress, and daily implements—from sickle to wooden plow and threshing sledge—hardly seemed to have changed since the days of the Bible.

Here was the heart of the Holy Land. Here the Canaanites had offered human sacrifice to their god Moloch; here Joshua had called upon the sun to stand still in the heavens in order to lengthen the day of battle. Here Deborah sang her exultant song of victory, and the Jewish kings, David and Solomon, built the city of Jerusalem and its Temple; here the prophet Amos, "who was among the herdsmen of Tekoa," proclaimed his message of universal peace and justice. Here Hillel and Akiva laid the foundations of the Talmud. Here Jesus was crucified; here the Romans massacred the Jews, the Persians massacred the Byzantines, the Crusaders massacred the Saracens, the Turks massacred the Arabs. Less than a century earlier, Napoleon had fought and lost to the Turks, who now, in the late 1800's, maintained a loose control over the country.

THE PEOPLE OF PALESTINE

When the first new settlers from Russia and Rumania, the Lovers of

Zion, began to arrive in 1881, a small Jewish community was already there. The Jewish community of Palestine—even after its defeat by Rome—had never ceased to exist. Jews had always lived in Palestine.

Most lived in the "four holy cities": Hebron, Safed, Tiberias, and Jerusalem. They were partly supported by charities, partly engaged in small business and in a few crafts, such as printing, weaving, and dyeing, which seem to have been almost Jewish monopolies. In the middle of the nineteenth century they became the target of frantic but fruitless efforts by missionaries to convert them to Christianity.

Living in small, closed communities, fanatically orthodox, the old Jewish community was suspicious of all change. Above all the old community was suspicious of political Zionism, which it regarded as a sinful attempt to force the hand of God, who had promised to redeem His people in their land. A remnant of this community survives to this day

Through all the years of exile Jews always lived in Safed, a center of Jewish study and mysticism.

in the Meah Shearim quarter of Jerusalem and is called *Neturei Karta* ("Guardians of the City").

Just as the old community rejected the pioneers and their secularism, they in turn were rejected by the newcomers. To the newcomers they represented the fossilization of Judaism and the passive acceptance of social injustice.

Yet a group of orthodox Jews had also broken away from the confines of their life in Jerusalem to try their hand at farming. They purchased a stretch of swampy land in the coastal plain close to the malaria-infested Yarkon River, 8 miles from the Mediterranean coast. The settlers were warned by a Greek doctor in Jaffa against settling in the swamp. "Over this entire blue and silent expanse of land I did not see a single flying bird," wrote the doctor; " . . . the place must be so bad and rotten that even birds of prey, always obeying the inner instinct, take care not to approach the spot." The settlers ignored this warning. In 1879 they named their settlement Petaḥ Tikvah (literally, "Gate of Hope," from Hosea 2:17). It was the first modern Jewish settlement. Today it is a city of more than 100,000 inhabitants and a part of metropolitan Tel Aviv.

But when Salman David Levontin, the first of the new Lovers of Zion from Russia, landed at Jaffa only three years later, in March 1882, Petaḥ Tikvah lay abandoned; Turkish officialdom (which had been deeply suspicious of this enterprise) and recurrent attacks of malaria combined to make life so miserable that the settlers, who were not used to farming, quickly gave up.

related themes

Study, Prayer, and Ḥalukah When the first Zionist colonists landed in Palestine in 1882, they found a Jewish community of 24,000 people already living there. A few Jews (no more than 500) were working in agriculture; others worked as clerks, craftsmen, and shopkeepers. But the vast majority of the Jewish men spent their entire lives in study and prayer. Over the course of the seventeenth, eighteenth, and nineteenth centuries, most Palestinian Jews were supported by the contributions of their fellow Jews from abroad. This practice was known as *Ḥalukah* (from the Hebrew word for "distribution" or "sharing"). Ḥalukah was, in turn, the work of *shliḥim* ("messengers") sent from Palestine to Jewish communities the world over. The shliḥim were persistent and energetic, leaving behind them small tin collection boxes, called *pushkas*, into which families and communities could place their donations for *Eretz HaKedoshah*. Before long, the collection box had become a permanent fixture in traditional Jewish homes.

The Bilu Manifesto   The first Biluim arrived in Palestine 15 years before the First World Zionist Congress met. Few Jews around the world were aware of what they were doing; even fewer knew why they were doing it. But the Biluim believed that their dream was crucial for the Jewish people as a whole. So at the beginning of their Aliyah, they issued a manifesto to explain their action to the Jewish people and to the world at large.

> We want a home in our country. It was given to us by the mercy of God. It is ours as registered in the archives of history. . . . We hope that the interests of our glorious nation will arouse our national spirit . . . and that everyone, rich and poor, will give his best labors. . . . We beg the Sultan of Turkey [to create a state in Palestine], and if it be impossible . . . [we hope] to possess it as a state within a larger state. . . .

The Biluim believed that eventually the whole Jewish people would believe in their cause. They understood that their dreams would have to be founded on practical politics; that is why they appealed to the Turkish Sultan. Finally, they were moved by a sense of desperation at the plight of the Jewish people. They concluded, "Hear, O Israel, the Lord our God, the Lord is One . . . and our Land of Zion is our only hope."

issues and values

Controlling the Future   The Biluim and most Orthodox Jews were bitterly divided over the issue of who should control the future of the Jewish people—man or God. The orthodox insisted that the Jewish people should sit still and patiently wait for the coming of the Messiah, who would gather them up from the corners of the world and bring them to Israel. The Zionists were, in Bialik's words, "obeying the call of their heart, streaming from the four corners of the earth to this land for the purpose of redeeming it from desolation and ruin . . . prepared to pour all their aspirations and longings into the bosom of this wasteland in order to revive it . . . plowing rocks, draining swamps, and building roads amid singing and rejoicing. . . ." In a sense, this question can be applied to all Jewish life in the Diaspora. Is your life shaped largely by forces beyond your control, or are there steps that you can take which will change your future?

A People of the Book   In his essay "The Law of the Heart," Aḥad Ha'am sharply criticizes the Jewish people for being so preoccupied with the *do's* and *don't's* of ritual observance that they lose sight of the Law's deeper meaning:

> But "a people of the book" . . . is a slave to the book. It has surrendered its whole soul to the written word. The book ceases to be what it should be, a source of ever new inspiration and moral strength; on the contrary, its function in life is to weaken and finally to crush all spontaneity of action and emotion, till men become wholly dependent on the written word and incapable of responding to any stimulus in nature or human life without its permission and approval.

Aḥad Ha'am is not criticizing the Bible itself, but only the tendency of the "people of the book" to ignore its larger values. Can Aḥad Ha'am's criticism be applied to Jewish life today?

EDUCATION IN ISRAEL

Photo Essay   In the fall of 1889, in the new colony of Rishon le-Zion, a dozen or so small children were huddled around wooden tables in a little stone house. Behind them on the wall there was a picture of Baron Edmond de Rothschild, the Jewish philanthropist who was the main support of the colonists in their new land.

A tall, bespectacled teacher entered the room and announced, *"Boker tov, yeladim, hayom nilmad ḥeshbon"* ("Good morning, children, today we will study arithmetic"). For all we know, it was the first time that a secular subject was being taught to Jews in the Hebrew language. Up until that time, Hebrew had served almost exclusively for prayer, holy studies, and an occasional poem. Yet the schoolroom in Rishon was no isolated experiment. In a half dozen new settlements in Jaffa and Jerusalem, young enthusiasts of the newly revived Hebrew tongue were engaging in similar efforts. Their inspiration came from Eliezer Ben Yehudah, the "father of modern Hebrew," who had settled in Jerusalem a few years earlier.

From those strange experiments—which, at the time, were widely criticized as unrealistic, even dangerous for the children—Hebrew education in Israel developed into its present form: a great national network of kindergartens, elementary schools, high schools, and universities. The school system has been a major instrument in the process of absorbing hundreds of thousands of new immigrants, who arrive speaking dozens of different languages from countries on five continents.

Education in Israel is compulsory and free to children between the ages of five and 15. Because sufficient public funds

Tel Aviv municipal kindergarten.

Elementary school library.

Utilizing educational television to teach trigonometry.

High school track team.

Bezalel Art School in Jerusalem.

are lacking, some forms of secondary education require tuition fees, but a considerable number of students, particularly those from Oriental communities, are granted scholarships. Some 80 percent of elementary school pupils continue their studies after the age of 14. Approximately half of them go to schools of vocational training.

Although Jews from African and Asian countries now make up over half of the population of Israel, there are still fewer Oriental secondary school students than students from European backgrounds. Usually this is because of the lower living standards and different cultural heritage of Jews coming to Israel from the Oriental countries. Special programs have been launched to resolve this problem; for example, children of Oriental origin need not attain marks as high as other children in order to advance from grade to grade.

Until 1951 the Hebrew University of Jerusalem was the only university in Israel; a small branch was maintained in Tel Aviv. In addition, there were the Haifa Institute of Technology (called the Technion), where engineers were trained, and the Weizmann Institute of Science, a postgraduate scientific institution in Rehovot. After 1961, four new universities sprang up, and today thousands of students attend Bar Ilan University (outside Ramat Gan) and the Universities of Tel Aviv, Haifa, and Beersheba. The Universities of Tel Aviv, Jerusalem, and Bar Ilan maintain additional campuses in the Galilee, in the Jordan Valley, in the Negev, and in Eilat. In Jerusalem there are also English-language colleges: Jerusalem College, and the Hiat Institute of Brandeis University.

In the early days of Zionism, the great Hebrew writer Aḥad Ha'am propounded the idea that Israel should become the "spiritual center" for world Jewry. Today that ideal remains uppermost in the minds of many Israeli educators.

Technion Institute, founded in 1952, today is housed in 55 buildings and has 9,000 students.

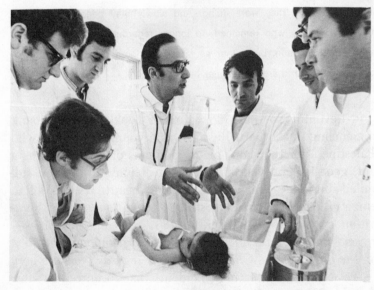

Israel's future physicians training in latest medical techniques.

Wind-tunnel testing at Technion's Aeronautical Research Center.

perspective

The achievements of the settlers of the First Aliyah were notable: they founded 18 settlements, began a number of projects aimed at draining the swamps, and initiated the use of Hebrew as a language of daily communication. But their efforts, particularly in later years, were bogged down by feelings of frustration and futility. There were so few of them and so many obstacles that had to be overcome. They were poor, struggling, endangered, and—perhaps worst of all—ignored. The rest of the world paid hardly any attention to what they were doing. And slowly they began to think of themselves differently. Those who remained no longer regarded themselves as the pioneers of a historic revolution, but rather as farmers trying to eke out a meager living and to cope with the world around them as best they could.

Salman David Levontin, 25 years old, a former bookkeeper and bank clerk in Kremenchug in southern Russia, was a young enthusiast who turned to Palestine after the shock of the pogroms of 1881. He was a sturdily built, good-looking young man, with dreamy large eyes, full lips, a trimmed mustache, and a bushy, round beard. He has left a moving memoir of his first year in Palestine (*To the Land of Our Fore-fathers*, written only two years later, in 1884). Its opening lines— "*'Sorry, sir,' said the hotel attendant in Kharkov. 'I cannot permit you to stay here, the orders of the Chief of Police as regards Jews are very firm . . .'*"—relates a humiliating incident that occurred a few months before his departure for Palestine. Levontin, on a trip to Kharkov, had been thrown out of his hotel room. A Jew from the Pale of Settlement could not remain in Kharkov even on a temporary visit!

Levontin had been sent to Palestine by the Lovers of Zion to purchase land from wealthy Arab landowners for a farming settlement. A few days after his arrival at Jaffa, an order was issued prohibiting the

ZIONISM AND
THE FIRST
ALIYAH
1881-1905

sale of Palestinian land to Russian and Rumanian Jews. The land purchased by the Lovers of Zion was therefore registered under the name of a British subject, Chaim Amsalag, a Jew from Gibraltar who at that time was acting as British vice-consul at Jaffa. Half the price of the land was paid by an elderly, rich relative of Levontin's; the other half was paid for by Levontin and eight other young Russian Zionists who had come to Jaffa independently of one another and then joined forces to settle on the land.

One of the young Lovers of Zion was Joseph Feinberg, a native of Sevastopol; he was 26 years old and a graduate of the universities of Heidelberg and Munich. Comfortably employed as a chemical engineer in southern Russia, he had been pressed into action by the pogroms of 1881. In Kiev he saw the czarist governor ride into town on his horse, greeting the rioters and being hailed in return. He too was shocked by the support the riots enjoyed among "cultured" Russians; he concluded that assimilation was impossible and that anti-Semitism was a law of nature. This sophisticated, educated child of a wealthy family, who spoke four languages fluently, was a professional to whom the entire world stood open. He might have gone, and probably would have succeeded, anywhere. In background he was not untypical of his fellow settlers. All had already broken out of the confines of ghetto life; all had been on the verge of assimilation; all were relatively well off. They paid for their half of the new land in cash.

RISHON LE-ZION

The new colony was named *Rishon le-Zion* (*"The first to Zion . . .* that bringeth good tidings to Jerusalem," Isaiah 41:27). The settlers loaded their packhorses with tents, tools, and supplies of food and drinking water and moved out from Jaffa early in August 1882, singing psalms and offering prayers of thanksgiving. Levontin, lying on his overcoat the first night and looking at the bright stars above, was seized with melancholy doubts. Already he "felt passionately in love" with the new place. It was, he wrote,

> the love of a prodigal son who returns to his home but finds that his father is gone . . . tears poured out of my eyes; my heart and soul trembled. My home and rest are in this place; here is the cradle of my youth . . . but my brothers, where are they? Will they really gather from the far places of the earth? . . . These hands of mine, used only to holding a pen and calculating profits and losses, will they be capable of handling a plow to produce bread for me, my wife and my children? Do I sacrifice my dear ones on this altar? Have I the right? Will I be at all useful. . . .

As he thus pondered, his servant and interpreter, a Jew from Jerusalem, interrupted his thoughts. He pointed to the tents which some Arab bedouin had pitched on a distant sand dune, and said: "When you build your houses and settle here . . . they will come, in the dark of night . . . to plunder and murder."

THE FIRST ALIYAH

Although it hardly seemed so at the time, 1882 was an eventful year in the history of the Zionist settlement of Palestine. Levontin and his group were only the first to arrive. Throughout the summer and fall, prospective settlers continued to reach Palestine. Petah Tikvah, abandoned three years earlier, was resettled by newcomers before the year was out. On the southern ridge of Mount Carmel a group of Lovers of Zion from Rumania purchased and settled Samarin, the future *Zichron Yaakov* ("Memory of Jacob"). Another group went farther north, to Upper Galilee, attractive to them because of its more European climate. After wasting much energy in quarrels with their Arab guides, they traveled through barren mountains on the backs of donkeys for almost a week, during which time one woman gave birth to a child. Finally the settlers reached a spot east of Safed and founded Rosh Pinnah (literally, "Head Stone"—the stone which "the builders rejected is become the *headstone* of the corner," Psalms 118:22). Other colonies were soon established in the north, the south, and on the coastal plain.

ELIEZER BEN YEHUDAH

Also in 1882, another young man who was to leave his mark on future events arrived in Palestine. Eliezer Perlmann, an obscure scholar from Lithuania, settled quietly in Jerusalem, returned his passport to the local Russian consul, and announced that Perlmann was dead. From then on he was to be known as Eliezer Ben Yehudah. This slightly built, 24-year-old philologist, whose health had been sapped by an early attack of tuberculosis but whose nature was as hard as steel, lived under the ruthless tyranny of an idea—the revival of Hebrew as a spoken language.

In his youth, Ben Yehudah had been an orthodox rabbinical scholar. He now began to search classic Hebrew literature for words to be used in a modern context. The very first word he created was *millon* (dictionary), a derivative of *milla* (word). Another early coinage was *leumiut* (nationalism). In his memoirs he noted that there was one thing that he regretted all his life: "I was not born in Jerusalem, nor even in the land of Israel."

Despite tremendous opposition from almost everyone he knew, Ben Yehudah succeeded in proving that Hebrew, the language of the Bible, dormant for centuries, could become a language fit for daily use. Sympathetic teachers in Jerusalem, Jaffa, and the new colonies joined his cause. Soon the children in all the new colonies spoke Hebrew fluently; although it was frequently a second language for them, after Yiddish, Russian, or French, it was nevertheless "alive."

NEED FOR FINANCIAL AID

Many new settlers who followed in the steps of Levontin and Feinberg were university students caught up by the double influence of Zionism and Russian socialism. They interrupted their studies to go off to settle in Palestine as farmers.

Actually, no socialist theories were put into practice at this early stage. The earliest settlers found Palestine a sobering experience. In reality, most colonies quickly gravitated to private ownership of land and the exploitation of cheap (native Arab) labor for profit-making purposes. Unfortunately, in less than two years, most of the inexperienced newcomers were close to bankruptcy and some were on the verge of starvation. It was Baron Edmond de Rothschild of Paris who came to their rescue.

BARON EDMOND DE ROTHSCHILD

Edmond de Rothschild (1849–1934), one of the least known descendants of a famous family of financiers, was inclined to leave the making of money to his brothers and cousins, preferring rather to spend it as he saw fit. Yet, through his support of some of the early Zionists, he played as great a role in history as any of his more famous namesakes. What seemed at the time an eccentric charity proved in the end a decisive political act. Were it not for his lavish support of the early settlers, the Jewish colonization of Palestine would have started much later, perhaps even too late to succeed.

In October 1882, Rothschild willingly responded to a plea by the settlers of Rishon le-Zion for a modest loan of 25,000 francs toward the digging of wells in the colony. He did so, as he later put it, as an "experiment," to see if it was possible to settle Jewish farmers in Palestine. The colonies soon became his main charity, surpassing even his generous support of French arts in general and the Louvre in particular.

Rothschild's total expenditure in Palestine has been estimated at £10 million. His properties there were later turned over to the colonists or earmarked for a foundation which today supports various educational enterprises, including instructional television.

Rothschild sought to influence every aspect of the colonists' life. He resented their wearing European clothes and wanted them to adopt local Arab dress; he insisted that they meticulously observe the Jewish Sabbath and the dietary and other laws of orthodox Jewish religion, which he himself—though not his pious wife—ignored. It is doubtful whether he ever hoped for a "Jewish state"; instead, he was interested in "creating centers where Jewish intellectual and moral culture could develop." He considered Zionism dangerous both for the Jews of Europe and for those in his colonies, since it exposed them to the accusation of not being "patriotic" Frenchmen, Russians, or Turks. Rothschild's attitude toward political Zionism mellowed in later years. Shortly before his death he said: "Without me Zionism would not have succeeded. But without Zionism my work would have been struck to death." He and his wife are buried at Rishon le-Zion.

HARDSHIPS IN PALESTINE

These first settlers soon abandoned their earlier utopian ideas. By 1902 they were thinking primarily of their own needs, and not exclusively of a Jewish national revival in Palestine. They had experienced the hardships of life in Palestine and had little patience for the advice of Zionists abroad, who, they felt, lacked the courage to come themselves. The romance of settling the Holy Land began to die. Disenchantment set in. Many of the settlers began to leave. Even Levontin, whose wife and mother had been against the entire venture, returned to Russia. (Twenty years later, he was to come back to Palestine as an employee of a newly created Zionist bank.)

Of those who left, some returned to Russia and Rumania. Others wandered as far as Kenya, America, South Africa, and Australia. The idea of leaving Palestine was hotly debated in the colonies. In the cemetery of Hadera, an early colony founded in the swampland of the Sharon, where many first settlers died of malaria, the tombstone of Peretz Herzenstein bears the inscription:

He was his country's loyal son
Until his final breath.
His dying words to his children were
Your country do not leave.

For years the Ḥuleh Swamps shown below were a source of malaria and disease. Between 1951 and 1958, the swamps were drained and transformed into fruitful fields.

Even Eliezer Ben Yehudah, the great fanatic of the Hebrew language revival, became a so-called "territorialist," a supporter of those seeking a territory in Uganda or Brazil as the site of the future Jewish national home.

related themes

The Meaning of the Land To the first pioneers the land of Israel was more than just a symbol of historic or spiritual importance. It was the first reality, the first sign that their dream was coming true. In 1846, Benjamin Disraeli, a Christian of Jewish origin who would later become the prime minister of Great Britain (and who always maintained his interest in the Jewish people), explored the real meaning of the land:

> The vineyards of Israel have ceased to exist, but the eternal Law enjoins the Children of Israel to celebrate the vintage. A race that persists in celebrating its vintage, although it has no fruits to gather, will regain its vineyards.

The prophetic vision of redemption is filled with images of a land, long neglected, being coaxed back to life. In the name of God, Amos says:

> On that day I will raise up the fallen tabernacle of David . . . and rebuild it as in days of old. . . . I will turn the captivity of my people and they shall rebuild the ruined cities and inhabit them. They shall plant vineyards and drink their wine, make gardens and eat their fruit. I will plant them on their own land, and they shall never again be plucked up out of the land which I have given them.

Hebrew and Modernity   Theodor Herzl once said "We cannot converse with one another in Hebrew. Who among us has a sufficient acquaintance with Hebrew to ask for a railway ticket in that language? Such a thing cannot be done. . . ." Yet Hebrew has become the spoken language of Israel. To understand how it was possible to revive the Hebrew tongue after 2000 years of nonuse, it is necessary to see how new words could be made up from old, existing roots. Thus, the Hebrew word for "telegram" is *mivrak*, which comes from *barak* (lightning). *Shevitah*, "labor strike," comes from yoshev (to sit down). *Ta'asiah* is the new word for "industry" and is derived from *la'asot*, the Hebrew verb "to make" or "to do." *Mesubach*, the modern word for "complicated," and *tasbich*, the word for a "complex" (for example, an inferiority complex), both come from the biblical word *svach*, which means "intertwined bushes or trees." Sometimes two words are added together to make a new third word. *Zeh* (this) can be added to *hoo* (he) to make *zehoot*, which means "identity." The two Hebrew words *mah* (what) and *hoo* can be added to make *mahoot*, which means "essence" (literally, "what it is"). And, similarly, *eich* (how) and *hoo* add up to *eichoot*, which means "quality" (or, literally, "how it is"). With just about 700 root words, the Hebrew language could easily be stretched to cover every situation. Herzl was wrong: no Israeli has any trouble asking for a railroad ticket from Tel Aviv to Haifa in Hebrew.

issues and values

"Why I Am a Jew"   The first pioneers broke away from the "confines" of Jewish life and were all on the verge of assimilation. Yet they returned. Herzl himself was an assimilated Jew, but he returned to his Jewish heritage after he witnessed the anti-Semitic spectacle of the Dreyfus trial. Another witness who was moved by that very same trial was Edmond Fleg, a French Jew. Fleg wrote a brief essay called "Why I Am a Jew."

> What is Judaism? What ought a Jew to do? How be a Jew? Why be a Jew? . . . I am a Jew because the faith of Israel demands of me no abdication of the mind; I am a Jew because the faith of Israel requires of me all the devotion of my heart; I am a Jew because in every place where suffering weeps, the Jew weeps; I am a Jew because at every time when despair cries out, the Jew hopes; I am a Jew because the word of Israel is the oldest and the newest; I am a Jew because the promise of Israel is the universal promise; . . . I am a Jew because, for Israel, the world is not yet completed—men are completing it. . . .

If you had to complete the sentence "I am a Jew because . . . ," how would you complete it? What, in your opinion, are the most essential reasons for remaining a Jew?

Sacred and Apart Baron de Rothschild's insistence that the Jewish colonists dress in Arab garb may have been a bit bizarre, but his demand that they observe orthodox customs and laws expressed a feeling shared by many Jews in the Diaspora: that Israel is a sacred land, and that Jews living in Israel have an obligation to recognize this fact and to fashion their society and their personal lives accordingly. In his essay "Religion Is the Source of Jewish Nationalism," the Zionist writer Yehiel Michael Pines writes:

> What is Jewish nationality divorced from Jewish religion? It is an empty formula, nothing but pretty phrases. After all, what is "nationality" if not a concept, or in other words a thought image? But a thought image which has no basis in reality is an illusion. What other basis in reality can there be for the thought image of Jewish nationality except the unity of the Jewish people with its Torah and its faith?

What role do you think the Torah and its laws should play in the Jewish state of Israel? Should religious laws be binding upon non-religious Israelis? Do you agree with Rothschild that Jews living in Israel have special obligations to tradition and to history that do not necessarily apply to Jews living elsewhere?

Tel Aviv in 1921, now Israel's largest city and commercial center.
The Arab city of Jaffa in the background merged with Tel Aviv
in 1949.

FROM DREAM
TO REALITY
1905-1948

perspective

For all of their differences of background and outlook, Theodor Herzl, the father of modern Zionism, and David Ben-Gurion, Israel's first prime minister, had much in common. Both had an unshakable vision that the Zionist dream would one day come to pass, an ability to move and persuade large numbers of followers, a healthy appreciation of the "nuts and bolts" requirements of state building (raising money, organizing groups, engaging people of power and influence, "wheeling and dealing" when necessary), and a willingness to immerse themselves in these activities totally.

In 1905, at a low point of Zionist morale, a second wave of migration began to reach Palestine from Russia. Inspired by the pogroms in 1903 and the unsuccessful Russian revolution of 1905, this new influx was the Second Aliyah. Its people and ideas were to change the course of events in Palestine.

This second wave lasted nine years, until 1914. Yet compared to the massive exodus of Russian Jews to America during the same period, the pioneers who came to Palestine represented a mere trickle, a few thousands as against 1½ million. Clearly, a personal and active commitment to Zionism was seen as a solution to the Jewish problem by only a small minority of Eastern European Jews.

THEODOR HERZL

A powerful cause of this second wave of pioneers was the creation, a few years earlier, of the World Zionist Organization under the brilliant leadership of Theodor Herzl. Herzl was an assimilated Viennese Jew, a well known journalist and playwright who had been driven to Zionism by the open anti-Jewish feelings displayed at the Dreyfus trial in France and by the ugly anti-Semitism he saw in Austria and Germany.

In 1896, Herzl published his famous tract *The Jewish State,* in which he urged the orderly departure of Jews from the lands of perse-

FROM DREAM
TO REALITY
1905-1948

70

cution to their own country. Herzl had never visited Eastern Europe. He had never read Pinsker or Lilienblum, and he arrived at his conclusion quite independently of those thinkers.

But where Pinsker had failed to attract worldwide attention, Herzl succeeded. He was a brilliant writer, a dramatic speaker, and a forceful personality. His main contribution to the creation of a Jewish state was the establishment of the World Zionist Organization, which first met on August 29, 1897 and continued to meet in annual congresses.

Herzl entered into negotiations with the Turkish sultan and the British government. His aim was to obtain a "charter" allowing the settlement of Jews in Palestine. His diplomatic efforts proved fruitless, but in the short span of eight years—between the publication of *The Jewish State* and his death in 1904—he created an international movement, laid the groundwork for various institutions that would express and carry out the movement's ideals, and forged a recognized role for Zionism in European and world politics.

DAVID BEN-GURION

Among the pioneers of the Second Aliyah was a young man named David Gruen (soon afterward, he changed his name to Ben-Gurion). In 1906 the 20-year-old David defied his father and announced that he was leaving Plonsk, a small Russian-controlled shtetl 40 miles from Warsaw, for Palestine. A short time earlier he had written: "We take with us [to Palestine] young and healthy arms, the love of work, an eagerness for free and natural lives in the land of our forefathers, and a willingness toward frugality." He wanted to "redeem" and build Palestine with his own hands, there to create "a model society based on social, economic and political equality."

With only a small knapsack on his back, he traveled by fourth-class train to Odessa, continued by ship across the Black Sea and down the eastern shore of the Mediterranean. Three weeks after his departure from Plonsk, travel-stained and weary, he was finally rowed ashore at the rocky port of Jaffa.

Ben-Gurion's journey was not an isolated instance. In the small towns of White Russia, the Ukraine, and Russian-controlled parts of Poland, hundreds of young men and women were packing their little bags. They bid their parents farewell, or simply ran away from home. Their departure was scattered and disorganized. No man, no ministry planned it. Individuals and small groups of friends just started moving. They embarked at Odessa or Trieste, and in Constantinople or Port Said they changed for slow cargo vessels or for occasional passenger ships bound for Jaffa in Turkish-controlled Palestine.

THE SECOND ALIYAH

They found the first wave of immigrants, or those who remained of it, slowly settling into the life of the country. Tiring of Zionist ideals, they lived with the Arabs as colonial employers. The new arrivals, inspired with socialist ideas, protested this "exploitation of Arab labor." They said that Jews must build their homeland with their own hands and not draw capitalistic profits from the employment of strangers.

The newcomers were young and mostly unattached. Few married or bore children during their first 15 years of settlement. They were filled with the burning excitement of Russian revolutionism, which they applied to Zionism with an enthusiasm such as had never fired the settlers of the First Aliyah. They had been educated in a different political school; they produced leaders; they had "ideologists." They were burning to work on the land, but an even greater concern, at least among the leaders, was the organization of political power to put their ideas into practice. Almost from the moment they set foot on land, they began to form overseas branches of their Eastern European–based political parties.

The Hebrew Social Democratic Party, *Poale Zion*, the party of Ben-Gurion and Ben-Zvi, considered itself as international and revolutionary. "We are the party of the Palestinian working-class in creation, the only revolutionary party of the Jewish worker in Turkey," ran an announcement published in Jaffa a short time after the first two dozen members disembarked at Jaffa. The men and women of Poale Zion considered themselves engaged in a "class struggle" in Palestine, although the country had little industry, hardly any workers, and few capitalists.

Of all the political groups which competed for membership among the newcomers, Poale Zion was probably the farthest left. But it was only a matter of degree. The majority of the pioneers of the Second Aliyah were advocates of social revolution. Revolution was a hope, a mood, a dream, a program; as the new settlers traveled from Russia to Palestine, they carried their revolutionary ideals in their knapsacks. Perhaps the revolution, which had failed so miserably in Russia, might succeed in one of the more destitute corners of the Ottoman Empire—a safe haven for Jews, and a new social paradise to boot. They would not quite achieve their dream, but in the course of trying they created a unique reality!

related themes

The Dreyfus Affair It all began when a cleaning lady at the German embassy in Paris found an unsigned letter containing information about French military operations in one of the embassy's wastebaskets. Somewhere in the French military was a traitor! The "evidence" pointed to Alfred Dreyfus, son of a rich Jewish family—a captain in the French army who wanted more than anything else to be known as a French patriot. Based on some hazy circumstantial evidence and the feeling that a Jew could not be loyal to one country, Dreyfus was convicted of treason, drummed out of the army in disgrace, and imprisoned on Devil's Island. Two years later, in 1896, a second letter containing military secrets was intercepted by a French intelligence officer. Comparing the handwriting on this second letter with the first, he found that both were written by the same man. An officer named Esterhazy was the probable culprit. A new investigation was launched, but in a new trial Esterhazy was found innocent.

This time, however, there was a public outcry, spearheaded by the French novelist Emile Zola. Zola wrote an open letter to the president of the French Republic (the letter was printed in newspapers around the world with the headline "J'accuse"—"I accuse"). Zola was convicted of libel and fled. Nevertheless, the cover-up became so obvious that the French government reopened the case. Dreyfus was retried in 1899, but again he was convicted; the verdict was the result of political pressure from those who felt that an admission of error would damage the army. Finally, in 1906, Dreyfus was exonerated, found innocent and restored to his former rank. Twelve years had passed since his first trial. The government, by way of compensating Dreyfus for the years of hardship on Devil's Island, awarded him the Legion of Honor medal; but Dreyfus himself was a broken man. What did it all mean for Jews? In an enlightened and progressive country, where Jews had enjoyed citizenship rights for nearly 100 years, anti-Semitism was still widespread, uncontained, and highly dangerous. It was with this insight that Herzl noted in his diaries, "What made me into a Zionist was the Dreyfus case."

Herzl's Impact Theodor Herzl was not the first Zionist. His Jewish

Theodor Herzl: Father
of Political Zionism.

background was sparse; he knew little Hebrew. He did not consider
Israel as the only possible site for a new Jewish state. His ideas were
not new (Eastern European Zionists had been saying the same things
for many years). Why then is Herzl honored as the father of modern
Zionism? In his autobiography *Trial and Error*, Chaim Weizmann offers
insights into Herzl's impact upon Eastern European Jewry:

> [His pamphlet] was an utterance which came like a bolt from the blue. We
> had never heard the name Herzl before. . . . Yet the effect produced by
> *The Jewish State* was profound. Not the ideas, but the personality which stood
> behind them appealed to us. Here was daring, clarity, and energy. . . . What
> had emerged from *The Jewish State* was less a concept than an historic per-
> sonality. What has given greatness to his name is Herzl's role as a man of
> action, as the founder of the Zionist Congress, and as an example of daring and
> devotion.

issues and values

Guilt by Generalization   In his diaries, Herzl, writing about the Dreyfus case, recalls ". . . the howls of the mob in the street . . . still ring
unforgettably in my ears: 'Death! Death to the Jews!' Death to Jews all
because this one was a traitor? . . ." From what happened in France,

it would seem so. Following the trial, petitions were drawn up demanding the expulsion of the Jews from France. Legislation was introduced to deprive the Jews of the right to vote. Newspapers and magazines urged employers to fire their Jewish workers. Public figures who spoke in defense of Dreyfus found themselves shouted down by their audiences. In sum, the Jews of France became victims of "guilt by generalization," whereby the crime of one Jew became the crime of all Jews. Have you ever heard an entire group blamed for the faults or sins of one of its members? Do you ever find yourself tempted to apply this sort of reasoning? What are some of the stereotypes that have been applied to Jews, blacks, Irish, and Italians because of this approach?

The Rejection of the Galut   One of the major goals of the Zionist revolution, in David Ben-Gurion's view, was the ultimate disappearance of the *galut* or Diaspora (meaning any Jewish community outside of Israel), as the world population of Jews moved to Israel. In a speech called "The Imperatives of the Jewish Revolution" (1944), Ben-Gurion said, "Galut means dependence—material, political, spiritual, cultural, and intellectual dependence—because we are aliens . . . rootless and separated from the soil, from labor. . . . Our task is to break radically with this dependence and become master of our fate. . . . To have survived in galut despite all odds is not enough; we must create . . . the necessary conditions for our future survival as a free and independent people. The meaning of the Jewish revolution is contained in one word—independence! Independence for the Jewish people in its homeland! . . . the goal of our revolution is the complete ingathering of the exiles. . . ." Do you agree with Ben-Gurion's evaluation of the galut? Do you personally feel a lack of roots? Would it be best, in your opinion, if all Jews lived in Israel?

perspective

To the members of the Second Aliyah, Zionism was a dream with all the intensity of a religion. They saw their coming to Palestine as an act of fulfillment and affirmation. For these young pioneers, labor on the land served as the crucial link between the vision and its practical implementation. They injected a richness of meaning, a sense of far-reaching significance into their work. Labor represented, in A. D. Gordon's words, "not a means, but an end in itself." Every gritty task, every menial chore, became part of a process of personal and national redemption.

The men and women of the Second Aliyah were a different breed from today's Israelis. They were true believers. Never were people more sure that they were on the right track. They viewed the world in a simple fashion; their unselfish idealistic beliefs were frequently divorced from reality. Contemporary Israelis are motivated by self-interest and recognize the realities of power. The early pioneers were dreamers. Their innocence gave them great strength; courage came from inexperience. They accomplished their tasks with an energy made possible only by a sense of total righteousness and an awareness of a higher purpose.

Arrival in Palestine in 1906 was often depressing. Embarrassing scenes frequently occurred in Jaffa. Groups of arriving pioneers, enthusiastically coming ashore, at times even kissing the dusty ground as they fell upon it, would mistake the people assembled on the dock for members of a welcoming party. In fact, the latter were simply preparing to embark on the same ship to go back to Europe.

Some contemporaries have put the number of those who left Palestine at 60 to 70 percent of the recent arrivals. David Ben-Gurion even spoke of 90 percent. We are concerned with those who remained, and who eventually came into power; the toughest who managed somehow to hold out.

They were marked by a terrible sincerity. On a summer night in

FROM DREAM
TO REALITY
1905-1948

1910, Joseph Chaim Brenner, a writer, who arrived with the pioneers of the Second Aliyah, was walking with some friends on the farm at Ben Shemen where they worked. Suddenly Brenner bent to the ground. He clutched in his fists a few clods of earth, kissed them, and with tears in his eyes exclaimed: "Land of Israel, will you be ours? Will you really be ours?" The ideal was never questioned—only the ability of weak and petty humans to achieve it.

Some pioneers of the Second Aliyah have described their decision to emigrate to Palestine in almost mystical terms: "Everything was suddenly crystal clear; the fog parted, my entire body shook with excitement. . . . It was as if I had suddenly awakened from a bad dream. I knew what I had to do. Nothing else mattered." Others claimed that the very moment they set foot in Palestine they were "reborn." Ben-Gurion started to count his years afresh from that date on, considering everything that preceded it a waste of time.

The poet Bialik wrote to the pioneers: "The very dust will come alive under your bare and sacred feet." This indeed was how they felt in the enthusiasm of the first months or years, even before the barren fields they had sown turned green, or the virgin hills they had cleared of boulders were covered by forests.

THE REBIRTH OF HEBREW

Although most of the pioneers had hardly more than an elementary command of the language, they were fanatical Hebraists. Disembarking at Jaffa, Ben-Gurion and many others—like Ben Yehudah in 1882— vowed never again to use a foreign language, but to speak only Hebrew. While such solemn vows were frequently impractical and often broken, they were sometimes kept with a stubborn will that bordered on the extreme. In a makeshift clinic for malaria-stricken pioneers, a girl patient who spoke Russian in a delirium was rudely chastised by the nurse for not using Hebrew.

Hebrew was more than a language. Using it reflected an attitude to life, history, and society. The proper term for the newcomers was immigrants. But the new arrivals rarely used that word. Instead they called themselves *olim*, which means "those who ascend," who rise above earthly desires.

Immigration into Palestine was called *aliyah* (literally "going up"), just as being called to the *bimah* to read from the Torah is called Aliyah. Those olim who went into agricultural work were called *halutzim*, a word similar to "pioneers," but with a much broader emotional meaning. It included the ideas of ecstatically serving the goal of rebuilding Zion, of hard work on new frontiers. The quality of being a ḥalutz was well reflected in a popular Jewish song:

> We are, we are, we are
> Pioneers, Pioneers! (Ḥalutzim! Ḥalutzim!)
> On burning fields
> On barren fields of waste.
> The first to arrive
> Like swallows in spring
> We believe . . .
> We'll cover the stony fields
> With golden bloom.

THE DIGNITY OF LABOR

For many young men and women who arrived with the Second Aliyah, physical labor was the highest ideal.

> Work is our life's elation
> From all troubles the salvation,
> Yah-ḥah-li-li labor mine!

The great prophet of the religion of labor was Aaron David Gordon. His influence was considerable and lasted for decades, long after his death in 1922. When already an adult, Gordon abandoned his family in order to commune with nature and the soil. At the age of 47, a weak and ailing man with a flowing white beard, he became a manual laborer in the fields of Palestine. He quickly attracted a large following among the young pioneers who called him *hazaken*, the old man.

Gordon preached that man could be made holy only through hard physical labor. He called upon his fellow pioneers not to live by their wits but by their sweat. Gordon slaved by day in the fields. At night he would join the young workers in dancing the *horah*. Intoning a monotonous Yiddish refrain, *"Frailich! Frailich! Frailich!"* (Joy! Joy! Joy!), he would whip himself and his fellow dancers into a state of near ecstasy. He wrote:

> In my dream I come to the land. And it is barren and desolate and given over to aliens; destruction darkens its face and foreign rule corrupts it. And the land of my forefathers is distant and foreign to me, and I too am distant and foreign to it. And the only link that ties my soul to her, the only reminder that I am her son and she my mother, is that my soul is as desolate as hers. So I shake myself and with all my strength I throw . . . the [old] life off. And I start everything from the beginning. And the first thing that opens up my heart to a life I have not known before is

labor. Not labor to make a living, not work as a deed of charity, but work for life itself. . . . And I work. . . .

Many pioneers of the second wave were idealistic to an extreme. Food was deliberately plain, consisting mainly of bread, olives, vegetables, and soup, prepared in communal workers' kitchens. Clothes were unadorned, Russian-style workers' garments. One well-known figure of the period, Israel Giladi, refused to wear shoes and walked barefoot as a matter of principle. His feet were covered with scratches and nasty wounds, but he insisted that: "our feet must get used to the soil of the Land."

There was, at the same time, a remarkable sobriety. In the wine-growing areas where many of the new pioneers worked, wine and other alcoholic beverages were cheap, frequently free for the asking. Nevertheless, there was apparently very little drinking. Most of the pioneers were young men and women in their late teens or early 20's. They led free lives, and frequently shared living quarters. Yet, with few exceptions, despite the near-absolute freedom under which they lived, casual relationships were rare. Long and rather melancholy friendships, accompanied by the exchange of poems and emotional letters, were common. Few pioneers married before 1922.

related themes

A Process of Spiritual Rebirth   The Hebrew word for immigration is *hagirah*, yet, as the chapter points out, the act of coming to live in Israel is called aliyah, or ascent. From the very beginning of Jewish history, immigrating to the land of Israel has been associated with a process of spiritual rebirth. For example, Abraham was commanded to go forth to the Promised Land because he had accepted the idea of One God and would soon enter into a sacred covenant with God. The Children of Israel were compelled to remain in the desert for 40 years until the older generation, born into slavery, would die out and a new generation, reared in the tradition of freedom, would arise to take its place. Later the Prophet Isaiah foretold a messianic era in which the Jewish people would be returned to their homeland, a time in which the nation would achieve a peak of moral perfection and, would be governed by a king who "with righteousness shall . . . judge the poor" (Isaiah 11:4). So too the Zionist pioneers came to Israel not only to achieve political independence but also to create an ideal society in which they would be spiritually reborn. A popular song of the period summed up these early Zionist hopes: *Anu banu artzah, livnot u'lihibanot bah*—"We have come to the land to build and to be rebuilt by it."

A Language of Idealism   Sometimes you can tell much about a people by the words and phrases of its everyday language. The modern Hebrew vocabulary has a number of words which have grown directly out of the country's involvement with pioneering, and have no real equivalents in English. For example, *hagshamah* (fulfillment) has come to mean a sense of fulfillment which comes from working together to achieve a shared dream, such as establishing a new kibbutz or *moshav*. The term *madrich* (literally, "a leader"; *madrich* comes from the root word *derech*, which means "road" or "way") is ordinarily applied to a leader in one of the Israeli youth movements, a person who tries to present or to help create a particular way of life by imparting values and inspiring commitment. And *dugmah hinuchit* (literally, "an educational example") has come to express the belief that one can only educate or lead others by setting a personal example. Thus, when Ben-Gurion wanted to encourage young people to settle in the Negev (south) of Israel and "make the desert bloom," he himself, at the age of 67, joined Sdeh Boker, a young struggling desert kibbutz.

issues and values

Dreams and Realities   There were times during the Second Aliyah when dreams met realities head-on. Rachel Yanait Ben-Zvi describes such a meeting in her autobiography *Coming Home:*

> Suddenly a thin young man pushed his way through the crowds on deck. . . . I was overjoyed to meet this first haver [Zionist comrade] . . . had he come to welcome us? He did not answer. . . . I heard him talking to a sailor, pleading to be allowed to return to Odessa . . . shocked at what I had overheard, I asked for an explanation. He poured out all the bitterness in his heart about unemployment, malaria, hopelessness. I hurried off the deck, not wanting to hear any further slander of the Land. He kept on talking. . . . I wished he would leave me alone.

What is your personal definition of faith? Have you ever met anyone you would call a "passionate" believer? Is there any single ideal or goal that you would commit yourself to wholeheartedly?

The Value of Work   A. D. Gordon described a new kind of work for the Zionists of the Second Aliyah, "not labor to make a living, not work as a deed of charity, but work for life itself. . . ." It is in the values of kibbutz life that this is most clear: ". . . To this day, ability to work and attitude toward work still constitute the most single important factor in our judgment of the individual [on a kibbutz] . . . this has nothing to do with production or volume. A person whose abilities are limited, but who works to full capacity . . . will gain complete acceptance and respect. Not so the shirker" (from Joseph Criden and Sadia Gelb in *The Kibbutz Experience: Dialogue in Kfar Blum*). So student groups coming from abroad to spend a period of time on the kibbutz are advised to work conscientiously, for the first question that a kibbutz member will ask about them is "How do they work?" What do you think is the purpose of work in American society? Do you get personal satisfaction from working? Do you agree with A. D. Gordon's definition of work?

American volunteers work on a kibbutz.

perspective

Revolutions have a way of attracting a number of anti-establishment types, and Zionism was no exception. A variety of eccentrics passed through the port of Jaffa during the early pioneer days. Some were gifted. Some were brilliant. Some even remained to become solid citizens and members of the new Israeli establishment. All of them shared the excitement of being free and on their own, thousands of miles from the pressures of society and the supervision of their parents. However, they soon came to realize that their new ideals called for an even greater discipline than before—that freedom had to be won through years of struggle.

It was natural that the early Jewish colonies should attract a considerable number of colorful personalities with pet solutions for the ills of mankind. Almost all came from that vast reservoir of desperate hopes created by the political disorder of Eastern Europe. There were nationalists and internationalists, Marxist socialists and non-Marxist socialists, followers of every political trend in Russia at that time. Only czarists were not represented. Everywhere among the newly arrived workers in the colonies one found copies of underground Russian magazines; at night the dim, kerosene-lit tent encampments would resound with deep male voices singing melancholy Russian songs of revolution.

A NEW LIFE, A NEW NAME

Choosing a Hebrew name became the rule among the ḥalutzim. It is interesting to note the names people pick when the choice is theirs. Thus David Grien became David Ben-Gurion (son of a lion cub).

Many new names were simply translations from the German or Russian into Hebrew. Silber (Silver) became Caspi, from the Hebrew כסף for silver; Stein (Stone) became Avni, from the Hebrew word

אבן for stone. But many a settler changed his or her name to one having inspirational content, recalling some biblical association, or referring to a place in Palestine. Inspirational names such as Amiḥai (my people lives), Ben Ami (son of my people), and Ben Artzi (son of my country) are common in Israel today. Names denoting heroic stature were also popular choices: Oz (strength), Tamir (towering), Hod (splendor, majesty). Some settlers changed their names as they had changed their lives. For example, "city" names became "farm" names like Karmi (of the vineyard), Kimḥi (flour), or Sadeh (field). In other countries, mountains have been named after men. In Israel the reverse was true; men were named after mountains—Sinai, Ḥermon, Atzmon, Gilboa, Tabor. Other local place names were also popular: Galili (Galilee), Sharon, Yerushalmi, Eilat, Elon.

For many settlers the new surnames were symbols of a personal and collective rebirth. The widespread adoption of names of local plants and places reflected the desire of the settlers to become one, in body and name, with the landscape of their regained homeland, its rivers and mountains, its trees and even its thorns.

NEED FOR ADVENTURE

In addition to their idealism, the pioneers were also full of a wholesome thirst for adventure. This is immediately apparent in the immigrants' voluntary flight from their often relatively comfortable surroundings, their illegal border crossings, their constantly changing homes in the still undeveloped land of their dreams.

"We left home in the happy feelings of floating on the waves of real life," wrote David Horowitz, the future president of the Bank of Israel, in a letter to his parents soon after his departure from Lvov, Poland. "Of wanting to give a lot to life and take a lot; to scrape as much of it as possible, to worship the God of youth and its ecstasy, to approach life with the eternal demand—all or nothing. We thirst for strength, tension, overflowing life, liberty and intoxicating beauty."

A NEW STYLE OF LIFE

Many pioneers were teenagers, barely 19 years old. In Palestine, beyond rendering service to an idea to which many felt passionately committed, there was also a chance to get out from under the pressure of parental authority and live independent lives, or so it seemed. Many from cold, dismal little towns in the Pale of Settlement loved to sleep outdoors, to gaze up at the brilliant stars spread out across the dark sky

During summer vacation, kibbutz children work in the fields.

and revel in the soft breeze that came in from the sea. Most memoirs of this period are full of moving passages praising the glories of the eastern nights. Natives of grim Polish provinces and the cold, landlocked Russian steppes rejoiced in the fine, white, sandy beaches that were as yet unspoiled by tar and urban sewage.

In their dress, as in their way of life and manner of work, they displayed a strong vagabond or bohemian quality. Yitzḥak Ben-Zvi, the future president, and his girl friend Rachel (he formally married her more than a decade later) lived in an abandoned ruin on the outskirts of Jerusalem. In this ruin the Central Committee of Poale Zion held its meetings; Ben-Gurion, a frequent visitor, would engage Ben-Zvi in heated discussion.

The household consisted of a straw mat and a few wooden crates. "What does a man need more?" Rachel Ben-Zvi writes in her memoirs, describing life in Jerusalem prior to World War I. "Why should we tie ourselves to a routine way of life? Why bother to cook and amass furniture? . . . our household does not require too much bother. In a minute the straw mat is aired, the tin cups are rinsed, everything necessary is done and we are at full liberty. . . ."

A BETTER SOCIETY—THE KIBBUTZ

The appearance of the kibbutz at this particular time is noteworthy. It was not based on any blueprint or dogma. The kibbutz was born almost by accident, as a way to solve the labor problems facing the settlers. By sharing both their labor and the benefits they reaped from it, the settlers hoped to achieve the vague, undefined goal of a "better society." Communal societies dedicated to an ideal—from the Essenes of antiquity to the Doukhobors of Russia, the Mormons of America, and the "flower children" of the 1960's—have appeared regularly in history at times of crisis, and most have disappeared. In the case of the kibbutz, however, varying practical and ideological factors combined to give it a permanence and a position in the general community seldom achieved by utopian experiments elsewhere.

More than any other group, the men and women of the kibbutzim would come to symbolize the new "Israeli" Jew. Members of kibbutzim have never numbered more than 8 percent of the population. But they have lived the ideals of labor Zionism which were major themes of Israeli nation building: the reconstruction of a land and creation of a haven for the persecuted, and the establishment of a good, just, even morally perfect society.

related themes

The Staying Power of the Kibbutz   The kibbutz was not the only system of communal living set up to be an ideal community. Yet the kibbutz has remained a working institution for nearly 70 years, while most other experiments in communal living have failed. Naturally, one must ask the question why. Murray Weingarten, in a book called *Life on a Kibbutz,* offers one explanation:

> The kibbutz has much in common with all these communities, but it is basically different . . . the kibbutz movement is part and parcel of Jewish national rebirth . . . it is rooted deeply in that movement and in a whole Jewish world of tradition and values . . . the kibbutz is as much an outgrowth of the needs of Zionist colonization as it is the product of a specific social point of view possessed by its builders.

In other words, the kibbutz is unique because, unlike other attempts to form a communal society, the kibbutz is a part of the mainstream of a national life and cultural tradition. Indeed, the kibbutz has been regarded (in Weingarten's words) as "the crest of the wave of Jewish rebirth in Israel."

The Meaning of Kibbutz Equality   Most people agree that the kibbutz offers a large degree of equality to its members. But what does equality mean? Can one speak of equality in terms of looks, brains, physical strength, or the ability to get along with people? Does the kibbutz elect its leaders solely on the basis of equality—that is, by rotation—or are a person's qualifications for the job taken into account? Aren't some kibbutz members socially sought after and respected, while others are not? Of course, there is no such thing as perfect equality, even on a kibbutz. No one can produce a uniform standard of brains, beauty, talent, popularity, or ability. What the kibbutz strives for is not assembly-line equality, but rather the assurance that inequalities will not be rewarded or punished in terms of basic needs such as food, shelter, education, and social services. Thus, every kibbutz member, regardless of individual talent, social status, public esteem, or the importance of the job he or she holds, receives the same housing, clothing, furnishings, recreational facilities, medical care, vacation time, personal allowance, child care and education allowance, and provision for aging parents who live on the kibbutz.

Women in Zionism   When Golda Meir became Israel's prime minister in 1969, there was no fuss, no agonizing speculation over the fact that the new head of government happened to be a woman. Israelis accepted it as a matter of course—just as they have always accepted the practice of girls being inducted into the army at the age of 18. The idea of women being full participants in the creation and sustenance of the Jewish state goes back to the days of the first pioneers, when women labored side-by-side with men, sharing the hardships and dangers, asking—and receiving—no special favor in work assignments. These women were not just the girl friends and wives of pioneering men, they were pioneers in their own right.

Their equal status came about as no accident. It was from the first a matter of philosophical design. The liberation of women from their traditional roles and dependencies was a deeply rooted and cherished ideal of Zionism. It found particular expression on the kibbutz. Lionel Tiger and Joseph Shefer, in their book *Women in the Kibbutz,* remark

. . . all the major household services are collectivized. Meals are served in communal dining halls and prepared and served by all kibbutz members on a rotation basis. Therefore women in principle are required no more than men to cook, serve, wash dishes . . . there is no individual shopping for food. A collective laundry cares for all the washing, a collective store does all the ironing and mending . . . children of 90 percent of the kibbutzim who are younger than 14 live in dormitories, starting at the age of two-to-six weeks. They are cared for by trained nurses and teachers. . . . Men and women are economically independent of each other. Each adult member of a kibbutz works within a general labor assignment scheme, and rarely, if ever, do families or couples work in the same branch . . . social status does not depend on marital, legal and economic status . . . No woman need depend on her husband, father, or any other man. Economic support and legal status are hers by virtue of membership in the collective . . . power is highly diffused; up to 50 percent of the membership serve on governing bodies. There are no impediments to male or female participation in politics.

issues and values

Rejection of Materialism The generation of the early Zionists was a generation of immigrants. Many came to the United States and a small number turned to Palestine. Those who went to Palestine rejected materialism, the attention to or emphasis on material objects or considerations. They were like Rachel Yanait Ben-Zvi, who asked, "What does a man need more? . . . our household does not require too much bother. In a minute the straw mat is aired, the tin cups are rinsed, everything necessary is done and we are at full liberty. . . ." On the other hand, those who emigrated to America found themselves in a truly materialist society, a consumer-culture, in which success was measured by one's accumulation of money and goods. In what ways is your life influenced by your ancestor's choice of a new homeland? Do you think that you could be happy living in the manner of the Ben-Zvis?

Embracing the New Eastern European Jews who immigrated to Palestine expressed their desire to become a part of their new surroundings and to put as much distance as possible between themselves and the ways of the old country. At the same time, their relatives, friends, neighbors, and other fellow Jews who had gone to the United States were adjusting to *their* new environment. Just as the Zionist pioneers gave themselves new names in Hebrew to symbolize their break with the old country, so many Jewish immigrants to this country gave themselves more American-sounding names. In a story called "Cycle of Manhattan," Thyra S. Winslow tells of the progress of the immigrant family of Abe Rosenheimer as he stepped up the social and economic ladder. With each step his name became more and more "American," until finally it was A. Lincoln Ross. The ways in which the immigrants to America and Palestine tried to blend into their new surroundings were similar. Were their reasons similar? Were the results similar?

Arthur Balfour: 1848–1930.

THE BALFOUR DECLARATION

Photo Essay Theodor Herzl's great aim had been to convince the great powers to issue a "charter," anchored in international law, for the establishment of a Jewish national home in Palestine.

Herzl's negotiations with the Turkish, German, and British governments were unsuccessful. He died in 1904 a broken man, convinced that his life was ending in failure. But even though his own effort was cut short, like a pruned tree it provoked new life. Thirteen years after Herzl's death, during World War I, the long-sought charter was proclaimed by the British government. It came to be known as the Balfour Declaration and was issued at a time when British expeditionary troops coming up from Egypt had just defeated the Turkish garrison of Palestine and were approaching the gates of Jerusalem. The British charter was in

the form of a letter from British Foreign Secretary Arthur Balfour to a distinguished Jew:

November 2nd 1917
Dear Lord Rothschild:
 I have much pleasure in conveying to you, on behalf of His Majesty's Government, the following Declaration of sympathy with Jewish Zionist aspirations which has been submitted to, and approved by, the Cabinet:
 "His Majesty's Government view with favour the establishment in Palestine of a national home for the Jewish people, and will use their best endeavours to facilitate the achievement of this object, it being clearly understood that nothing shall be done which may prejudice the civil and religious rights of existing non-Jewish communities in Palestine, or the rights and political status enjoyed by Jews in any other country."
 I should be grateful if you would bring this declaration to the knowledge of the Zionist Federation.

Yours,
Arthur James Balfour

In the Balfour Declaration, for the first time since the Romans destroyed Jewish independence in the year 70 C.E., a great world power recognized the Jews as a people, one people, a people like all other peoples, entitled to a national home. Some Zionists were worried by its vague wording. They were reassured by Lord Balfour, who said privately that the British government favored the establishment of a Jewish state in Palestine. It would be as Jewish as England was English.

Although it had been addressed to Lord Rothschild, the declaration had been secured largely through the efforts of a little-known biochemist at the University of Manchester, Chaim Weizmann. Weizmann was 43 years old at the time. He was a native of Motel, near Pinsk in Russia, which was in his words "the darkest and most forlorn corner of the Jewish

Pale of Settlement." He had been a devoted Zionist since his early youth, and a delegate to several early Zionist congresses. When Herzl died in 1904, even though Weizmann was in the lower ranks of the Zionist leadership, he wrote to his bride Vera, "I feel that a heavy burden has fallen on my shoulders." As he proved in later years, this statement was not just an impertinence.

Weizmann had settled in Manchester in 1905. There he met Arthur Balfour, member of Parliament for Manchester. He converted Balfour to Zionism after a long discussion. The high point of this talk was when the men discussed the Uganda scheme, which the Zionist Congress had rejected.

"Why don't you want to set up a Jewish national home in Africa?" asked Balfour. "Britain is offering you Uganda! Take it, and settle the homeless Jews there."

"Mr. Balfour, supposing I were to offer you Paris instead of London. Would you take it?"

Balfour sat up, surprised. "But Mr. Weizmann, we have London."

"That is true," said Weizmann, "but we had Jerusalem when London was a marsh."

Balfour leaned back, stared at Weizmann, and said, "Are there many Jews who think like you?"

"Millions," said Weizmann, "whom you will never see and who cannot speak for themselves, but with whom I could pave the streets of Russia."

"If that is so," said Balfour, "you will one day be a force."

The idea of a Jewish restoration in Palestine had been popular in England—especially among Protestant clergymen—throughout the nineteenth century. Nevertheless, the Balfour Declaration was issued not merely out of deep and widespread sympathy for the persecuted Jews of Russia but for a variety of other reasons as well. First, as a lever against the French. France (as the traditional "protector" of the Christian churches in the Holy Land) claimed Palestine as war booty. By proclaiming Palestine a Jewish national home, the British hoped to control it. Second, the Russian Revolution had taken place, and many of its leading figures were Jews. The British statesmen

Balfour (left) visits Weizmann (center) in Tel Aviv, 1925.

Lord Balfour formally dedicates the Hebrew University on
Mount Scopus, Jerusalem, April 1, 1925.

felt that a pro-Zionist declaration would
make the Bolsheviks in Russia pro-British
and keep Russia in the war. Third, it was
hoped that the declaration would encourage America's participation in World
War I.

The Balfour Declaration aroused considerable enthusiasm. Most people did
not realize how vague the language was.
Nor was it immediately noticed that simul-
taneous, equally vague promises had
been made by the British government to
the Arabs. The British government may
have hoped that these promises would be
forgotten after the war, like so many other
wartime statements. This was not to be.

Arabs and Jews alike emerged from
World War I convinced that Palestine had
been promised to them by the victorious
English. English officials, politicians, and
public opinion were themselves divided.
Weizmann was one of the few who recognized as early as 1918 that the Balfour
Declaration would remain a worthless
piece of paper unless the Jews did something about it.

The first thing would be to emigrate to
Palestine in great masses. But despite the

tremendous dislocations caused by World
War I and the Russian Revolution, less
than 200,000 Eastern European Jews
migrated to Palestine, whose gates had
been opened by the declaration. They
were not the millions Weizmann had
hoped for, and the gates did not remain
open for long.

Moreover, there was an acute shortage
of funds to settle even those Jews who
were arriving. The annual budget of a
middle-sized Jewish community in Western Europe or in the United States was
still larger than that of the entire Zionist
settlement program.

Meanwhile, Arab opposition to the Balfour Declaration grew steadily; in 1920
and again in 1929 this opposition erupted
into large-scale violence. The international situation which, apart from pure
sentiment, had prompted the British government to issue the Balfour Declaration
was also changing rapidly. It became
easier for successive British governments
to gradually back away from the idea of a
Jewish restoration in their ancient homeland. By 1939, Britain had in effect abandoned the declaration.

Foreign Office,

November 2nd, 1917

Dear Lord Rothschild,

I have much pleasure in conveying to you, on
behalf of His Majesty's Government, the following
declaration of sympathy with Jewish Zionist aspirations
which has been submitted to, and approved by, the Cabinet.

His Majesty's Government view with favour the
establishment in Palestine of a national home for the
Jewish people and will use their best endeavours to
facilitate the achievement of this object, it being
clearly understood that nothing shall be done which
may prejudice the civil and religious rights of
existing non-Jewish communities in Palestine, or the
rights and political status enjoyed by Jews in any
other country"

I should be grateful if you would bring this
declaration to the knowledge of the Zionist Federation.

Yours,

Arthur James Balfour

The Balfour Declaration.

13/ THE ḤALUTZ

perspective

Israel's pioneers, the Ḥalutzim, wanted a society in which there would be a balance between the individual and the group. They saw the group as a collection of individuals organized for the benefit of each of its members. At the same time, they saw society as more important than any single member. On the one hand, they were seeking what they called *hagshamah atzmit* (self-fulfillment) within the group; on the other hand, their pioneering ideals included the establishment of a community and a state which would outlive them as individuals.

Consider, then, the early Zionist pioneers, the ḥalutzim of the second wave of immigration (1905–1914), hardworking and argumentative, obstinate, enthusiastic young men and women in their late teens or early 20's, isolated within their communities, slowly making headway and developing a way of life that only few could accept. Looking back one notices a number of curious parallels between the ḥalutzim and the "hippies" who made their appearance more than half a century later in the industrial societies of the West.

ḤALUTZIM AND HIPPIES—A COMPARISON

Of course, like all oversimplifications of this type, the comparison cannot be driven too far. The hippie-style rebels of an earlier age became the Israeli establishment of a later one, and a rather rigid, conservative establishment at that. At least half the members of the first Israeli Constituent Assembly in 1948 were veteran ḥalutzim; a third were members of kibbutzim, although the kibbutz population at the time hardly exceeded 5 percent.

Most ḥalutzim came from middle-class backgrounds. But like the hippies, they deliberately left established society in pursuit of a new life based upon a seemingly impossible dream. In addition to their Zionist aspirations, many ḥalutzim sought a community in which their own identities could be redefined and where social and personal relations would be based on love. Theory was not always put into practice, but there is no reason to doubt the genuineness of their dreams, hopes, and ideals.

They often rejected such externals of the old life as alcohol, tobacco, movies, dancing, and even decent table manners. As they rejected some habits, they ritualized others. This was especially true in their dress. The role of dress in the history of revolt goes back to Adam and Eve and is well known in modern times, from Gandhi's *dhoti* to the Mao jacket. The ḥalutzim despised suit jackets and dresses as the abominable symbols of the decadent world they had escaped. The men wore rough cotton shirts, sometimes embroidered at the neck in the Russian peasant style, over bulky shorts or trousers. Many women wore trousers. Men's neckties were banned.

Totally committed to politics, the leaders often displayed an amazing lack of personal sentimentality. Yitzḥak Ben-Zvi married his wife in between two sessions of the party's Central Committee. Ben-Gurion, expelled from Palestine by the Turks at the outbreak of World War I, went to America to make speeches for his political party, Poale Zion. He met and married a young nurse in New York in 1918, only to abandon her almost penniless and in the sixth month of her pregnancy in order to volunteer for the Jewish Legion, which was being organized by the British to assist in the occupation of Palestine. Later he wrote to her:

> . . . I did what I had to do, for your sake too, and I assure you, my dear Paula, that a time will come—and it is not far away—when you will share this feeling and you will understand.
>
> I did not want to give you a *small, cheap, secular* kind of happiness. I prepared for you the great sacred human joy achieved through *suffering and pain*. To the greatest joy of my life, I have become convinced *that you were born* for such happiness . . . to suffer together with me for a great cause and you deserve that I bow my head before you. *Therefore* I love you so dearly. . . . I know you were not ready for the suffering and hard test . . . but I know you well enough to be certain that you will carry this heavy burden. . . . in tears you will arise to the high mountain from which one sees vistas of a New World, a world of gladness and light, shining in the glow of an eternally young ideal of supreme happiness and glorious existence, a world only few will be *privileged* to enter, for only rich souls and deep hearts are *permitted* entry there. I know that your soul is rich and your heart great enough for the superb world and the superb life that I want to prepare for you.

Three months later, when Paula gave birth to a daughter, he named her Geula (literally, "salvation").

Such sentiments were shared, as we have seen, by many pioneers of the Second Aliyah. They disdained "small, cheap, secular" kinds of happiness and desired to open glorious vistas of a "superb life" in a new Jewish community in Palestine, based on a messianic blend of Zionism and socialism. These messianic sentiments became even more pronounced with the arrival of the third wave of immigrants, between 1919 and 1924.

THE THIRD ALIYAH

As a mass movement the Third Aliyah was mainly a result of the Balfour Declaration of 1917. The British declaration, and its subsequent endorsement by the League of Nations, gave international legality to what had been, since 1881, the haphazard experiment of a few enthusiastic amateurs. However, it was not the only reason for the coming of the Third Aliyah. The financial problems, boundary changes, and general European disorder following World War I caused many Jews to seek a new life elsewhere. Russian Jews, in particular, felt a growing disappointment with the results of the Russian Revolution of 1917, to which they had pinned their hopes for social justice and equal opportunities. The revolution and its immediate aftermath inflicted terrible suffering on all Russians, but most historians agree that the Jews in the former Pale of Settlement suffered more than the population in general. In the Ukraine alone the number of Jewish casualties as a result of the revolution has been estimated at between 60,000 and 130,000. There and elsewhere, the revolution was accompanied by a series of pogroms, led by peasants and soldiers, that were far more devastating in ferocity, number of victims, and destruction than any previous riots under the czar. Some Russian Jews began to realize that the ideology of the Russian Revolution would not solve the Jewish problem, and they sought to emigrate.

The spirit of the third wave of immigration into Palestine was passionately anti-authoritarian. The new ḥalutzim were opposed to formal government by professionals. They wanted to be free people, operating in loosely associated, voluntarily established communes of like-minded enthusiasts, subject to the most direct, grassroots kinds of democracy imaginable. No one person should be master; all must have an equal share in government.

WHAT IS A ḤALUTZ?

And yet, these liberal ideas frequently clashed with rigid principles of .

service and rules of personal behavior. These rigid rules were imposed by majority decisions and were sometimes so intolerant of minority views that people holding even slightly different opinions often found it impossible to live in the same settlement. There is little that can so restrict an individual's freedom as service to an extreme form of self-government. The demands of ḥalutzism must have come as a terrible burden to all but the strongest spirits. Its requirements were defined in a typical 1923 statement:

> *Halutzism* is not sacrifice but Fulfillment. It is the marriage of innermost, subjective strivings and objective values.
>
> The *halutz* is an "Individualist." His act satisfies his very own, basic drives for a new life.
>
> The *halutz* is the socialist (commune-man) *par excellence*. He wants the commune, because without it he could not be an individual; for only within the commune can the "new life" flower, *among* humans, not merely *within* them.
>
> In the *halutz* individualism and collectivism unite in a natural-organic manner, not in an ideological one. And so is proven, that the "contradiction" between individual and commune is a European lie . . . as he fulfills himself, the *halutz* fulfills the Idea. Within him is abolished the polarity of individual and commune, as well as the polarity of Body and Spirit, Being and Value.

related themes

Opposition to the Balfour Declaration   When the Balfour Declaration was issued in 1917, many Jewish young people from Eastern Europe were encouraged to emigrate to Palestine. The knowledge that the British government would help them in creating a Jewish state spurred them on. But at the same time, Jewish anti-Zionists began to fear that the creation of a Jewish homeland would undermine their political status and expose them to accusations of dual loyalty. Though these anti-Zionists in Britain were unable to keep the declaration from being issued, they did manage to get its wording watered down: the original draft of the declaration was much more specific and unconditional in its promise of a homeland to the Jews. The *Times* of London observed that "only an imaginative nervousness suggests that [the founding of a Jewish state] in some form would cause Christendom to turn around on the Jews and say 'Now you have a home of your own, go to it.'"

Quiet Protest While the Jews of the Second and Third Aliyot used their action and their work as a social protest, the Jews remaining in Europe protested in much quieter ways. Much of this quiet protest was carried on in the Yiddish literature which developed during this period. In his story "The Calf," Mendele Mocher Seforim, the father of Yiddish literature, bitterly cries out at the lot of the poor Jewish students in the European houses of study. "Almighty God," he writes, "is it really your will that a human being be cooped up like a goose from childhood, never to see the world, and to stuff his mind with such nonsense as mine is stuffed with?"

Sholem Aleichem, the most famous of the Yiddish writers, spoke with sad humor of poverty and the way in which God allowed the Jews to suffer it. "We have so many poor people in our town, God bless them, that if you really went at it you could distribute Rothschild's fortune among them. . . . I am, as you know, a trusting person, and I never question God's ways. Besides, if you do complain, will it do any good?"

And the writer Y. L. Peretz's classic story "Bontche the Silent" is a model of quiet protest. In one scene Bontche is brought to heaven and informed that for his saintly acceptance of his suffering on earth all paradise is his. Bontche replies, " 'What I would really like, your excellency, is to have every morning for breakfast a hot roll with fresh butter.' A silence falls upon the great hall, and slowly the judge and the angels bend their heads in shame at the unending meekness that they have created on earth. . . ."

issues and values

The Individual and the Community Popular slogans among young people are "do your own thing" and "create a life-style that is really and truly *you*." The ḥalutzim, too, were seeking to create a life-style which would reflect their own values and needs. However, unlike the youth of America, the ḥalutzim believed that true individuality could only flourish in a framework of community involvement and responsibility. Aḥad Ha'am, the great Hebrew writer, expresses this feeling in his essay "Flesh and Spirit." There he writes: "The existence of a man who is a Jew is not purposeless, because he is a member of the people of Israel . . . this attitude to life . . . lifts the individual above the love of self and teaches him to find purpose in the well-being of the community." How would you define "doing your own thing"? Is your personal fulfillment strictly a private affair?

Rebels Against the Establishment The ḥalutzim were rebels against the establishment. Yet they were by no means the first Jews to rebel, even against the Jewish establishment. Long before, the prophets had openly defied the "establishment" of the first Hebrew Commonwealth because they felt that the kings and priests were distorting the spirit of the Law with their social injustice and moral indifference. The Ḥassidic movement which arose in the middle of the eighteenth century in Poland and the Ukraine rebelled against the elitism and the dry formalism of the Talmudic scholars (who were the Eastern European establishment) and sought, instead, a piety marked by joy, religious ecstasy, and a sense of ongoing intimacy with God. Both Reform and Conservative Judaism came into being as efforts to redefine Jewish tradition along lines that would reflect its true essence—the creators of these movements believed that the "establishment" Judaism of the time had grown too rigid, too frozen, and too ritualized to meet their needs. If you had to define the Jewish "establishment" today, who or what do you think it is? Do you feel that you are a rebel against the Jewish establishment in any way? Do you think you are leading basically the same kind of life as your parents, or do you try to make specific changes?

perspective

Israel's earliest folk heroes were farmers and construction workers. There were no miracles, no instant transformations, only the prospect of work—and the promise that tomorrow would bring more of the same. Nevertheless, the experience of the Labor Brigade was marked by an enthusiasm that flatly refused to give way to despair. More than courage was involved, more even than the capacity to endure; the pride of participation in the building of a new way of life stood fast and firm against the impact of hardships and setbacks.

In the early 1920's the ḥalutzim sought a project to honor the memory of Joseph Trumpeldor. Trumpeldor, a prominent pioneer, had been shot to death in 1920 by Arab marauders while defending Tel Hai, the northernmost Jewish settlement in the Galilee. The death in action of this former pacifist and onetime military hero, who had even expressed his abhorrence of killing by becoming a vegetarian, gave the young Jewish community in Palestine—and Zionists everywhere—their first heroic legend.

THE LABOR BRIGADE

A group of ḥalutzim formed the Joseph Trumpeldor Labor Brigade, aimed at turning the entire country into one great kibbutz, owned and self-governed by members engaged in agriculture and industry. They felt that under this plan there would be little need for government, since people would enjoy unheard-of freedom through independent, loosely federated, collective and cooperative bodies owned and directly controlled by their members. The men and women of the Labor Brigade frequently shared their income and all their personal possessions. They lived in tent encampments and hired themselves out as construction workers, road gangs, and swamp-drainage teams.

FROM DREAM
TO REALITY
1905-1948

Newcomers frequently arrived at camp straight from the boat. A laborer on one of the road gangs later described his first days:

> We found [a tent] with torn flaps. Beds in those days were two iron bars tied to a wooden board. Even those were luxuries to us, for we had none. So we gathered a few pieces of broken plywood and put them on the ground. I remember how jubilant we were when one day we found a whole piece of plywood which could serve as a real bed. . . . Within a few days our [European city] shoes were disintegrating in the mud. They were not made to protect the feet of road workers. It was impossible to get other shoes . . . soon most of us moved about with feet bound in cloth rags. . . .

Many Labor Brigade members later found their way to the kibbutzim. At least one of the present three great kibbutz movements—*HaKibbutz HaMe'uhad* (the United Kibbutz), with a membership in 1970 of close to 26,000—is a direct descendant of the Labor Brigade. Membership in the brigade never exceeded 665 at one time, but the total number of *halutzim* who passed through has been estimated at 2000. Many later achieved considerable prominence in Israeli politics.

THE EFFECT OF THE BRIGADE

The romance of the Labor Brigade and its road gangs lingered on for years. It was considered a status symbol to have one's address at a certain point on this or that road under construction, where one of the labor communes of the brigade had pitched its tents. In later years, even brief membership in the select fraternity of men who had paved, say, the Haifa-Jedda or Afula-Nazareth roads became a note of distinction and frequently a key to political advancement. In 1954, 30 years after the event and six years after Israel had attained independence, almost half the leading politicians in the ruling Labor Party and a third of all senior officials in government, the trade unions, and the union-owned industries had been, in the 1920's, construction workers, laborers in road gangs, or members of idealistic communes. Few would have suspected in these individualists the beginnings of a future "establishment."

related themes

Joseph Trumpeldor Joseph Trumpeldor was born and raised in the rugged mountains of the northern Caucasus. It was there he acquired the physical strength and the courage which were his trademarks ever after. Trumpeldor was always a man of action. In the Russian army he became the first Jew ever to be commissioned as an officer; he won a medal for bravery and had his arm amputated after receiving a battle wound in the Russo-Japanese War. Trumpeldor left the Russian army in time to witness the pogroms of 1905. These anti-Semitic outbursts made him determined to leave Russia. He organized and prepared a group of young people to start a new life as farmers in Palestine; once there, he used his army background to train the settlers to defend themselves.

When World War I broke out, Trumpeldor along with Vladimir Jabotinsky organized the first Jewish military force in nearly 2000 years—the Jewish Legion (which was first given the name "Zion Mule Corps")—fighting as part of the British army against the Turks.

In 1919, Trumpeldor began the task of creating a system of defense for the Jewish settlements in the Upper Galilee, to protect the settlers from the constant Bedouin raids. Somehow, despite a critical shortage of food and weapons, the Jews held their own and even managed to do some farming. But in March 1920 a band of Arabs came to Kibbutz Tel Ḥai on the pretext of a visit, and once inside they attacked the unarmed kibbutzniks. In the course of this battle, Joseph Trumpeldor was fatally wounded. Through his life of action and through his personal strength and courage, Trumpeldor helped establish the principle of self-defense in the Jewish community of Palestine.

Hashomer Although Trumpeldor was a key figure in the defense apparatus of the early Zionist settlements, he was not its creator. *Hashomer* (the Guard), the official defense agency of the Yishuv, was founded in 1907 by a small band of pioneers (among them David Ben-Gurion and Yitzḥak Ben-Zvi) who helped establish new settlements and assumed responsibility for the safety of Jewish villages located in heavily populated Arab areas. The members of Hashomer believed that security could be neither begged nor bought, but had to come from within the community. The older Jewish farmers and landowners (the Biluim) strongly disagreed. They opposed Hashomer for two reasons. First, they did not wish to offend the Arab guards they were employing (and who sometimes opened their gates at night for the Arab marauders to come in), for the guards were in a position to make trouble. Second, they doubted that the Jewish guard would be able to defend them when it came to actual fighting. But the farmers were wrong. Hashomer effectively protected the Jewish settlements until

Hashomer: Defenders of the Yishuv.

1920, at which time it was replaced by the larger *Haganah,* which was to serve as the defense arm of the Jewish community in Palestine until 1948, when the State of Israel was established and the Israeli army came into being.

issues and values

Working and the Labor Brigade The ḥalutzim were like pioneers everywhere; they had to face the realities of everyday work to bring their dreams to life. It is hardly surprising that a person who knew how to germinate a seed, when to fertilize, or how to graft a vine gained rapid respect. One modern kibbutznik wrote:

> The truly respected person is the one who has mastered a trade or an agricultural skill. . . . The experienced and hard-working orange-grower, vegetable gardener, tractor driver, mechanic, carpenter or poultry raiser is the real backbone of the kibbutz in his own mind and in the minds of his fellow members . . . the children in the school will respect a teacher who, they know, could have been a good tractorist had he so desired, and tend often to sneer at other teachers not so gifted. The sneering is slowly giving way to an appreciation of these responsibilities too, but the underlying concentration on physical labor as the prime status factor still remains. . . . (Murray Weingarten, *Life on the Kibbutz*)

Given this need and this attitude, it is hardly surprising that the Labor Brigade became so important and, above all, so cherished. In America, by contrast, we seem to have the idea that "the cleaner the hands, the more respectable the job." Do you share this view? Which profession or line of work do you think is most cherished or prized in American society? What needs do you think that profession or line of work fulfills?

Normalizing the Jew   For a variety of reasons, the majority of Jews in the Diaspora are businessmen, professionals, intellectuals, and small tradesmen; they are rarely found in the spheres of agriculture and heavy industry. The early Zionists believed that this was an abnormal state of affairs. A. D. Gordon wrote an essay called "People and Labor," in which he said:

> The Jewish people has been completely cut off from nature and imprisoned within city walls these 2000 years. We have become accustomed to every form of life except to a life of labor. . . . It will require the greatest effort of will for such a people to become normal again. A vital culture, far from being detached from life, embraces it with all its aspects. Culture is whatever life creates for living purposes. Farming, building, road-making—any work, any craft, any productive activity . . . is the foundation and stuff of culture. We must ourselves do all the work . . . the dirtiest and the most difficult . . . then and only then shall we have a culture of our own. . . .

Do you agree with Gordon that for a people to be normal and vital, it must engage in all forms of labor? Are there any lines of work or profession in this country which you would describe as being particularly Jewish or non-Jewish?

perspective

The dreamers of Bittania were, by any measure, fanatics; some of their practices bordered on the bizarre. Though passionately antireligious, they infused their daily life with a quality of feverish mysticism, seeking through their experience to be propelled to heights of joyous abandon. They viewed their leader as a combination guru and father-confessor. And still, for all their radicalism, the people of Bittania believed that their community signified not a breaking away from the Jewish people (whose ghetto life they despised and whose rituals they rejected) but a means of liberating them.

One of the most fascinating of the brotherhoods which sprung up in the early 1920's was that of Bittania. The commune of Bittania was located in the Jordan Valley, romantically perched on a dry, stony hilltop overlooking the Sea of Galilee. It is hard to imagine a softer, more peaceful landscape. Here, in the first century A.D., according to the Jewish historian Josephus, the area surrounding the lake had been a virtual Eden of fragrant flowers, fruit trees, and fountains.

In Bittania proper there was nothing picturesque whatsoever. It was a dismal, slumlike conglomeration of dirty tents and shabby, wooden huts surrounded by a few dreary vegetable patches. The men and women of Bittania—the commune numbered some 40 or 50 members—came mostly from Galicia. There they had belonged to the Zionist youth movement *Hashomer Hatzair* (Young Guard).

The men and women of Bittania called themselves an *eddah* (congregation). "To remain pure we must extricate ourselves from the abyss of conformity," began a Hashomer Hatzair statement:

> Perhaps we shall be the first torrent of youth to remain young forever; humanity's first chance to escape failure. Let us go far between mountains and deserts to live in simplicity, beauty and truth. Perhaps our

new *eddah* will be the nucleus of a new culture of new relationships between humans leading communal lives. We shall be the pioneers who shall carry the revolution through to the masses of miserable Jews, who will stream to the country to live by our principles. Let us create a new land of Israel free from the shackles of European capitalism and of the diaspora. . . .

MEIR YAARI

The members of Bittania were mainly of solid middle-class origins. Some had been to college; nearly all had completed good Polish or Austrian *gymnasiums,* and most spoke two or three languages fluently. Their leader was a slim young man by the name of Meir Wald, who soon Hebraicized his surname to Yaari. He was simply called Meir by his disciples. He was a man of extraordinary intellect, personal magnetism, and suggestive power; his lean face was pierced by a pair of fiery eyes; a shock of black hair fell over his high forehead. He was the unchallenged guru of his group. His followers sat at his feet in concentrated admiration, a charmed circle.

David Horowitz, one of the few who broke away, later recorded his reminiscences. He compared Bittania to a "monastic order without God." It was no simple matter to be accepted as a member; candidates passed a trial period, a kind of initiation. Horowitz likened Bittania to a "religious sect . . . with its own charismatic leader and set of symbols, and a ritual of confessions in public. . . ."

THE SIHAH

Although the men and women of Bittania spent from ten to 14 hours a day working hard in the fields, such labors of the body were considered as sidelights to the "real life." Everyone knew, says Horowitz, that the real life at Bittania "began in the evening." After a frugal meal in the communal dining shed, members engaged in the *sihah* (literally, "conversation"). In reality, it was a prolonged session of monologues and near-hysterical public confessions where members bared their innermost secrets, yearnings, and doubts.

Daily sessions usually began with a half hour of silent contemplation at which Meir Yaari presided. "Who art thou, Man?" a participant once called out to Yaari, according to the published record, "you who have such power and daring to force me this very minute to step out of my soul—one step above it and myself!"

Another exclaimed: "I beseech you, I beseech you, brethren, teach me true love! True love! I want to be sacrificed on its altar." A kind of

Meir Yaari: Leader of
the Bittania commune.

release was achieved by this obsessive sharing. Members "sat up til dawn . . . we confesed to each other. It was like pure prayer bursting forth from heart to heart. . . ." On one occasion they called it their "night of atonement." On another, a member exclaimed that "in Bittania a book was opened to us which was different from the usual; it was the soul of man."

The land they tilled they called their bride; they were its "bridegroom who abandons himself in his bride's bosom . . . yes, thus we abandoned ourselves to the motherly womb of sanctifying earth." And Yaari summed up: "In this last hour of usage, before our wedding night, we bring as holy sacrifice to you, earth of our fulfillment, these our very lives, our daily lives in the Land of Israel; our parents, children, brothers, our poverty and wealth. . . ." Speakers sometimes fainted from excitement at the rostrum; girls seized by sudden fits of hysteria jumped to their feet and ran from the room crying. "There were times when I feared that collective madness would seize this lonely congregation," Horowitz writes.

BITTANIA—ONE AMONG MANY

In retrospect, the commune of Bittania certainly seems more bizarre than the others. But was it? The men and women of Bittania were on the whole more outspoken than the rest of the pioneers. They left a revealing written document testifying to their inner struggles and debates; members of other communes, less outspoken or more reserved, have not.

People commonly considered to be "in their right senses" would scarcely have settled as pioneers in Bittania or in one of the other early communes. Weizmann, although he was not a socialist, was fascinated by the communards. ("To be a Zionist it is not necessary to be mad, but it helps.") He often said that he felt better among the communards than among the Jewish settlers in the towns. To Weizmann, the search for a "new, just society" in the communes seemed one guarantee that the Zionist enterprise would not end as "just another nation-state."

THE PIONEERS

The physical and psychological strains of creating a new society based on justice and love were enormous. The ḥalutzim were mostly young men and women in their 20's. In photographs, however, they look much older—weary and slumped over tin plates in shabby communal dining rooms, or bravely smiling into cameras out in the dusty fields. It is hard to imagine today the environment in which they lived; it has since been so completely reshaped. Large stretches of country were still barren, traversed only by dirt tracks. Traffic moved slowly, much of it on camelback or by "diligence," a horse-drawn wagon similar to those used in the American West a few decades earlier. Medical services were improving, but disease was still rampant. There was hardly a ḥalutz who escaped malaria. Levi Eshkol remembered fever-stricken nights which gave him terrible nightmares. With recurrent attacks, the whole body weakened and became less resistant to other diseases. Dysentery, rheumatism, typhoid, and skin and eye diseases were all common.

Among those who remained in the kibbutzim, the single most important compensation for enduring such hardship was the deep sense of satisfaction and of personal achievement which came from participation in an extraordinary drama.

related themes

Jewish Tradition and Nonconformity   "To remain pure, we must extricate ourselves from the abyss of conformity," the *Hashomer Hatzair* statement read, and it touches a central nerve in Jewish history and tradition. By remaining aloof from the evil ways of their neighbors, Lot and his family became moral nonconformists in Sodom. When the other spies presented a hysterical report to Moses, Caleb and Joshua, who had been sent with them to scout out the Promised Land, told the truth instead and were then singled out for praise and reward. The concept of a Chosen People, a people charged with the mission of learning, living, and imparting God's Law, was, in effect, a command to be "a nation not like other nations"—that is, to nonconform.

Perhaps the greatest source of danger to Judaism and the Jewish people has been the impulse to conform. When the people wanted a king, Samuel bitterly criticized them for wanting to fashion a society like all the other societies around them. He described for them all the evils which a king would work, and with the creation of a kingdom, all these predictions eventually came to pass.

Finally, the largest threat to Jewish life in the Diaspora has been the phenomenon of assimilation, which comes directly from the impulse to conform to the way of life of the non-Jewish majority.

Cowboys and Ḥalutzim   It is interesting to compare and contrast the ḥalutzim and the people who pioneered the American frontier in the nineteenth century. Both groups broke away from the established centers of civilization. Both had a desire for adventure, a willingness to endure hardship and danger, a need to explore uncharted territory, and the hope of taming a wilderness. Both cowboys and ḥalutzim became the folk heroes of their respective cultures.

But for all the similarities, there were crucial differences. The American pioneers were essentially loners; their basic drive was to cut loose from all organized society. The rancher, the homesteader, the prospector, and the trader may have come together for purposes of mutual profit or mutual protection, but they were really rugged individualists. The cowboy is portrayed as a rootless wanderer, drifting from job to job, most at home on the isolated stretches of prairie and plain. The "Wild West" was wild because the rule of law—the basic component of community—did not prevail in many places.

The ḥalutzim, on the other hand, were interested in new forms of community life, forms that would express their new principles. They were deeply aware of their connection to the Jewish people as a whole. Even so radical a commune as Bittania is described as an eddah or congregation—"the nucleus of a new culture . . . we shall be the pioneers who shall carry the revolution through to the masses of miserable Jews. . . ."

issues and values

Past and Future   In some ways the Bittania experiment was an attempt to escape from the past into an ideal future. In his essay "Revolution and Tradition," Berl Katznelson explains:

> There are many who think of our revolution in a much too simple and primitive manner. Let us destroy the old world entirely, let us burn all the treasures that it accumulated . . . and start anew. . . . But a renewing and creative generation does not throw the cultural heritage of the ages into the dustbin. It examines, scrutinizes, accepts and rejects.

Katznelson goes on to show what he means, using Passover as an example.

> I know no literary creation which can evoke a greater hatred of slavery and love of freedom than the story of the bondage and exodus from Egypt. . . . I know of no other remembrance of the past that is so entirely a symbol of our present and future. . . .

Do you study history as a "required course" or as the "interesting" and "colorful" events of the past? Or do you try to see how history relates to the present, how current events have been shaped by the past? Are there any events in Jewish history which have special meaning for you today?

Center and Spirit of World Jewry The settlers of Bittania also wanted to cut themselves off from the Diaspora. Not all Zionists felt this way. Many felt that the new Jewish state should play a central part in the shaping of world Jewry and Judaism. Aḥad Ha'am expressed this view in his essay "The Jewish State and the Jewish Problem":

> We may . . . establish a Jewish state; it is possible that the Jews of that state may increase and multiply until the land is filled with them, but even then the greatest part of our people will remain scattered on foreign soils . . . this Jewish settlement [in the land of Israel] . . . will become in the course of time the center of the nation [world Jewry] . . . then, from this center, the spirit of Judaism will radiate to the circumference to all the communities of the diaspora, to inspire them with new life and to preserve the overall unity of our people. When our national culture has attained that level . . . Israel will be not merely a state of Jews but really a Jewish state.

What is the difference between a state of Jews and a Jewish state? In what ways does the State of Israel affect you personally?

THE
STATE
OF
ISRAEL

perspective

The kibbutz and its way of life are above all an affirmation, a proclamation of faith in the future. Here a community has been created where none existed before. The land has been brought to productive life. Values and ideals have been given active expression. And yet, beneath the surface, there are memories of a bitter past— of pogroms, Arab marauders, children huddling for safety in underground bunkers, battles fought, and people killed. Kibbutz Yad Mordechai is a particularly moving case in point.

South of Ashkelon, alongside the Mediterranean Sea, the narrow coastal road winds through orange groves and cotton fields toward the town of Gaza and the old Egyptian frontier. There are vineyards and banana plantations; the fields are dotted with beehives and plastic-covered hothouses. Along the way are two dozen or so new villages and kibbutzim. Some of the villages have been settled by Jewish refugees from the Arab countries. Others have been settled by Eastern European survivors of the Holocaust, and still others by second-generation Israelis, youngsters from older towns and settlements in the north. Everywhere there are huge cowsheds and chicken farms, orchards and vegetable beds. The area, which prior to 1948 was a dusty plain, is now largely under artificial irrigation. Part of the water is pumped up from artesian wells; part flows down to this southern region from the north, through the pipes and open channels of the Jordan River Project, completed in 1963.

Few Israeli landscapes reflect the changes of the past quarter century as visibly and dramatically as this coastal strip. Ashkelon is a new city of gleaming white houses; two-thirds of its population consists of immigrants from Morocco, Tunisia, and Iraq. Founded in 1953, the new town stands on what had been a barren sand dune scattered with

THE STATE
OF ISRAEL

110

archaeological remains. In antiquity, Ashkelon had been one of the five strongholds of the Philistines; successively Greek, Roman, Byzantine, Arab, and Crusader, it was destroyed and had been abandoned since 1270.

Farther south along the coastal road, a few hundred yards before the 1947 Egyptian-Israeli border at the Gaza Strip, a ruined water tower lies on its side, surrounded by luxuriant gardens, with benches under flowering oleander trees around a small artificial pool. The scene is dominated by the shell-pocked tower, a remnant of the Egyptian-Israeli war of 1948. Nearby the giant bronze statue of a man rises above the treetops, a rough-cut figure in shirtsleeves and baggy pants. The bronze statue represents Mordechai Anilevicz, the 22-year-old commander of the desperate Warsaw Ghetto uprising of 1943.

The nearby kibbutz is named after the dead hero: Yad Mordechai. Its little houses, clustered around a pleasant communal dining room, are set in a wide expanse of tree-shaded lawn. Yad Mordechai was founded in 1943 by one of the last groups of Zionist pioneers which managed to escape Poland on the eve of World War II.

Yad Mordechai, for all its calm and pleasant exterior, is burdened with its heavy memories of the Holocaust. To this inheritance was added the crucial role the kibbutz played in Israel's War of Independence.

THE PARTITION OF PALESTINE

In November 1947 the United Nations General Assembly decided to partition Palestine into an Arab and a Jewish State. If left to themselves, the two states within partitioned Palestine might have clashed initially, but they might have worked out a bearable solution to their differences. In the beginning, hatred and suspicion would have overshadowed everything. But gradually, the two sides might have evolved a kind of grudging coexistence.

But they were not left alone. On May 14, only one day after British rule over Palestine formally came to an end, the regular armies of five neighboring Arab states invaded the country. We now know that they expected a quick victory, an easy military operation that would last only a few days. We also know, at least in the case of Egypt and Syria, that their chief aim was not to safeguard the rights of Palestinian Arabs but to carve out for themselves sizable chunks of territory in a country suddenly abandoned by the British. Only the Jews of brand-new Israel stood in their way.

The invading Egyptian force comprised roughly 10,000 men. Their infantry was supported by a small air force, heavy artillery, and tank and armored units. The new Jewish state was unequipped with anything but the most primitive weapons. Israel was hardly prepared to meet an invasion. The Egyptians, relying upon their vast superiority in manpower and equipment, hoped—not without reason—to reach Tel Aviv within a few days.

THE BATTLE OF YAD MORDECHAI

Yad Mordechai, at the Gaza end of the main coastal highway to Tel Aviv, was one of the first Jewish settlements to bear the full brunt of the Egyptian attack. The settlement had prepared some fortifications: a barbed-wire fence, trenches, a few dug-in concrete positions. These were not designed to withstand an attack by regular forces supported by tanks and artillery; nor had Yad Mordechai given serious thought to such an attack. Only a few weeks before the war, the men of Yad Mordechai had been told by "reliable sources" in Tel Aviv that Egypt was not planning an invasion. "You will have to hold out only against bands of Arab irregulars and armed villagers from the immediate neighborhood." When, contrary to expectations, the Egyptian army advanced toward Tel Aviv, Yad Mordechai became the scene of battle. It was neither the longest nor even the bloodiest battle in that short and awful war. Yet it was, in all likelihood, one of the most decisive.

There were barely over 100 men at Yad Mordechai, including boys of 14; only about 75 or 80 men and boys were capable fighters. Armed only with rifles (some of them antiquated), 3,000 rounds of ammunition, 400 hand grenades, two machine guns, and two 2-inch mortars with 50 shells, the defenders of Yad Mordechai effectively blocked the advance of an entire Egyptian brigade for a full six days. Teenagers with homemade "Molotov cocktails" (bottles filled with a burning liquid, usually gasoline) threw themselves upon Egyptian tanks and armored vehicles. The settlement was surrounded and under constant artillery fire, and it was repeatedly bombed from the air. The water tower was blown up on the second day. Twenty-four men—nearly one-third of the active defending force—were killed; another 30 were wounded. On May 22, the fourth day of Egyptian attack, Yad Mordechai sent this signal to the settlements to the north: "The men's morale is sinking. . . . They approach exhaustion . . . the settlement must be reinforced or abandoned. . . . It is vital that women and wounded be evacuated immediately."

On May 23 the last machine gun had become unserviceable. Late that night the men of Yad Mordechai decided to abandon their burning settlement. Even as they crawled out of their bunkers, choking from the nauseating stench, and even though morale was extremely low, they argued among themselves over the decision to retreat. Some of them passionately demanded that they imitate the Warsaw Ghetto uprising and fight until the last man had died. Fortunately they were overruled. The survivors managed to infiltrate through the Egyptian lines and reach the neighboring settlement of Gvar Am, a few miles north.

Yad Mordechai was lost. Nevertheless, the battle had a profound military and political effect. During the six days that it lasted, Jewish units farther north were able to set up a line of defense. The advance on Tel Aviv was arrested. The new state was not destroyed.

RECLAIMING YAD MORDECHAI

A United Nations cease-fire went into effect on June 11, 1948, but it did not last long. When the firing resumed a few months later, the tables were turned; Yad Mordechai was recaptured by the Israelis. The Egyptians were pushed back to the Gaza Strip and to their own frontier, and remained there until 1967. Yad Mordechai was rebuilt nearly from scratch in 1949; only the shattered water tower was left as a reminder.

Writing of Yad Mordechai 15 years after the battle, Chaim Laskov, a former Israeli general and chief of staff, quoted an anonymous English poet:

> The race is not to him that's got
> The longest legs to run,
> Nor the battle to those people
> That shoot the longest gun.

related themes

The Warsaw Ghetto Uprising   Kibbutz Yad Mordechai is named for Mordechai Anilevicz, leader of the Warsaw Ghetto uprising, which is usually regarded as the most dramatic act of Jewish resistance to take place during World War II. When the ghetto was first established by German order, more than 500,000 Jews were crowded into its small area. The leaders of the various parties and factions within the ghetto were confronted by the agonizing question of how to deal with the German demands. To cooperate might buy time. They had heard rumors of the death camps, but the Germans had taken great care to mislead them and keep them unsure by giving them constant reason to hope for the best. They knew that, whatever the future might hold, resistance would only bring death. But by February 1943, German intentions were no longer in doubt; for the Jews, not to resist now would be to cooperate in their own extermination. There were only 60,000 Jews left in the ghetto; the rest had been "relocated" to various concentration camps, where they were either put to death or used as slave labor. The Jews remaining in the ghetto decided to fight back. When the Germans entered the ghetto to begin the final process of Jewish deportation, they met with savage resistance and were forced to retreat. They tried again, this time using tanks, artillery, and flame-throwers against the Jewish uprising, but they were driven back by home-made bombs. On the eve of Passover, April 19, 1943, the Germans, ordered by their superiors to destroy the ghetto at all costs, began their final attack. A fierce bombardment commenced. The fighting was street to street, house to house. The German commander reported that "the resistance put up by the Jews and bandits could be broken only by relentlessly using all our force and energy day and night. . . ." When the streets were lost, the ghetto fighters took to the sewers and continued the battle from there. In all, the fighting lasted 28 days and ended with the blowing up of the ghetto synagogue. More than 56,000 Jews were killed. Nearly 100 managed to escape through the sewers and lived to tell the world what had happened.

The Burma Road The War of Independence was marked by the Israelis' ability to improvise in the face of desperate odds. One of the most spectacular acts of this kind was the construction of the Burma Road,* which broke the siege of Jerusalem. Jerusalem had been encircled by Arab forces by March 1948, cut off from the outside world except for a small, single-engine plane and a makeshift airstrip. In Jerusalem there was no fuel and no running water (water had to be brought to families by truck and was severely rationed), and electricity was a "sometime thing." The city was regularly bombarded by Arab artillery. Food rations were running dangerously low; there was a strong possibility of famine. On May 28, the Jewish quarter of Jerusalem's Old City fell to Transjordan's Arab Legion, led by British officers. With the road blocked at Latrun, the Israeli army had to construct a new way through the Judean hills to Jerusalem—and quickly. This route, known as the Burma Road, was carved out of the rocks of the hills in total secrecy. Every night engineers, bulldozers, and stone-

* A road extending from Burma to China, which was used during World War II to supply Allied military forces in China.

cutters hacked a path through the mountains; they succeeded in creating a barely passable road that spanned the entire distance, except for a final steep and dangerous stretch 1½ miles long. Urgency forced the men to improvise. Hundreds of men walked the mile and a half to the supply trucks from the coastal plain, each carrying on his back a 45-pound sack of flour, holding on with one hand to the shirttail of the man before him. Gradually the last stretch of distance was bridged, and by the time of the first truce, the siege of Jerusalem had been broken.

issues and values

Spiritual Resistance   The Jews of Europe resisted the Nazis spiritually and intellectually as well as physically. Newspapers were circulated within the ghettos and in the concentration camps. Systems of mutual aid and responsibility were established. Torah scrolls were rescued from the ruins of synagogues. Works of history, literature, and philosophy were widely read and discussed. People made drawings, wrote poetry, and attended lectures, concerts, and dramatic presentations.

Even in the Warsaw Ghetto students continued their Jewish studies.

There were marriages and Bar Mitzvah ceremonies. Diaries were kept —and later discovered—painstakingly documenting the details of the tragedy that was taking place. A group of Jewish physicians within the ghetto even initiated a number of studies on the pathological aspects of starvation; these were found and published after the war. And finally, as an ultimate expression of their will to live, in direct defiance of Nazi edict, the Jews persisted in teaching their children—extensively and at all levels. One Israeli teacher recalls that she learned to read Hebrew in Bergen-Belsen, and that her teacher, in the absence of books and writing materials, scratched the Hebrew letters on the ground. What were these Jews trying to achieve? The majority of them were put to death. Wherein, then, lay the importance of what they did?

The People Factor   By every law of statistics, the newborn State of Israel should have been overrun by the Arab armies within a few days. Yigael Yadin, chief operations officer of the Haganah, gave the following evaluation of the military situation on May 21, 1948:

> The regular forces of the neighboring countries—with their equipment and their armaments enjoy . . . a great superiority at this time. Our air force cannot even compare with theirs. We have no air force. The planes have not arrived yet. . . . To sum up, I would say that the outlook at this time seemed delicately balanced. Or—to be more honest—I would say that their superiority is considerable.

At the beginning of the war, the Israeli air force consisted of four Piper Cub single-engine planes. The Arabs had modern warplanes supplied by Britain. Israel did not have a single tank, and its artillery consisted of five howitzers made in France in 1873! And yet, as in Yad Mordechai, the Israelis held their ground, resisted the Arab invaders, and went on to win a most remarkable victory. Yadin said:

> . . . Evaluation of the possibilities cannot merely be a military consideration . . . the problem is to what extent our men will be able to overcome enemy forces by virtue of their fighting spirit. . . . It has been found in certain cases that it is not the numbers and the formation that determine the outcome of battle, but something else.

The Warsaw Ghetto, the battle of Yad Mordechai, the Israeli War of Independence, and the spiritual resistance of those caught up in the Holocaust are all examples of a people's ability to stand up to an enemy despite great odds. Have you ever come across an instance in which the "people factor" worked to transcend seemingly insurmountable obstacles?

perspective

As the members of Kibbutz Yad Mordechai busily raise their children and cultivate fields, the Arab refugee camps nearby stand as a grim reminder of the continuing tragedy and ever-present danger that cloud their lives. It is a moral dilemma that touches all Israelis to one degree or another. The kibbutzniks feel that they have earned the right to the land on which they live: they have worked for it, developed it, fought for it, and inherited it as their birthright. Morover, they know that they are not responsible for the creation and continuation of the Arab refugee problem. Yet this problem exists. As long as the refugees remain in their camps, hopeless, feeding on hatred and visions of revenge, regarding Palestine as their rightful home, the Israelis will never enjoy complete ease of mind—or conscience.

YAD MORDECHAI NOW

Today Yad Mordechai is a thriving little community of some 300 adults and 200 children. Its hothouses produce long-stemmed roses that are exported by air to Europe. Its beehives produce up to 40 tons of honey each year. Agriculture—citrus groves, dairy farming, cotton, and barley—is fully mechanized, and a canning plant manufactures jams and juices. As in all Israeli kibbutzim, the poor life of earlier days has given way to a measure of comfort. At first, some of the bare cement houses destroyed by the Egyptians were repaired in order to accommodate the returnees; these structures have since been replaced by pleasant cottages in which each family has a two-room apartment with a private kitchen and bathroom. There is a library of 24,000 volumes.

The land which Yad Mordechai cultivates today is almost three times the pre-1948 area. Like all the older kibbutzim, Yad Mordechai inherited the land abandoned in 1948 by inhabitants of the neighboring Arab villages. The kibbutzniks had been on quite friendly terms with the Arab villagers before the war. The villagers' land is now leased to Yad Mordechai by the Custodian of Abandoned Arab Property. The Gaza Strip, to which most of the Arab villagers fled, is only a few hundred yards away. From the rooftops of their kibbutz, the men and women of Yad Mordechai can see the refugee camps where most of the villagers and their descendants have lived since 1948. In turn, the Arab refugees can clearly see the men and women of Yad Mordechai tilling the soil to which they themselves cannot return.

THE PEOPLE OF YAD MORDECHAI

Let us take a look at the Yad Mordechai kibbutzniks as we stand on the narrow strip of sand dunes separating them from their former neighbors. The view is disturbing to many Israelis, as it is to outsiders. It reveals the crushing force of circumstance, the terrible irony of history. The kibbutzniks of Yad Mordechai were swept to the shores of Israel by the worst kind of disaster—the Holocaust. The displaced Arab villagers were victims of the unfortunate political aims of the neighboring Arab leadership. Both groups were pawns moved on the board of history by forces beyond their control.

The kibbutzniks of Yad Mordechai originally bought land for themselves and settled on it. They had no intention of pushing out their neighbors. A detached outsider might accuse the kibbutzniks of hardheartedly ignoring the problem of the Arab refugees. But such an accusation would ignore the true sequence of events—the Arabs' invasion of 1948 in opposition to the United Nations resolution, their refusal to make peace with Israel, the continuation of a state of war ever since.

The mood of the men and women of Yad Mordechai who give this subject serious thought can best be described as deep and tragic. It is the mood of individuals caught in a situation where, morally speaking, no alternative was entirely satisfactory.

What alternatives did exist for these people? Should the men and women of Yad Mordechai have remained in Poland in 1939? Palestine was one of the few countries to which they could go. Even here there were strict immigration quotas. Many of their friends and relatives who wanted to join them were refused entry and perished in the Holocaust. In 1943 the settlers began to create a new existence for themselves at Yad Mordechai. It was a hard and difficult life, but one which, at the time, held a promise of freedom and security.

When the Egyptians attacked, should they have surrendered? If so, where could the Egyptians have sent them? Who would have taken them? If they surrendered, they might have been massacred, as were the kibbutzniks in the Etzion bloc. What could or should they have done in the years that followed, as the Arab threats of war continued and Yad Mordechai became a target for attacks by saboteurs from across the nearby Egyptian border? In the meantime, a new generation was born and was growing up, fully at home on the new lawns of Yad Mordechai. The irony is deepened by the fact that the men and women of Yad Mordechai belonged, as they still do, to *Mapam* (Hashomer Hatzair), the most moderate Israeli political group. Hashomer Hatzair had opposed the establishment of an all-Jewish state and had advocated a binational solution, an Arab-Jewish entity.

TWO DISPLAYS

At the foot of a low hill south of the kibbutz, where some of the worst fighting took place during the siege of 1948, the kibbutzniks, aided by military historians, have attempted a careful reconstruction of the battle of Yad Mordechai. Human figures cast in metal, together with Egyptian tanks, armored vehicles, and pieces of artillery, represent the assaulting force at a particularly difficult moment for the defenders— May 24, a few hours before the retreat. The display gives a good idea of events during the last hours of battle and makes one wonder how the defenders held out as long as they did.

Another display at Yad Mordechai suggests one possible explanation for the defenders' stubbornness. Not far from the "battlefield," across a small park and newly planted forest, the people of Yad Mordechai, aided by public funds, have built a small museum. This ultramodern structure recounts recent Israeli history within the wider framework of the Jewish tragedy in modern times. In a cavelike entrance hall, a few graphic displays depict the eclipse of Jewish life in Europe under the Nazis:

> In this place—
> Seek and look, for what can be seen no more,
> Hear voices that can be heard no more,
> Understand what is beyond all understanding.

A harrowing image is evoked of Jewish life in Eastern Europe before 1939, a rich, rooted civilization that is now alive only in the memory of the survivors.

Next are rooms commemorating the deportations and extermination camps, the Warsaw Ghetto uprising, and Jewish partisans in the forests of Poland and the Ukraine. There are the yellow stars, Nazi deportation lists, execution orders. Through a window cut into the bare concrete wall, the visitor looks out upon the nearby battlefield and the statue of Anilevicz next to the shattered water tower. The haggard faces of survivors in the displaced persons camps after the war look down from the darkened walls. There are pictures of the great exodus from Europe of 1946–1947. Portrayed is the desperate struggle of the refugees to reach the shores of Palestine by all means available—their arrival at night in illegal boats on desolate beaches, and the first Jewish settlement built in the northern Negev on Jewish-owned land but in defiance of British restrictions.

Finally, the visitor reaches a semicircular hall where models, maps, photographs, and documents convey glimpses of the history, trial, and final triumph of Yad Mordechai itself. It is one of the most instructive museums in the country, conveying a sense of continuity between past, present, and future.

related themes

No Place to Go   The British closing of Palestine to Jewish immigration came as a blow. As it was, there was practically no place for Jews to go even when they could get out of Europe. Most countries (including the United States) had strict immigration quotas, for reasons ranging from internal politics to bureaucratic red tape. Thus, in October 1934, a ship bearing over 300 Polish and Czechoslovakian Jews could find no port to accept it because its passengers had no visas. In 1939, 68 Jewish refugees were sent back to Germany from Argentina because their temporary visas had run out. In June 1939, a boat bearing 900 Jewish refugees sailed along the American coastline for three weeks. The United States would not admit its passengers, and it was finally compelled to return to Europe. In December 1941, the *Struma*, a converted yacht carrying 769 Jews, arrived in Istanbul, but the Turkish authorities refused to admit the refugees to Turkey, and the British government refused to allow them to enter Palestine. Finally, after long negotiations, the two countries agreed to permit the children on board to enter Palestine. But Turkey decided to send the ship away before this decision could be carried out. On February 24, 1942, it was learned that the *Struma* had sunk—probably torpedoed by a German submarine. Only one passenger survived.

Annexation of Palestinian Land   Until the War of Independence, the country that is known today as Jordan was called Transjordan. The

"Trans-" indicated that the sovereign territory had only extended to the East Bank of the Jordan River. During the war, the Transjordanians captured territory on the West Bank of the Jordan, including the Old City of Jerusalem. Transjordan held on to this territory (which had been granted as a Palestinian state by the United Nations in its partition plan of 1947) and to Old Jerusalem, formally annexing both territories on April 4, 1950. Egypt seized the Gaza Strip, which had also been earmarked as part of the Palestinian Arab state by the UN, and like Jordan, refused to give up control of the newly acquired areas. In 1967 both territories were captured by the Israeli army. One of the great ironies of the Palestinian problem is that the land being demanded by most Arabs was in Arab hands from 1948 to 1967, and yet they refused to discuss peace with Israel even then!

issues and values

A Tradition of Mistrust   There is a long-standing tradition of mistrust between Israel and the Arab nations. The Arabs consider Israel a "Western export," a state created by strangers, which is bent upon expansion at their expense. The Israelis have been forced to live for years under the threat of destruction from Arab nations. The Arab-Israeli agreements of 1949, which ended the 1948 war, were supposed to be a first step toward a final peace. The Egyptian delegate declared that the agreements were "tantamount to a non-aggression pact . . . a provisional settlement that could only be supplemented by a peace settlement . . . [which] bound Egypt to assurances and commitments not to resort to force, or even plan or threaten to resort to force." Shortly thereafter, the Arab governments openly announced their intention to prepare for a "second round" with Israel. The Egyptian newspaper *Al Akbar* observed that " . . . in the last analysis, the difference between peace and unrest in our region depends upon Israel's annihilation." What steps must be taken to heal this tradition of mistrust? If you were an Israeli leader, what conditions would you ask for as a test of Arab goodwill? How would you argue against accusations of Israeli expansionism?

The Law of Return   One of the fundamental principles of the State of Israel is that every Jew has the right to settle there. In 1950, the Law of Return gave legal status to this principle, granting unconditional and automatic citizenship to all Jews who want it. In 1948, on the day of its creation, Israel had a Jewish population of 650,000. By 1951, 754,800 new immigrants had come to settle. And by 1972 the number of Jews who had immigrated to Israel since 1948 was 1,400,000, out of a total population of 3,164,000. Absorbing so many newcomers would pose an overwhelming challenge to any country. The Oriental immigrants (who numbered over 650,000) often came with no personal belongings, as the Arabs forced them to leave everything. Many had no occupational skills. Integrating these immigrants posed numerous problems, many of which still persist. But four factors contributed to the success of the absorption process: (1) the fact that all immigrants regard Israel as their home; (2) the common Jewish heritage; (3) the willingness of the Israeli government and the people to engage in this task with all their energy and resources; and (4) the help of Americans and other Jews of the Diaspora. America has been described as a nation of immigrants. In what ways is the absorption of immigrants in this country different from the process in Israel? Are you aware of being from a different homeland—that is, do you still carry the marks of immigration to this country? In what ways?

Operation Magic Carpet, 1949–1950, brought 46,000 Yemenite Jews to Israel.

perspective

Israelis still live with memories of the Holocaust. Many of its survivors are citizens of Israel—witnesses to, and reminders of, what took place in Europe. There is a grim awareness of the lonely role played by the Jews of Palestine in the rescue and rehabilitation of European Jews, and of the fact that the international community largely stood by and let the Holocaust happen—doing nothing, saying nothing. Most Israelis have come to believe that they live in a world serenely indifferent to the fate of Israel and of the Jewish people.

ALONE IN THE MODERN WORLD

Since Israel became independent in 1948, Israelis have lived in a state of geographic and political isolation unusual in the modern world. Almost every country is linked to others by military and political pacts or alliances. Most countries today share common markets, or at least open borders and a common language or religion, with another country. Israel has none of these. Apart from its geographic isolation, it is probably the only country in the world that is engaged in constant military conflict and yet belongs to no military, political, or economic alliance.

Against the background of the Holocaust, the effects of isolation have given rise to a pessimistic sense of encirclement and of being utterly alone in the world.

When our children under the gallows wept,
The world its silence kept. . . .

The sentiment in these lines, from a well-known poem by Nathan

Alterman, is shared by many Israelis. It is a basic cause for attitudes which the outside world frequently sees as stubbornness. Criticism by foreign governments has little effect. For in Israeli eyes, since the Holocaust the civilized world has little moral right to tell Israel what it should and should not do.

THE HOLOCAUST REMEMBERED

The Holocaust remains a basic wound within Israeli society. It is impossible to exaggerate its effect. It was a hell that exterminated one-third of the Jewish people and caused the destruction of Eastern European Jewry. The early pioneers had rebelled against that world, but they were its cultural heirs nonetheless.

The ever-present awareness of the Holocaust accounts for a great sense of loneliness, a main characteristic of the Israeli temperament. It explains the Israelis' overwhelming urge for self-reliance at any cost, for a world which permitted the Holocaust to happen could easily look the other way as the Jewish state was destroyed. The lingering memory of the Holocaust makes Arab threats of annihilation sound plausible.

Even the typical bustle and liveliness of Israeli life may be a way Israelis have of covering up a deep and basic sadness. All over the country many private and public monuments to the Holocaust keep alive the bitter memory which lies at the center of Israel's self-image. In vast areas, many thousands of trees are annually planted in memory of lost Jewish communities and individual victims. In Israel, tree planting and building are acts of faith in the future, serving a purpose similar to religious ceremony and prayer in previous ages.

Yad Vashem, the great memorial center in Jerusalem, is dedicated to the gigantic task of tracing the fate and registering the name of every single man, woman, and child among the 6 million who died. It, too, is an expression of faith. Surrounded by young trees, Yad Vashem (Martyrs and Heroes Remembrance Authority) is a massive building set on a vast paved terrace facing the pink hills of Judea. In the semidarkness of the interior hall, the names of dozens of Nazi death camps, carved in stone, are dimly lit by a single torch. Close by is a research center. In the rituals of government and diplomacy, Yad Vashem is given a solemn role. There are military cemeteries in Israel, but in Israeli protocol, Yad Vashem occupies the place of monuments for unknown soldiers in other countries. It is here that wreaths are laid on national anniversaries and during visits by foreign dignitaries.

Jews, of course, are not the only people who live under the shadow

Yad Vashem in Jerusalem: A memorial to the six million who died.

of a traumatic past. The systematic plan for the extermination of the Armenians, which led to their end in 1915, is perhaps the closest parallel. Their "unremembered genocide," as one Armenian writer has commented bitterly, "was perpetrated almost thirty years before that term was coined." The Japanese were profoundly affected by the first atomic blast at Hiroshima—not just the *hibakusha* (the actual survivors of Hiroshima) but the entire Japanese people, even youngsters who cannot remember the war. Nor were the Jews Nazism's only, or most numerous, victims. Millions of Poles and Russians were slaughtered or gassed by the Nazis. But if others were struck by Nazi barbarism, the Jews nevertheless seem different—and not merely in their own eyes—because they were singled out for extermination as a *people*. They were singled out, not because of what they did, or refrained from doing, and not because of their politics, but simply because they were there, they existed. They were a symbol the Nazis could not bear.

EFFECTS OF THE HOLOCAUST

The impact was so overwhelming that in Israeli eyes it has taken the form of fate. Young Israelis, especially, have come to believe that the singling out of Jews for extermination was possible only because the Jews had no country of their own. Six million perished not because they lacked courage, but because they lacked any way to put such courage into practice. It is possible to conquer and exterminate a people even in its own sovereign state. But with the possible exception of nuclear warfare, there is no form of mass extermination that cannot be resisted in some way by its intended victims. In the eyes of the younger generation of Israelis, the Holocaust seems to confirm one of the basic beliefs of Zionism: without a country of your own, you are the inevitable prey of beasts.

As with all traumatic memories, the urge to forget and suppress the Holocaust runs parallel to the urge to remember, lest forgetfulness lead to further pain and agony. Alternating between remembering and forgetting, some Israelis have come to the conclusion that the only way to attain any peace of mind is to succeed in doing both.

The result is that many young Israelis are torn between honoring the martyred dead and being ashamed of what they think is a past of weakness. At one moment they are filled with awed remembrance; at the next, they reject any identification with the past.

Older settlers, many of them prominent in Israel's public life, bear some feelings of guilt. Perhaps, somehow, they might have done more to save the Jews of Europe. Maybe they did not cry out loudly enough to persuade the Western Allies to save the Jews. Perhaps they should have undertaken more of their own rescue operations.

Leaders of the Jewish underground security force, Haganah, in one instance developed a plan to parachute hundreds of young Palestinian Jews into occupied Europe. Their aim was to encourage resistance among those doomed to die, and to organize underground routes of escape. It was a fantastic plan and might easily have become a suicide mission. But there was hope that a few parachutists might succeed in blowing up a gas chamber, or at least a railroad track leading to one. The plan was vetoed by the British. The Zionist leaders have never been sure that they acted rightly in obeying the veto. A few parachutists were sent—Hannah Senesh and Enzo Sereni among them —but all were captured, some tortured horribly, and all put to death.

At the trial of Adolf Eichmann in 1962, the attorney general spoke for many when he said that this question "will continue to plague our national conscience." Dr. Nahum Goldmann, former president of the World Jewish Congress, admitted that "we are all guilty of not having gone to all lengths." Goldmann himself had pleaded with the American Secretary of State Edward Stettinius in 1944 to respond to a specific German offer to exchange Jewish lives for American or English trucks. Stettinius refused for reasons of military strategy. "We were too impressed," Goldmann later admitted bitterly, "with the argument that the [Allied] generals should be left in peace to fight the war." Israelis came to agree with a statement once made by Hitler himself, that the democracies which "ooze sympathy for the poor tormented Jews . . . remain hard and obdurate themselves when it comes to helping them."

A number of incidents immediately after World War II, some of them trivial, tended to reconfirm the bitter lesson in Israeli eyes. Early in 1946, tens of thousands of Eastern European Jews, survivors of the camps, were streaming westward, trying to "get out of Europe"—which to them was a graveyard—and into Palestine, where they hoped to assume a new identity. Not only were the gates of Palestine closed to them, but a British general—in a famous interview—chose to describe these refugees as well-fed, healthy, and robust, their pockets "bulging with money." In London, British Foreign Secretary Ernest Bevin publicly complained that the Jews were always pushing themselves to the head of the line. It is impossible today to convey the sense of rage that such statements, coupled with restrictive immigration policies, aroused at the time.

THE EICHMANN TRIAL

The Eichmann trial of 1961–1962 had a deep effect upon Israelis. As the tale of Nazi horror unfolded daily in the courtroom, it served as a first opportunity for many to face the past squarely. Reactions toward the Holocaust deepened considerably. After the Eichmann trial, Chaim Guri, a poet of the younger generation, wrote that, from now on

> . . . free men will turn from time to time to look at their receding past without freezing into pillars of salt. They will be wiser. They will not evict from their souls this chapter in the chronicles of life but will live it fully, unashamed. Only then will they endow their liberty its truest meaning: that it is not self-evident.

After the trial was over, many felt that painful emotions had been released and that the nation had been relieved of the psychological burden of the Holocaust. But this has not been the case. The effects of the Nazi Holocaust upon the national psychology reached a new peak in the weeks preceding the Six Day War of 1967. Israelis, including many young people who were not yet born when the Holocaust took place, were seized by dreadful fears. Many were certain that another massacre was being prepared for them by the rulers of Egypt, whose bloodthirsty statements were resounding hourly on the radio.

Repeated Arab threats continue to obstruct the sense of "normalcy" that had been one of the major aims of the early Zionists. Precisely because the memory of the Holocaust is so alive, Arab threats of annihilation arouse a cultural reflex in many Israelis. The Arabs do not realize that in the Israeli arsenal, this reflex is a more powerful weapon than the toughest tank. It is an unrecognized gift presented to the Israelis by their enemies, adding to their normal talents an extra measure of resolve, inventiveness, devotion, cohesion, vigor, and determination.

related themes

The White Paper   The Holocaust was not totally unexpected. Before the outbreak of World War II, many Jews wanted to flee from Europe. As early as 1936, Chaim Weizmann declared: "There are six million people doomed to be pent up where they are not wanted, and for whom the world is divided into places where they may not enter. . . ." Among those places in 1939 was the land of Israel. For three years (1936–1939), violence and rioting were organized by the Arab leadership in Palestine; finally, in response to Arab demands, the British issued a White Paper in 1939. The White Paper limited Jewish immigration to 75,000 persons, to be admitted to Palestine over the course of five years—only 15,000 immigrants a year! The Permanent Mandate

Commission of the League of Nations, which had granted the British a mandate to rule Palestine, declared that "the policy set out in the White Paper was not in accordance with the interpretation placed upon the Palestine Mandate." But the British government enforced the White Paper until 1948, and the doors of Palestine were officially closed to Jewish refugees throughout World War II.

The Jewish Brigade   With the outbreak of World War II in September 1939, the Jewish Agency declared that, despite the White Paper, " . . . the war which has now been forced upon Great Britain is our war, and all the assistance that we shall be able and permitted to give to the British army and to the British people, we shall render wholeheartedly." But for a while, at least, the Jews of Palestine were not allowed to give any assistance. The British were afraid that if they accepted Jewish assistance, the Arabs would join with Germany. In order to convince King Faruk I of Egypt to join the Allied cause, the British placed a ring of army tanks around his palace. It was not so easy to gain the support of the Palestinian Arabs. One of their most powerful leaders, Haj Amin el-Husseini, the grand mufti of Jerusalem, openly sided with the Nazis. He was invited to visit Germany and was given a "tour" of Auschwitz. For a while, the other Arab leaders remained neutral, but when Italy joined the German side in 1940—bringing an Axis power into the Mediterranean—the British consented to allow a program of limited Jewish enlistment, with the understanding that the volunteers would be attached to separate army units. It was not until 1944 that a special Jewish division, called the Jewish Brigade, was created. The Jewish Brigade fought in Belgium, Holland, Austria, Italy, and Germany. The members of the brigade had two purposes: to contribute to the victory of the Allies against Nazi Germany, and to search out the surviving remnants of European Jewry and help them in whatever way they could.

issues and values

Epidemic Potential   Anti-Semitism has been described as an infectious disease with the potential to become an epidemic. Barely one year after Hitler came to power in 1933, Germany's anti-Jewish laws were being imitated by Poland, Lithuania, Latvia, Rumania, and Hungary. In Poland, Jewish stores were picketed, Jewish professionals and university students were discriminated against, and the Polish foreign minister declared that his country had a million Jews too many. The government took over industries known as Jewish to impoverish its Jewish citizens. In Rumania, Jewish employees were dismissed from factories. Those Jews left were compelled to work on the Sabbath. And in Hungary, a systematic expulsion of Jews from the economic life of the country was officially initiated in 1939. What are the reasons for this epidemic potential in anti-Semitism? Do you believe the potential still exists today? Does this belief affect you personally in any way?

"Ordinary" People The Holocaust was not the work of sadists and fanatics alone. Thousands of "ordinary" Germans took part in the "Final Solution of the Jewish problem." These Germans were guards, drivers, technicians, laborers, clerks, businessmen, and physicians (who, in addition to their regular duties, performed "scientific" experiments upon Jewish prisoners, and determined who was fit for slave labor and who should be put to death immediately). Most Germans claimed that they were just "following orders." They argued that they were so involved with their specific duties that they were unaware of—and therefore not responsible for—the larger picture. The following letter illustrates the way in which the mass murder of human beings was placed into normal, workaday perspective:

> . . . Following our verbal discussion regarding the delivery of equipment of simple construction for the burning of bodies, we are submitting plans for our perfected cremation ovens which operate with coal and which have hitherto given full satisfaction.
>
> We suggest two crematorial furnaces for the building plant, but we advise you to make further inquiries to make sure that two ovens will be sufficient for your requirements. We guarantee the effectiveness of the cremation ovens as well as the durability, the use of the best material and our faultless workmanship. Heil Hitler.
>
> (signed) C. H. Kori

Do you think that Mr. Kori's "business as usual" response was a typical instance of human behavior in the face of inhumanity, or an exception? In the light of this letter, what values do you think were uppermost in Kori's mind?

perspective

The Israeli yearning for peace has been expressed again and again—in novels, short stories, plays, poetry, films, popular songs, essays, and private discussions. Visitors to Israel are constantly amazed at how little pride Israelis take in their military victories, and how little hatred they bear toward the Arabs. And yet, the Israelis have had no choice but to become a nation of soldiers—experts in the art of war, who can never afford the luxury of letting their guard down, for a defeat could well mean the destruction of their state.

In Chapter 3 we observed the role of Zionist ideology in Israeli history. Early Zionism was based upon faith in peaceful change. But the Zionist ideal of the redemption of the Jewish people on its land has become intertwined with the reality of violence. The resulting clash of the bright and the depressing, the hopeful and the tragic, is a main characteristic of Israeli society.

For almost its entire existence, Israel has been in a state of war or semiwar. For almost its entire life, it has been under military attack and partial political and economic siege. The bloodiest and most dramatic stage in this perennial siege occurred in the years after Israel was granted independence in 1948. But the bitter struggle between Arabs and Jews over the area known as Palestine had begun much earlier.

EIN BRERAH

The first serious clash between the groups took place as early as 1886. Because they could no longer graze their cattle in the swampland, Muslim *felahin* (peasants) from Yahudiya, an Arab village a few miles south of Petaḥ Tikvah, broke into the new colony in broad daylight,

PERMANENT
STATE
OF
SIEGE

131

when most of the men were out in the fields. Five settlers were injured; one later died of her wounds.

From the earliest days of settlement the settlers struggled daily for security. The struggle has now lasted for almost a century and its end is not in sight. Israelis are fond of saying that in this long conflict with forces that have often been superior, their main weapon has been an awareness of *ein brerah,* "there is no choice." "Ein brerah" deserves to be inscribed as a motto on Israel's national coat of arms.

Israelis often say, "Yes, we live dangerously. Ein brerah! There is no choice! But we are free!" They rarely pause to think that this may be a contradiction in terms. The early pioneers never aimed at the establishment of a fortress-state in which citizens would spend much of their adult lives under arms; and yet this is precisely what circumstances have forced them to do. The Zionist dreamers envisioned a safe haven in Israel for persecuted Jews everywhere. But in Israel today, Jews, as Jews, live in greater danger of their lives than anywhere else in the world. There is a bitter irony in this, and yet it is not uniquely Jewish. History often defeats people by fulfilling their wishes in an unexpected form or by answering their prayers too completely. History cannot be programmed.

THE SOLDIER CITIZEN

Living dangerously—at war, or under considerable tension—has become a way of life. The average, native-born Israeli has known nothing else for his or her entire life. He or she has been a soldier in and out of uniform since a 17th or 18th birthday. Premilitary training may have begun at the age of 14 or 15. If he or she is 45 years old, he or she most likely has been in Israel's active service in four wars. Each year the citizen is called to active reserve duty, and has also undoubtedly participated in some of the numerous, bloody skirmishes that have taken place between the all-out conflicts. While still in the teens, he or she became accustomed to life in a city divided by sandbagged positions and manned by armed volunteers. Gunfire at night was as regular as the full moon; travel between settlements was safe only in daytime, and then only in armored buses or car caravans under guard.

This picture applies to the more than 50 percent of Israelis who are native-born, yet the immigrant to Israel can often be included in it as well. If the immigrant arrived in the country during the years of pioneering before World War II, his or her life has been marked by civil strife and war almost as much as the sabra's has. If the immigrant came later, from war-torn Europe, it is even more certain that death and destruction were close companions of his or her earlier years.

A good illustration of what this can mean to the Israeli can be found in the personal memoir of a native-born Israeli writer, Moshe Shamir. In 1968 he wrote:

> My son is named after my brother who fell in the War of Independence. This was exactly twenty years ago, when the almonds of 1948 were in full bloom. I am named after my father's brother, who fell in the ranks of the Red Army at the gates of Warsaw. This happened in 1920. My father was named after the brother of his father, who was murdered in the Ukraine during a pogrom by rampaging peasants. This was in 1891. . . . Are we now still at the beginning of the road? At the middle? At the end? I only know this: in this half-century in which I live and breathe, fear of death has never left our house. . . .

THE SIGNS OF DANGER

In a nation of refugees and survivors of disasters, one expects to find a kind of feverish tension and drama. Many foreign visitors arrive in Israel expecting to find signs of current crisis. More often than not, the dangers must be pointed out to them. Unless they travel in certain exposed border regions or in the Arab territories occupied by Israel since the 1967 war, where the problems are of a special nature, visitors often search in vain for signs of the toll that such tension has taken. Faces are not more pallid than elsewhere; looks are not more anguished. Gestures and manners are not more nervous.

There are, of course, numerous external aspects of the war that nobody can miss. The front lines that are likely to erupt in full-scale battles are distant and closed to civilians, but city streets are dominated by large numbers of young (and some middle-aged) men and women in drab army uniforms. The highways swarm with fully armed soldiers hitchhiking home or back to the front. Air-raid shelters are everywhere. Vicious and unpredictable terrorist attacks impose a heavy burden on cities large and small in outlying regions, as in Jerusalem and Tel Aviv. At the entrance to museums, movie houses, theaters, supermarkets, and department stores, ladies' handbags and gentlemen's briefcases are checked by aging civil defense guards for hidden explosives. Evil-looking iron bars and barbed- or meshed-wire fences enclose the campus of the Hebrew University of Jerusalem, and even the Western Wall on High Holy Days, as a protection against saboteurs.

Before 1967 the heaviest burden of war was felt in the border settlements. After 1967 their burden was still the heaviest, but the deadly conflict had also penetrated the interior of the country. Now there were occasional acts of sabotage in centers of civilian life—a supermarket, a student cafeteria, a main square in Jerusalem, a crowded bus station in Tel Aviv, a residential section, a hotel, an airport, a movie house, a street market.

And yet, despite such disruptions, the country never seemed more self-confident than in the years after the 1967 war. The country's economic growth rate soared. Industry and building boomed, and the rate of investment grew. Education, tourism, the social services, and even the arts expanded as never before. More books were written and sold. The number of art galleries rose by a third. Never had there been so many nightclubs, fancy restaurants, fashionable boutiques, beauty parlors, and discotheques. In Tel Aviv alone there were almost twice as many theaters in 1969 as there had been three years earlier. An ambitious program was launched in Tel Aviv for slum clearance, urban renewal, and beachfront development. A new university—the seventh in the country—was opened in Beersheba. A green strip of parks and walks was built around the medieval walls and ramparts of the Old City of Jerusalem, whose battered stones were illuminated nightly. More immigrants were arriving in the country from affluent and "safe" countries than ever before in Israeli history. Even Russia, under world pressure, suddenly permitted some Jews to emigrate to Israel.

But in the absence of peace, the general state of military preparedness continued. Psychologically it is no small matter to live under a constant threat of annihilation, and no one really knows what the emotional cost is.

OF PEACE AND WAR

The ordinary Israeli man who has already finished his regular, compulsory period of two and one-half or three years' army service remains a reservist until he is 54. Let us assume that he is 30 years old, married, with children. He has thus been through two hard wars; and, in addition to his regular army service, he has been called up for reserve duty ten or 12 times, for periods of service varying from 90 days to four months. He must periodically bid his family good-bye, leave his job or studies, and go off to rejoin his army reserve unit.

He was either born in the country or brought to Israel at a young age. He is neither refugee nor immigrant. He is a product of life in the new country. His character and outlook have been fashioned by its peculiar challenges and demands. In school—frequently in his youth movement as well—he was nurtured on ideals of social justice, Jewish values, tolerance, comradeship, and above all, respect for the sanctity of human life. In school he recited lines by Rachel, the popular poetess of the Second Aliyah, herself a pioneer in the Jordan Valley before World War I. She wrote in "My Country":

לֹא שַׁרְתִּי לָךְ, אַרְצִי,
וְלֹא פֵּאַרְתִּי שְׁמֵךְ
בַּעֲלִילוֹת גְּבוּרָה,
בִּשְׁלַל קְרָבוֹת;
רַק עֵץ – יָדַי נָטְעוּ
חוֹפֵי יַרְדֵּן שׁוֹקְטִים,
רַק שְׁבִיל – כָּבְשׁוּ רַגְלַי
עַל פְּנֵי שָׂדוֹת.

I haven't sung your praise
Nor glorified your name
In tales of valor
And in wars.
Only a tree my hands have planted
On Jordan's bank,
Only a path my feet have tracked
Across the fields.

He probably still knows those lines by heart, as well as the words and lively tune of another famous song:

אָנוּ בָּאנוּ אַרְצָה
לִבְנוֹת וּלְהִבָּנוֹת בָּהּ

We have come to the country
To build and be rebuilt by it.

He remembers them fondly; to build, not to make war. But on the day he is called up again by the army, on the day that he kills, as occasionally he must, he realizes in a bitter moment of truth that it is not enough to plant trees and cut paths in the fields. Whatever was built has been paid for with unjust deaths. Such knowledge matures him considerably; he becomes noticeably sadder. It is hard for the outsider to realize the depth and extent of this sadness.

related themes

An Early Understanding   Because of their colonial ambitions in the Middle East, Great Britain and France thwarted Arab nationalist aims, and, in the process, destroyed any possibility of Arab-Jewish cooperation. Today it seems that Arab and Jewish nationalism are inevitably in bitter opposition to one another. But for one brief moment it seemed that an agreement might be reached. In 1918, Chaim Weizmann met with Emir Faisal, who was about to be crowned king of Syria. Later, after his coronation, Faisal made a statement which was quoted in the *Times* of London in December 1918:

. . . The two main branches of the Semitic families, Arabs and Jews, understand one another and I hope . . . each nation will make definite progress toward the realization of its aspirations. Arabs are not jealous of Zionist Jews and intend to give them fair play . . . and the Zionist Jews have assured the

PERMANENT
STATE
OF
SIEGE

135

nationalist Arabs of their intention to see that they, too, have fair play in their areas. . . .

But in July 1920, France exiled King Faisal from Damascus, triggering a reaction by Arab nationalists which, among other things, resulted in their total opposition to the idea of a Jewish national home in Palestine.

The Arab Intention   The slogan *ein brerah*, "there is no choice," refers not only to living dangerously or having to fight, but to winning as well. Israel has no choice but to emerge victorious from conflicts with Arab neighbors; a single defeat would mean destruction. The Arab leaders have made this point time and again. In 1961, President Nasser of Egypt wrote a letter to Jordan's King Hussein in which he stated: "We believe that the evil [Israel] which was placed in the heart of the Arab world should be eradicated." In 1965, Nasser published a joint statement with the president of Iraq which declared: "The Arab national aim is the elimination of Israel." And on the eve of the Six Day War, President Arif of Iraq announced: "We are resolved, determined, and united to achieve our clear aim of wiping Israel off the map. . . . God willing we shall meet in Tel Aviv and Haifa."

issues and values

Aliyah   In a meeting with American Jewish students in the fall of 1970, Golda Meir, then prime minister of Israel, was asked how American Jews could best express their solidarity with Israel. She replied:

> What we need most of all is aliyah. And we need aliyah because Israel must have, should have, millions of Jews—not only for the sake of Israel, but for the sake of the Jewish people all over the world. We have received and absorbed hundreds and thousands of people without any skills whatsoever, but we need people to come and make a modern, progressive society out of this pressure cooker. That is what we need. That is what we want. There are many things of which we dream, but because of the shortage of people and because of the wars we have to fight, to our sorrow, we can attain these only with more people coming in. And since we believe Israel is important to all Jews, we are not ashamed to ask Jews to share the burden with us. And we need political support.

Do you feel an obligation to share Israel's burdens? How do you presently express your obligation, if at all? Do you think American Jews should be encouraged to consider aliyah?

Identity and Responsibility The continuing conflict between Israel and the Arab nations has given Israeli young people an inescapable sense of identity and responsibility. There is no choice for them but to be aware of who they are and what they must do, for their homes, their families, their lives, and their country are at stake. American Jews do not have the same feeling of connection or continuity. One reason may be that there is no sustained crisis to pull them together. The majority of Jewish young people in the United States today come from families that have been here for two or three generations and are largely middle-class. Every Jew under 25 was born well after the Holocaust and has never known a time in which a Jewish state did not exist. As Walter Ackerman points out in his essay "The Present Moment in Jewish Education,"

> Jews of previous generations had no problem concerning their Jewish identity. The home, the community and its institutions, the [routine] of religious observance and an intricate pattern of social relationships all contributed to the growing child's self-definition. . . . He was deeply conscious of the interdependence of all Jews and understood that "whatever happened to Jews as Jews anywhere had implications for Jews everywhere." The Jewish child of today, by contrast, grows up in a fragmented society.

Do you think that your Jewish identity is strong and well-defined? How could Jewish education help? Which subjects and activities do you think should be stressed in order to offer you a full Jewish heritage?

THE SINAI CAMPAIGN

Photo Essay In the Sinai campaign of 1956, Israeli troops defeated the Egyptian army and occupied the Gaza Strip and all of the Sinai Peninsula to the banks of the Suez Canal. The Israeli army code word for the campaign was Operation Kadesh (see Deuteronomy 13:26).

The Israeli attack was launched in the hope of causing the collapse of the regime of the Egyptian dictator Gamal Abdel Nasser. It may have been hoped that the Nasser regime might be replaced by a more moderate one, a regime more willing to live in peace with Israel. Another purpose was to destroy the bases of the sabotage units (*fedayeen*) which the Egyptian High Command had been send-ing into Israel during the preceding years. These saboteurs had caused the deaths of many Israeli civilians, including women and children. Most importantly, the Israelis hoped to end the constant shell-ing of Israeli villages by Arabs in the Gaza Strip.

There were political reasons as well. First, Egypt had violated the 1949 armis-tice agreement with Israel. In that agree-ment, Egypt had pledged to refrain from all acts of war against Israel as a prelim-inary toward full peace between the two countries. Egypt not only claimed that the "state of war" was continuing but also cited that state of war as a reason for blocking the Suez Canal and the Straits of Tiran (Sharm el Sheikh) to Israeli ship-ping.

Israel could live without shipping through the canal, but the closure of the Straits of Tiran blocked the port of Eilat,

An Israeli ship passes through the Straits of Tiran, liberated by the Sinai Campaign.

Israeli soldiers patrol the Gaza Strip.

cutting off Israel from all shipping routes to the Far East. This was regarded as unbearable.

Second, as a result of the Egyptian-Czech and Egyptian-Soviet arms agreements of 1955–1956, Egypt was well stocked with the most modern weapons of aggression, tanks and airplanes. Colonel Nasser openly announced that he intended to use these weapons one day to deliver a death blow to Israel. Other Arab politicians in Egypt and elsewhere spoke of "driving Israel into the sea." The Sinai campaign was a preventative strike by Israel against such a possibility.

The campaign was launched on October 29, 1956. Israel acted in conjunction with France and Britain, who had their own grudges against Egypt. They wished to undo Egypt's nationalization of the Suez Canal. Altogether, it was a strange and unnatural alliance. It linked two declining colonialist powers with a new nation which only eight years before had gained its independence from one of these powers, the British. But Israel could not afford to be choosy; in despair and isolation, it decided to make the best of an opportunity offered. As General Moshe Dayan said at the time: "Their aims are not ours, and ours are not theirs. We should behave like the cyclist who is riding uphill when a truck chances by and he grabs hold. We should get what help we can, hang on to the truck and exploit its movement. Where the route forks, we break off and we proceed our separate ways."

The Anglo-French-Israeli Sinai-Suez Campaign lasted barely 100 hours. Israel's *military* aim was achieved by the occupation of Sinai; British and French forces, however, surprised the world by completely failing in their assigned task, the seizure of the canal itself. The United States government was thoroughly opposed to the entire operation and furious at Britain and France, which had not previously consulted Washington. So angered was the United States that it joined with the Soviet Union in pressuring France, England, and Israel to withdraw their troops. England and France complied almost immediately. Israel withdraw from all occupied territories only after receiving assurances from the United Nations and the United States that Egyptian troops would not return to the Gaza Strip. United Nations troops would enter Gaza and be stationed at Sharm el Sheikh to safeguard Israeli shipping to Eilat.

The first of these assurances was violated by Egypt almost immediately. The second was kept for over a decade. Relative calm prevailed along the Israeli-Egyptian border. In 1967, Egypt's sudden request for the UN to remove all troops from Sinai and its decision to reimpose the blockade at Tiran led directly to the Six Day War.

Examining a Russian MIG captured from the Egyptian Air Force.

Moshe Dayan: b. 1915.

United Nations
observers near the
Syrian border.

142   The Western Wall, Jerusalem.

ISRAEL & THE ISRAELI: ENVIRONMENT AND PERSONALITY

perspective

Many visitors to Israel are struck by the blunt and matter-of-fact manner of the sabra. People often think of this as "toughness"—the sabra has grown up with danger, has had to fight four wars in 25 years, and this has left its mark. Nevertheless, a closer look reveals a character that lies mostly beneath the surface. It may be that the sabra's toughness is not due to an absence of emotion, but is just a way of keeping deep inner feelings under control.

Young men have gone to war four times and more within less than 30 years. Each war called for near total exertion; each war was fought in the firm belief that it would bring peace within reach, or at least a little closer. None has. On the contrary, year after year, war after war, the basic situation remains static. There are some Israelis (as there must also be Egyptians) who have four times in their lives fought over the same arid, desolate, godforsaken wadi * that controls a strategic point along the Egyptian-Israeli front. War after war, it has always been the same, dismal wadi, only a few miles long, yellowish-brown, under a thick dustcloud in the scorching heat of the desert sun. Israelis took it, then left it; they took it again and left it again. Nothing changes.

"When, my friends, have we last seen peace?" the poet Chaim Guri exclaimed some years ago in a short prose piece. "This soil is insatiable," he wrote bitterly. "How many more graves, how many more coffins are needed until it will cry out—enough, enough!"

EFFECTS OF WAR ON THE YOUNG

ENVIRON-
MENT AND
PERSONALITY

It is the younger Israeli who must bear on his shoulders and with his

* Wadi—a dry riverbed in the desert.

nerves the main burden of this seemingly endless emergency. One result has been a growing cult of toughness among younger people.

It does not go unopposed; there are frequent protests in the newspapers, by teachers, parents, and youth leaders who constantly battle against senseless military practices in youth movements and schools.

Frequent and prolonged periods of service in the army breed a matter-of-factness in the young that contrasts sharply with the emotionalism of their elders. Such directness is partly the natural reaction of the young to the ideological fervor and slogans of a previous age. But it is also a result of the kind of life they lead. The more puritan older settlers often grumble that young people are too selfish, too career-minded, not sufficiently responsive to traditional Zionist ideology. Yet younger Israelis have never shirked their responsibilities in time of danger. The belief in the power of ideas, which played such a great role in the lives of the founders, has been replaced among the younger people by an urge for self-preservation.

The language of younger Israelis is often abrupt, unmusical, and delivered in harsh staccato phrases. One reason is that "official" Hebrew is still too formal; the developing street slang that substitutes for what is missing or inadequate in the dictionary is still raw. Another reason may be more important. The abruptness that marks sabra speech may be a means of covering up perfectly normal emotions. For too many years there has been a relentless educational effort to produce a new, "manly" Israeli Jew.

THE SABRA

The novelist Yael Dayan draws a portrait of a young sabra hero in her *Envy the Frightened*. "Do you know what he is afraid of? To be afraid —this is the fear that masters him, until all other fears, human normal, healthy ones, are pushed aside and stop existing." Bruno Bettelheim, the psychologist, quotes an Israeli psychoanalyst who has devoted much of his professional life to the study of kibbutzniks: ". . . our children are ashamed to be ashamed, are afraid to be afraid. They are afraid to love, are afraid to give of themselves. . . . I am not sure whether it is a deficiency in emotion or a [fear] of feeling. . . ."

The letters written by young Israelis to their sweethearts are known to be dry, unimaginative, and frequently impersonal. They are often so skimpy in exclamations of love, devotion, or longing—indeed, of any feelings whatsoever—that a reader may suspect a near-total lack of sensitivity. Or else he may suspect that the young writers, if they have

feelings, are so frightened by them—or so ashamed and embarrassed—
that they have resolved to keep them permanently concealed. One does
not talk of feelings; one rarely admits that they exist.

The tendency to shy away from feeling, as from some dangerous
enemy territory, is a basic character trait among the new generation of
Israelis. It is well illustrated by a conversation in New York in 1967, a
few weeks after the Six Day War. Elie Wiesel, the Jewish writer, inter-
viewed Colonel Mordechai Gur, one of the celebrated heroes of the
war, who later became chief of staff of the Israeli army. Colonel Gur's
brigade, at considerable cost in human lives, had captured the Old City
of Jerusalem. The emotional impact upon Jews everywhere had been
tremendous. Between 1948 and 1967, Jews had been unable to visit the
Western Wall, the old Jewish quarter, the Temple Mount, and other
religious monuments within the ancient city walls, since all these places
were controlled by Jordan. The following questions and answers were
exchanged by the Jewish writer and the Israeli general:

> *Wiesel:* . . . you were the first up on the Temple Mount, weren't you?
> *Gur:* That's right.
> *Wiesel:* Were you excited?
> *Gur:* What do you think?
> *Wiesel:* Did you cry?
> *Gur:* No, I did not cry.
> *Wiesel:* Why not?
> *Gur:* I don't know. I don't like tears.
> *Wiesel:* Did you feel any?
> *Gur:* Of course. Like all the others. But I didn't cry.
> *Wiesel:* What *did* you feel?
> *Gur:* I don't think I can put it into words.
> *Wiesel:* Try.
> *Gur:* No, I don't think people should discuss their feelings.
> *Wiesel:* What should people discuss?
> *Gur:* Who says you've got to discuss anything? You don't have to.
> *Wiesel:* I beg to differ. It's a duty—and a privilege—to talk about
> this. . . .

THE MEANING OF WAR

Yet out of that same war came a document that did indeed give insight
into its effect on young Israelis. Soon after the war, a group of young
kibbutzniks went from kibbutz to kibbutz asking ex-fighters a number
of penetrating, highly personal questions. They tape-recorded a long
series of interviews with the young soldiers which were later published

under the title *"Siah Lohamim"* (*The Seventh Day* in its English version; the literal translation means "Conversation Among Fighters").

In this slender volume, young men and women talk about themselves. They touch upon deeply personal problems and ponder such controversial subjects as individual morality in wartime and the limits of duty, patriotism, and discipline. The reliability of the dialogues has been enhanced by the fact that they were recorded almost immediately after the 1967 war; many participants were still nearly in a state of shock and had not yet closed up emotionally.

The picture that emerges from this unusual document is far from uniform. Some of the participants in these dialogues seem close to an emotional breakdown from the harrowing blow of the war. To understand this anguish, it must be remembered that, despite the emphasis on "manly vigor," these young products of kibbutz society have been raised in a unique spirit of humanitarian idealism. Yet, at the same time, no group in the Israeli population has a better fighting record. Kibbutzniks represented only 4 percent of the population but 25 percent of the casualties in the 1967 war, and almost 30 percent of the casualties in the 1973 war were kibbutzniks. One young soldier in *Siah Lohamim* noted this fighting record and the high casualty rate among kibbutzniks. He concluded bitterly that the kibbutz, which was meant as a new way of life, was becoming a main reservoir for "specialists in making war." "We have always been taught to respect human life above everything else . . . and here we are turning living and breathing people into heaps of bones and tortured flesh. . . ."

None of the participants in these dialogues doubted the justice of their cause; it was a clear question of survival. None rejoiced in their victory. Few could forget the scenes of suffering, or overlook the price paid by both victors and vanquished. "What's the point of living?" asked one. "It is a tax we pay," answered another, "like income tax. And we must carry on."

One said: "I came back terribly depressed. Victory meant nothing for me. I couldn't even smile, although people were cheering us when we passed the Mandelbaum Gate [in Jerusalem]. I never want to go back there . . . we had to do it, I know. But don't let it happen again. If it never happens again, perhaps it was worth it. Perhaps. . . ."

"I am still trying to run away from it. No, I don't even want to think about it. . . . I feel like vomiting, an awful feeling of disgust whenever the subject comes up. . . ."

"There it was, the tank that a short time ago had attacked us. It was hit . . . going up in flames . . . a figure emerged from it . . .

all in flames moving towards an Israeli jeep in dazed agony, in flight in the wrong direction . . . a moving torch all ablaze . . . the men in the jeep killed him . . . he may have died anyway . . . his death was inevitable. But not to those who shot him. During the day, when they go about their work, they may forget him . . . but at night he will be there all right. He'll be there with them when they dream and when they wake. . . ."

"I would go to war willingly if I knew that it was the last war. But I know I am going to die for something which has no end. . . ."

QUESTIONS WITHOUT ANSWERS

"Maybe we really ought to have a lot of children; to have more and more children," said one.

"Why?" asked another, "so there will be a lot of soldiers?"

"No, so that if one dies he would not be missed so much."

"How can you raise children this way and show them flowers and all sorts of beautiful things and know at the same time that maybe in ten years, they, or their fathers. . . ."

They posed such questions again and again, and of course found no answers. But pervading their bitterness was a kind of determination, repeated often in these dialogues, not to let circumstances completely destroy their moral fiber.

One soldier told his interviewers that in one of the battles, after he had shot at an Egyptian, he discovered that he had missed. "I had to shoot," he said, "but I was glad that he got away." *

related themes

Superpower Arena   The Middle East has come to be considered one of the most dangerous places on earth, a setting in which there is a high risk of superpower confrontation that could escalate into an all-out nuclear war. Because of its oil resources and strategic geographic location, the Middle East is regarded by the United States and the Soviet Union as vital to their respective national interests, and their rivalry in the Middle East has been intense. The U.S.S.R. gained entry into various Arab states as a supplier of armaments and trainer of armies. Any Arab

* This is a classic Jewish dilemma. When Jacob returned from Haran he was threatened by Esau's army of 400 men. The Bible tells us that Jacob was "greatly afraid and distressed" (Genesis 32:7–8). As Rashi explained it, Jacob was "afraid" of death and was "distressed" that he might kill.

defeat, therefore, represents a humiliating setback to the Soviets. After the Israeli victory in Sinai in 1956, the U.S.S.R. threatened to rain rockets on Israeli cities. And during the Six Day War, Soviet Premier Kosygin called President Johnson over the Soviet-American "hotline" to warn that unless Israel stopped its advances, the Soviet government would be compelled to consider military intervention. President Johnson replied by dispatching ships from the American Sixth Fleet to the war zone. And directly after the Yom Kippur War—despite Soviet-American détente and the fact that a cease-fire had been brought about by a joint Soviet-American initiative—the United States placed its troops around the world on alert, because of the Nixon administration's belief that the Soviets were preparing to send seven airborne divisions (about 49,000 troops) into the Suez area.

Other Forms of War Wars are not always fought—or won—by the military alone. The Arab states have carried on their battle against Israel in a variety of ways. To begin with, they organized an economic boycott, designed to isolate Israel from world markets and sources of supply; companies that dealt with Israel were placed on the Arab blacklist. In defiance of international law, Egypt barred Israeli ships from use of the Suez Canal and, until 1967, harassed ships from other countries which carried goods bound for Israel. Until the Sinai campaign of 1956, an Egyptian blockade at the mouth of the Gulf of Aqaba and the Straits of Tiran denied Israel any direct access to African and Asian ports. (The reimposition of this blockade in May 1967 was one of the principal causes of the Six Day War.) The Arab nations took other measures as well: they opposed Israel's presence in international agencies, tried to persuade other countries to break off relations with Israel, and issued a constant propaganda barrage against the Israeli government and people. Most destructive of all, from the early 1950's onward, the Arab states created and trained terrorist groups, recruited mainly from the refugees, and charged these groups with the task of disrupting and demoralizing Israeli life by initiating random attacks on Israeli civilians.

issues and values

The Price of War Chaim Guri's lament, "How many more graves, how many more coffins are needed until it will cry out—enough, enough!" underscores a point noted by friends and enemies alike:

Israel's major disadvantage in fighting the Arabs has been that its citizens have never learned to accept the grim price of young people killed and wounded. The Israeli general Ariel Sharon once observed that the Arabs were chiefly afraid of starting a war they could not win, while the Israelis were chiefly afraid of casualties and the loss of human life. When an Israeli soldier is killed, his family is not informed by a telegram, as is the custom in most countries; instead, a representative of the army and, whenever possible, the victim's commanding officer or one of his friends personally convey the sad news. The Arabs are well aware of this Israeli "weakness," and they have not hesitated to exploit it. After the Yom Kippur War, the Egyptians traded under 250 captured Israeli soldiers for approximately 8000 Egyptian soldiers, and viewed this as a major concession for which they should receive something in return. Which major Jewish value is expressed in Israel's "weakness"? How else has Israel expressed this value?

Environmental Influences The native-born Israeli is called a sabra. This name is borrowed from a cactus-fruit that grows in the Middle East. The fruit is prickly on the outside and sweet on the inside. And while generalizations can be overdrawn, the sabras' reputed bluntness and uneasiness about expressing feelings openly may be characterized as responses to the challenges and dangers of growing up in Israel. Many character traits are responses to physical and cultural conditions; everyone is to some extent the product of an environment. What personal traits of yours do you feel are products of your environment? What kinds of challenges confront you as a Jew growing up in the United States in the final quarter of the twentieth century?

perspective

Israel has been described as being "not so much a small country as a large village," with everyone deeply aware of everyone else. Hope and despair, triumph and tragedy, are shared by all. There is a strong sense of intimacy, of the belief that "we are all in this together." And this very closeness causes the feelings of anxiety and persistent sadness, the products of living in the shadow of war, to feed upon themselves and grow ever stronger.

Distances are short in Israel. From a rooftop in Tel Aviv the outskirts of Jerusalem can be seen with the naked eye, and Tel Aviv is only an hour's train ride from Haifa. Within this small triangle lives close to 80 percent of the population. Such concentration increases contact among Israelis and brings with it both problems and advantages. In addition, a large part of the Israeli population (basically composed of immigrants) still lives among members of its own ethnic group, sharing a common mother tongue.

APARTMENT LIFE

Most Israelis live almost painfully close to each other, in small apartments, with little privacy. As in other Mediterranean countries, much of the drama and comedy of daily life happen out of doors in full view and hearing of everyone. Seven or eight months of the year, people leave their hot rooms to eat and play on the balconies attached to all apartments. Most Israelis live in small, cooperatively owned apartment houses that are managed (or mismanaged) by the tenants. The system nurtures a degree of neighborliness much more intense than that found in other cities around the world.

The typical Israeli institution is the neighborhood unit of near-identical, cooperatively owned apartments, the *shikun*. The shikun is often built as a planned housing development for people who already know each other well: for specific ethnic groups, for members of a single profession, even for members of a single political party. There are shikunim for Zionist veterans, for immigrants from Poland or the United States, for teachers, for needleworkers, for journalists, and for demobilized soldiers. Tenant owners can sell their flats to anyone, regardless of the "character" of the shikun; yet the atmosphere of togetherness remains. Because Israel is so small and its manners so informal, it is easier than it would be in bigger or older countries to know "practically everybody," from the prime minister to the latest soccer hero. There is, at least, a strong feeling that one knows many people. Chaim Topol, the actor, expressed it in a remark in 1969: "I know *everyone* of my age in Israel."

This is especially true in the case of kibbutzniks, of veteran settlers and their descendants. Veteran settlers still count the most. They form the political and intellectual leadership.

A SENSE OF UNITY

Under such circumstances, tragedy rarely strikes the family alone. In the kibbutz, with its basis in community, its communal dining room and similar collective arrangements for hundreds of members (really one large, loose family), this is obvious. But even in the towns, news travels fast and immediately affects apparent strangers. On a hot summer afternoon, it takes but a short while for most people in the shikun, or on the street, to know that the redheaded boy from Number 5, who was only 19, whose mother beats her rug on the balcony too early in the morning, whose father works as a tax collector for the city, was killed this morning by a land mine or during an artillery barrage on the frontier.

In the years between 1967 and 1970, almost every fourth or fifth speech by the minister of defense or the army chief of staff was a funeral eulogy. The days following the Yom Kippur War of 1973 were like one long funeral. Each death in action draws strangers closer to one another. In a country as small as Israel, even "limited" casualties are mourned by the entire nation. No one is spared the tragedy of a fallen or wounded soldier. It is at such moments that one notices in Israel a sense of unity so strong it makes the country seem more like a big village than a state.

FOLLOWING THE NEWS

The mass media powerfully dramatize this state of affairs. Israelis constantly listen to the radio news. It is almost like an addictive drug to them. No people in the entire world tunes in to the news as regularly.

Israelis are early risers. Most people are at work before half past seven in the morning. At six and at seven, the sound of "Here is the news, read by . . ." spreads from window to terrace, echoing through courtyards and streets from one end of the country to the other. "Today, in the early hours of the morning, a land mine . . . the minister of foreign affairs last night warned that if Syrian artillery guns . . . the body of corporal. . . ." Seven or eight additional times a day, at the sound of a radio news beep, most Israelis pause at whatever they are doing to hear whether there has been another battle or artillery exchange, or some new act of sabotage by Arab terrorists. Not infrequently, the names of the latest casualties are read out. ("My God, isn't that so-and-so's son?")

The habit of following the news so closely partly explains the sudden shifts in the public mood. Israelis easily fall from heights of joy to darkest gloom; from glowing hope for imminent peace to bleak despair that the war will never end. One day the great powers are ready to impose a settlement; next day they are in disagreement again.

Israeli buses and taxis are usually equipped with radio sets. Every hour on the hour, when the news comes on, it blares out over the noise of traffic, and the entire bus falls silent. There is an eeriness in scenes like this that is characteristically Israeli. In restaurants, sidewalk cafes, offices, workshops, and stores, the news is switched on a couple of times each day. Men on temporary reserve duty with the army take along small transistor radios. They carry the news with them, even as they make it, wherever they go.

JEWISH HUMOR IN ISRAEL

The traditional, fretting type of "gallows humor," once so dear to the European Jew, has become almost extinct in Israel. One finds it among older people, but even then quite rarely. Sabra humor—not a very developed art as yet—is different. It rarely touches upon the security situation. There are few Israeli-made jokes on the Arab-Israeli conflict.

But while much of the traditional Jewish humor seems gone, much of the fretting remains—the traditionally Jewish routine of complaining and griping that in Yiddish is called *kvetching*. The modern Hebrew equivalent, *ohev tzarot* (a love of trouble), is but a dim echo. Another Yiddish word, *kutter* (from the German *Kater*, or "tomcat"), has been for some years a sabra expression for "whining." It is noteworthy that Yiddish has entered the vocabulary of youngsters who do not otherwise speak that language, and one understands why four of the most common Hebrew expressions are *yehiyeh b'seder* (it will be all right), *b'li panikah* (don't panic), *al tid'ag* (don't worry), and *lo asson* (it's not a tragedy).

WORRYING AND NOT WORRYING

The other side of worrying is the constant reminder not to worry, that everything will be all right. But when a public speaker tells an Israeli audience that "things are not going to be easy . . ." or "we may soon find ourselves again in great trouble . . ." or "it is going to get very tough . . . ," a murmur of "I told you so . . ." usually rumbles across the hall.

But while Israelis automatically await the worst, they desperately go on hoping for the best—above all, for peace. A survey taken a few years ago showed that Israelis had a greater fear of war than of any other possible disaster. Much of the literature that is written by Israeli-educated or Israeli-born younger writers has as a main theme the experience of war, which has been the central experience in the life of the younger generation. Not a single novel, poem, or play praises the so-called glory of war. Victories are portrayed as terrible defeats. New Israeli literature has been marked by pacifism and by a desire to understand the "enemy."

POSITIVE RESULTS

Living under such difficulties and being faced with such challenges also has a positive side. Israelis respond to challenges with a vigor that is evident today in every corner of the land. Flourishing villages and lively towns have turned wide stretches of the country into one vast settled area; extensive forests cover the once rocky surface of the mountains. Vast irrigation projects have transformed the neglected, dusty landscape from yellow-brown to many shades of green. Cities and industrial complexes have sprung up in the desert, from Eilat (where the bare nothingness of 1949 has been turned into an important oil port and tourist center) to Arad (a desert industrial city of 15,000 inhabitants, where there were only rock and sand as recently as 1959) to Beersheba (which has become one of the country's university centers, boasting its own medical school). The Israeli landscape reflects an achievement that has probably not been equaled anywhere else in such a short period.

Absorbing the huge masses of immigrants who came to Israel out of necessity, and not because they shared the ideals of the pioneer

Arad: An industrial town surrounded by desert.

generation, has also required heroic efforts. It was not easy to assemble
a mass of immigrants, speaking dozens of different languages, all with
different traditions, educational backgrounds, and values, and to make
them into a unified nation. In this respect, Arab antagonism has been
a great help: facing a common enemy has kept all Israelis together, in a
sense of shared social purpose, when the initial pioneering enthusiasm
has long since waned.

NEGATIVE ELEMENTS

Despite the basic unity among Israelis, which is always more obvious in
a time of active Arab antagonism, serious internal conflicts have threatened Israel. There are conflicts between Oriental and European immigrants; these have been aggravated by the fact that the European
old-timers are usually better off economically than the Orientals, who
were later arrivals in the country. Moreover, immigrants from Europe,
because of their education and more valuable skills, usually advance
more quickly.

The conflict between religious Israelis and secular Israelis over the
separation of synagogue and state continues to be a serious issue.

State intervention in the economy, often needlessly heavy-handed,
has been another source of conflict which, under other circumstances,

could divide Israelis into two opposing camps. Furthermore, the widening generational gap between the zealous old-timers and the "pragmatic" sabras caused a near breakdown in communications between the ruling political elite—until very recently, one of the oldest in the world—and younger people.

Continued Arab enmity carries with it another threat to which Israelis are very sensitive. They recognize the possible danger of "militarization" in civilian life.

ARMY LIFE IN ISRAEL

Israel may be a fortress, but it is very far from being a military society. Between his frequent army call-ups, the average Israeli remains a dedicated civilian. An Israeli chief of staff once raised a public storm when he announced that Israelis were reservists on leave. He would have been closer to the truth had he said that the army is a body of civilians temporarily donning uniforms, for longer or shorter periods of time.

The average Israeli boy grows up in a free atmosphere. His tradition is antimilitarist, and the army reflects this tradition. The brutality of war takes its toll on him, of course. But there is a positive influence as well. Although the army has become a highly disciplined and professional body, the Israeli soldier is trained by teaching and example, not by order and punishment. In combat units the rotation of home leave is often determined by drawing lots among the men, not by orders from commanding officers.

The army is a citizen army, and the gap between officers and men is small. There are few privileges of rank. The Israeli military code bluntly states that officers have no privileges whatsoever—only duties. Officers are usually addressed by their first names.

Jews have never been admirers of an army career, and there is a certain amount of poking fun at "military forms" in Israel. There are no fancy uniforms, except for officers going abroad on representative missions; until 1974 there were no decorations except battle ribbons, distributed to all who served in any capacity during wartime. Medals for heroism are rather rare in an army that expects heroism from every soldier.

Job turnover among army officers is usually rapid, and the army is rarely a lifelong occupation. Most senior officers are weeded out soon after they reach 40. This practice has helped to prevent the establishment of a military class. Retired army officers are usually hired by industry, banks, investment firms, or government-owned development

March 12, 1974. A bereaved father studies booklet containing the names of the 2,522 Israeli soldiers dead or presumed dead.

companies, mainly because of their administrative experience, which they often develop further by returning to a university for a year or two after retirement.

Years of soldiering in war have made the so-called military virtues only slightly more attractive. A proposal to create high school military academies for boys planning an army career was vetoed out of fear that such academies might encourage undesirable "militarist" tendencies among young cadets.

related themes

"Everyone Returned . . ." The first question an Israeli asks when news comes of a military action, large or small, is not "What happened?" or "Who won?" but "Was anyone hurt?" This point is brought out in a personal account by an American student who visited Israel in 1968 at a time when there were clashes on the Jordanian border. The student wrote:

> I find this incident particularly encouraging in an age when politicians speak of "kill ratios," and when concern for human life seems to have hit an all-time low in many parts of the world. I was walking down Jerusalem's Herzl Boulevard. Up ahead, I saw a large group of people crowded around a car, listening to a news report on its radio. I was only able to hear bits and pieces of the report, something about military action on one of the borders. When the broadcast was over, the people dispersed quickly and quietly. I went up to one of the men and asked if he could tell me what had happened. He looked at me and said simply: "It's O.K. Everyone returned safely." And with that, having told me what was important, he walked away. Not a word about the action itself. Just "Everyone returned safely." Israelis tend to take this kind of thing for granted, but I find myself constantly amazed. . . . (*Judaean Leaves*, vol. 15, no. 6, 1970)

Israeli Humor   Israeli humor has a certain feeling all its own. At times it is a grim humor, ruefully aware of the illogic and absurdity that have become a part of the Israeli experience. In the year before the Six Day War, there was a mood of depression in Israel which was not helped by the fact that many were leaving the country to live elsewhere. One story told of a note tacked onto the bulletin board at Israel's international airport: "Will the last person to leave [Israel], please turn out the lights?" Earlier, in the period following the Israeli War of Independence, someone suggested that the way to solve Israel's monetary problems was to declare war on the United States. Then, as had been the U.S. custom in dealing with such defeated enemies as Germany and Japan, America would spend billions of dollars putting Israel back on its feet. To which one Israeli replied, "With our luck, we'd probably win!" Then there is the situation of Israel in the United Nations, where, Israelis insist, if an Arab delegate were to make a motion in the General Assembly that the world was flat, that motion would automatically receive a two-thirds majority vote. And finally there is Abba Eban's classic remark directly after the Six Day War, in the face of Russian and Arab demands for immediate Israeli withdrawal from captured territory. For the first time in the history of human warfare, he noted, "the victor sues for peace while the vanquished demands unconditional surrender."

issues and values

Do We Have It Too Good?   The continuing Arab threat has moved Israel to levels of national unity and creative achievement that it might never have attained in the absence of tension and pressure. Many Israelis wonder what might happen if peace were suddenly to become a reality. Would the country be able to sustain its feeling of cohesiveness, or would the process of depersonalization begin? American Jewish communal leaders have sometimes expressed a similar opinion about the need for external threats and crises to guard against the inroads of assimilation and to keep the Jewish community intact. "Having it too good," they observe, is not necessarily good for Jewish life in the Diaspora. Do you think that Jewish life requires an "injection" of crisis in order to function effectively? Does your attachment to Judaism depend upon such external threats as anti-Semitism or danger to Israel?

A Nation's Heroes   The "culture hero" of the Eastern European Jewish community was not a man of great physical prowess or the person who made the most money, but the scholar—the individual who proved himself able to comprehend the Talmud in its various meanings and applications. The scholar was honored, desired as a husband or son-in-law, and—if he happened to marry the daughter of a rich man—supported while he devoted his days to the study of sacred texts. A poor wife was often willing to be the breadwinner in the family so that her scholarly husband might be free to study. Modern Israel is still too young for us to speak precisely about culture heroes, but the most obvious hero yet to emerge is the ḥalutz, the pioneer. The value of *ḥalutziut* (pioneering) has been extended to include not only settling on new land and developing it, but pioneering in all walks of life. Who are the culture heroes of your society? What values do they represent?

David Ben-Gurion, Israel's first prime minister, typified the new "culture hero," the ḥalutz.

perspective

In Israel, the generation gap has been emphasized by differences in background, culture, and experience.

Native-born Israelis (or people who have been raised in Israel) have never been members of a minority, have never encountered anti-Semitism within their own culture, have never known the fears and troubles of Jews in the Diaspora. Their parents, who fled these troubles in the hope of finding new freedom, can hardly understand the new attitudes which a life of freedom has produced in their children.

In local newspaper cartoons, Israel is represented by two different images. One is the slightly haggard, stooped figure of an elderly man. He wears a dark, dust-stained, somewhat old-fashioned suit. His walk is a bit hesitant. His brow is furrowed, suggesting at once energy and weariness. The other figure is an eager teenager in khaki shorts, open sandals, and a *kova tembel,*° an inside-out sailor's hat that is popular in Israel. The little fellow, a kind of overgrown Dennis the Menace, seems to express innocence combined with childish cunning, charm mixed with a surprising talent for endurance.

The first character represents Grandfather Israel—the wandering, persecuted Jew who has finally come home. He stands for the original force behind the movement that led the Jews out of the Diaspora back to Palestine, where they hoped to find safety and rest. Grandfather Israel represents a deep-rooted history and tradition with a long past but an uncertain future.

The second figure is in some ways a response to the first. It represents the sabra—ignorant of the past or indifferent to it, responsive

ENVIRON-
MENT AND
PERSONALITY

° Literally, "foolscap." *Tembel* is Hebrew slang for "fool, buffoon." Of recent origin, *tembel* possibly derives from the English slang word "dumbbell."

only to the present, living every moment, keen, practical, "uncomplicated."

BETWEEN THE GENERATIONS

Our two figures sketch a portrait of Israel that reflects its inner conflict. Let us observe them more closely.

Both figures live in the present, but one looks back over his shoulder at the persecutions of the past; the other looks ahead to the uncertainties of the future. The past is Jewish; it harks back to the persecutions of the Diaspora, and the desperate passions generated by them. The future is Near Eastern; it reminds us of tomorrow's confrontation between Israel and the resentful Arab peoples surrounding Israel and, since 1967, in its very midst.

It is a sad landscape, even though everywhere one sees the marks of an enormously successful effort at human and physical reconstruction. For one sees not only flourishing new cities, universities, fertile fields, forests, and irrigation works, but also the marks of hatred, war, and human suffering.

There is nothing unique in conflict between the generations. It is to be found everywhere, and particularly in countries where the older generation is of immigrant stock. Compared to that of other Western societies, the generational conflict in Israel may even appear relatively mild. It is softened by the fact of war, the common danger shared by all. Yet it remains a reality. War itself—or the frustrating inability to put an end to it—may very well be a main cause of conflict.

This frustration was illustrated in the mid-1960's by the youthful reaction to an absurd, though appealing, incident. A Tel Aviv cafe owner, Abie Nathan, mortgaged his small cafe and flew a monoplane, *Shalom I*, to Egypt, on a one-man peace mission. The Egyptians turned him back; the Israelis in turn prosecuted him for illegally leaving the country. The enormous outpouring of popular sympathy for Nathan reflected the younger Israelis' weariness with an old leadership that was talking and talking peace but not achieving it. When Shulamit Aloni, one of the few members of parliament under 40, publicly kissed Nathan upon his return, she was scolded by her party leader, the elderly Golda Meir, who saw in Nathan no more than a misguided meddler.

FATHERS AND SONS

In this confrontation between generations, Grandfather Israel is a forbidding father figure. He stands for authority and experience, and he

FROM
ONE
GENERATION
TO THE
NEXT

161

frequently preaches the puritanism of the pioneering age. He seems overwhelmed by memories, and tends to view the history of Judaism solely as the tale of one prolonged and bloody pogrom. He sees the establishment and defense of Israel as one great act of compensation for Jewry's historic suffering in the Diaspora. Grandfather Israel is on his way out.

The blank-looking young fellow in his silly kova tembel is clearly the older generation's image of the young. The young fellow is much less touched by "ideas" or historical considerations than the older man. This could be merely a result of his youth and his still limited experience. Yet clearly there are deeper reasons.

His short lifetime has not fired him with that hope for a better world which lit the imagination of his elders. He senses that they were marvelous dreamers in their time, and he acknowledges their daring, though a bit grudgingly. But he finds it difficult to follow their dream. Face to face with the Arabs, he is both more extreme and more moderate than his elders. He might be more ruthless in action, but at the same time he is more flexible. When the founders of Zionism were confronted by the Arabs in Palestine who resented their arrival, they either averted their eyes or misinterpreted Arab opposition by making comparisons with European pogroms. Younger Israelis face their neighbors more honestly.

Moshe Dayan pointed out this difference between the older and younger generations in a talk to a Tel Aviv audience. "In my youth," he said, "I traveled a good deal with my late father, through the Valley of Esdraelon. We used to meet Arabs. At that time, especially in the winter, Arabs wrapped their faces in a *keffiye* until only their nose and eyes remained exposed. My father was not born in this country; he came from Russia when he was 17. He would say: 'Look, they have the eyes of murderers.' But these Arabs were not murderers . . . it only seemed to my father that in the eyes which peered through the keffiye's folds he saw the same look that he remembered from his Russian shtetl. But this did not make these Arabs into murderers."

UNDERSTANDING THE ARAB POSITION

Older Israelis were baffled and frightened by the Arabs. Younger Israelis are more rational and more inclined to look squarely at a situation which they did not create but into which they were born.

It is easier for young Israelis to see the Arab point of view. This makes them more dangerous opponents for the Arabs, but it also makes them more apt to compromise. Public opinion polls have shown a preponderance of young people among the "doves" (that is, those favoring far-reaching territorial compromises in return for peace), whereas older people tend to be "hawks." The "doves" might be far more numerous if the Arab spokesmen were not so unyielding.

The young Israelis find themselves locked in a desperate struggle which seems endless. They did not initiate that struggle; they inherited it. Yet they see themselves entangled in it, a position which a sensitive, small, but not uninfluential minority of the young regards with unease. The very existence of such a minority bears witness to the fact that the cruelty of permanent war has not eroded the nation's moral fiber. This unease may spread, partly because of battle fatigue. As the toll of casualties mounts, the question *Mah yehiyeh hasof?* (What will be the end?) is asked with increasing frequency. This is, of course, a very Jewish question, a part of the hope for peace that for Jews is almost second nature.

related themes

"An Army that Sings" One American correspondent during the Six Day War called the Israeli soldiers "an army that sings." In many ways it could be said that the present younger generation has turned to song to express its deepest hopes and fondest dreams. Many of the songs have arisen from the Israeli war experience and reveal a deep longing for peace. "Tomorrow," one of the popular songs of the Six Day War, says "Tomorrow, maybe the ships will sail from the shores of Eilat to the Ivory Coast; / And the old battleships will glisten with the gold of oranges . . . / All this will happen tomorrow, if not today; it is as clear as the light at noon . . . / And if not tomorrow, then the day after. . . ." This expression of a wistful longing for peace goes back to the first days of Israel's creation. During the War of Independence, young Israelis used to sing, "It may be possible that . . . already tomorrow . . . in the passing jeep the soldiers will have whispered: 'It's over!' " And another song, "Those Were the Days," imagined a future in which " . . . today you can no longer recognize anything. In place of fortifications there is a city. Maybe—because of those days."

The Sabras To the early settlers, their children were "on the drawing board" as much as their new country was. They hoped for children who would be free and proud, raised in a land and culture of their own, unburdened by the fears that have haunted Jews living in Diaspora

FROM
ONE
GENERATION
TO THE
NEXT

163

countries. In short, the pioneers envisioned a "new Jew." Yet when the sabras finally came into being, the older generation grew nervous—not because their children did not develop according to plan, but because they did. The sabras were very different from their parents. They did not brood about anti-Semitism and pogroms, because they had never experienced these things. They were not inclined to express their revolt against injustices they had never known. So, numerous articles began to appear which spoke of the "normalization" of Israeli youth, of their lack of commitment and lack of sensitivity. The older generation began to call them *Dor Bitzua* ("Generation of Implementation"), meaning that the young were content to do what the old planned for them, instead of creating new goals of their own. Later, in the 1950's, they were called *Dor Espresso* ("Espresso Generation"), a name which compared Israeli youth to a cup of espresso coffee—a machine-made brew which comes out lukewarm and somewhat tasteless. By now the older generation has outgrown many of its fears, and has come to understand that its sons and daughters are idealistic, heroic, and sensitive, in their own way. But the earlier doubts of the elders pointed up the extent of Israel's generation gap.

issues and values

"Thinking Narrow" Many Israelis of the younger generation decided to "think narrow." They wanted to define themselves strictly in national and geographic terms: as Israelis rather than as Jews, with no significant ties or commitments to the world Jewish community. Their concern was with the here and now, rather than with the tragedies of the past. This tendency became known as *C'na'anut* (from Canaan, the name of the land of Israel before it was settled by the Hebrew tribes). *C'na'anut* was a kind of thinking in which the 2000 years of dispersion and persecution were forgotten; Israeli youth took a long leap backward to identify themselves with their ancient national heritage. Two events changed their attitude: the Eichmann trial and the Six Day War. Through the Eichmann trial, the horrors of the Holocaust were relived by the sabras, who had never personally experienced them. And in the tense weeks of waiting before the Six Day War, as it seemed more and more obvious that most of the world's nations would stand by quietly while Israel was being destroyed—and later in the discovery that the Jewish Quarter had been destroyed and the ancient Jewish cemeteries desecrated during the Arab occupation of the Old City—a new sense of identity with the Jewish people emerged, as the Jews of Israel realized that their only true and constant friend was the world Jewish community. Do you feel a part of a world Jewish community, or are you only concerned with what happens to Jews in this country? Has recent Israeli history shocked you in any way?

Youth in the Kibbutz   The gap between the sabra and the generation of older settlers is not as great on the kibbutz as it is in the cities of Israel. As Sadia Gelb and Joseph Criden point out in *The Kibbutz Experience: Dialogue in Kfar Blum:*

> We have learned to bridge the gap between the various age groups, young, middle aged and older. Believing as we do in the principles of democracy, we have found that by giving each generation freedom of expression, we have obviated the need for rebellion . . . and we have been able to work together on activities and programs that benefit all age groups . . . both physically and psychologically the younger generation has always had room in which to move around. . . . The wide spaces in which we live have also made for freedom of expression, and whatever friction occurs is usually with peers rather than with the older generation. Our children have few inhibitions about expressing themselves. A six-year-old has no compunction about telling his kindergarten teacher: "You are wrong." . . .

Do you feel that there is a Jewish generation gap between people your age and the age of your parents? What differences are there? Could the approach which has been taken by the kibbutz help to bridge the generation gap in other settings?

Jewish graves in Jerusalem desecrated by Arabs.

FROM
ONE
GENERATION
TO THE
NEXT

165

perspective

The solution to the problem lies in forces beyond Israel's control. The Israelis know that on this issue the Arab politicians have been cynical and ruthless, using the refugees as a means of furthering their own ends. Yet because the Israelis are themselves a nation of immigrants and refugees, and because of the strong moral quality of the Jewish tradition and Zionist pioneering ideals, Israel's past achievements and future hopes are shadowed by the presence and plight of the Palestinian refugees.

After the 1967 war, when victory brought new strategic borders but, frustratingly, no solution of the conflict, there were impassioned appeals to make an immediate, one-sided effort to resettle those Arab refugees who were now under Israeli jurisdiction in captured territories. Suggestions were also made to encourage the establishment of an independent Palestinian state in the newly captured areas. Nothing came of these suggestions, mainly because there was no significant response on the part of the Arabs, but partly because the Israeli cabinet, exhausted by the war and challenged by internal problems, shut itself to new ideas and fresh approaches.

A CRISIS OF CONSCIENCE

The crisis of conscience that emerged after the 1967 war was rooted in a number of causes. There was, first and foremost, Israel's new sense of strength and security. Equally important was the first opportunity, provided by the war, for younger Israelis to face the mass of defeated Arabs in the occupied towns and villages of the West Bank and to see for themselves the dismal refugee camps of the Gaza Strip.

    The attitude of most Israelis to the tragic problem of the Arab refugees has always been complicated. Themselves a nation of refugees

ENVIRON-
MENT AND
PERSONALITY

166

and children of refugees, Israelis have often thought of themselves as sympathetic to the plight of the Arab refugees. In a nation besieged, such sympathy has had its necessary limits. But in the 1967 war, when Israeli forces overran some of the worst refugee camps in Jordanian territory, statistics suddenly took on human form.

REMEMBERING THE HOLOCAUST

"I had a terrible feeling during the meeting with the civilian population [in the occupied territories]," a young kibbutznik soldier is quoted as saying in *Siah Lohamim:*

> "Kids, three or four years old, already knew how to raise their arms [in surrender], to walk about town with their arms above their heads. I remember that old men and women came to implore. It was an awful feeling, awful. It's a horrible feeling to have to explain to these women that nobody intends to kill their husbands. Horrible, and I can't free myself from it."

The soldier was relating an intensely personal reaction to an incident probably witnessed by many; yet his description comes as a shock to most Israelis, who immediately transfer the image to the photograph, well-known to every schoolchild, of a terrified Jewish child in Poland, with his arms raised high above his head, on his way to a concentration camp. The two situations are, of course, different and incomparable, but the connection is unavoidable.

Chapter 16 described the terrible impact of the Holocaust on the national psychology of Israel, especially during times of war or danger. The effects of such a group experience lead to a determination to win in war, but also to compassion and empathy with the loser. If the Arabs were able to develop even a fraction of that empathy toward Jews and Israelis, real peace would be within reach.

The moving confession of another young soldier quoted in *Siah Lohamim* illustrates this point. In the early days of confusion following the 1967 war, masses of civilian Arabs fled the territories suddenly occupied by Israel. The young soldier, remembering this terrible exodus, testified to his sense of personal identification: "If I had [in this war] a clear association with the . . . Holocaust, it was in a certain moment, when I was going up the Jericho-Jerusalem road and the refugees were streaming down (toward the River Jordan). . . . I felt directly identified with them. I almost saw myself carried by my father . . . [my] identification was precisely with the other side, with our enemies." Still another soldier bitterly admitted that when he entered

Arab refugee camp in Gaza.

an Arab refugee camp in order to put down a disorder, he felt "like a Gestapo man. . . . I thought of home, I thought my parents were being led away. . . ."

REMEMBERING ZIONIST DREAMS

Many Israeli soldiers were surprised, and some were deeply disturbed, to discover among the refugees the living memory of a lost homeland to which they were passionately attached, just as the Jews had remained attached to Zion during the Diaspora. The education of these young soldiers—some were born after the establishment of Israel—little prepared them for a discovery such as this. Entering a refugee camp, one young soldier discovered that the inmates were still living in small clans or neighborhood units organized according to the villages, towns, and even the streets they had lived in before 1948. These villages and towns were now thoroughly Israeli—Beersheba, Zarnuga, Ramle, Lod, Jaffa, Rehovoth. He described his confused reaction in *Siah Lohamim.* "I remember it made me boil," he said at first.

> *Question:* Why?
> *Answer:* I remember I couldn't grasp it. [After all] nineteen years had passed. . . . How dare you say that you are from Beersheba . . . that you are from Rehovoth. [At first] it made my blood boil.
> *Question:* And now?
> *Answer:* Now I think I understand. First and foremost they have preserved some glimmer of hope to return. I think this war was a result of

this hope. . . . I can [no longer] be angry with them. . . . I can only pity them. In reality, for them these nineteen years have been a waste of time . . . nineteen lost years, in inhuman conditions, for a hope that will not come true.

Question: You didn't have some respect for people who remained loyal to their homes, to the place where their forebears were born? After all there is the same element in us. "Our hope is not yet lost, to return to the land of our forefathers." * We were also educated on loyalty to place, home, soil and to a lost country. The myth of the lost country is really our own myth. Didn't you connect these things?

Answer: When I try to clarify these things to myself today, I say that . . . it's clear, their tragedy is a real one . . . and in my view today there does not seem to be anything more to prevent them from living alongside us. . . . Again I don't know if . . . that's already a political problem, the more basic problem of how to establish links among people, between two nations. But I see no reason, even today . . . yes, why shouldn't there [again] be Arabs in Zarnuga and Beersheba . . . and let them say they are Zarnugians and Beershebans.

DEALING WITH MEMORIES

This uneasiness is not widespread among all Israelis. It is, however, felt in influential places: in the university, in the kibbutz, and very much among young writers and poets who, in every society, frequently serve as the conscience of the group.

The young writers reveal their own torn emotions and the moral dilemmas they face. A good example is in the story "Facing the Forests," written by A. B. Yehoshua, one of the most popular and respected young writers in Israel, who is dean of students at Haifa University. This story tells of a young student who is hired to guard a forest. It is a new forest, representing the rebirth, the recultivation of Eretz Israel, and it has been planted over the ruins of an Arab village. The student's job is to watch for fires in the forest, and yet he stands by while a demented Arab—a relic of the village—burns the trees down. As his eyes drift over the smoking hills, he lowers his brows and "there, from within the smoke and fog, arises before him the small village, reborn in a few basic lines, as in an abstract drawing, like every sunken past."

The work of Amos Oz also deals with the Arab-Israeli entanglement. His best-selling novel, *My Michael*, hailed by many critics as a great work, deals with a Jewish woman's fantasy about a pair of Arab twins she had known in her youth. It delves into her feelings of love

* From the early version of *Hatikvah* (The Hope), the Israeli national anthem.

and hate toward them, and into the guilt that makes her self-destructive.

Many Israelis share a sense of ambivalence—both sympathy and hostility—toward the Arabs. At the same time, one must not forget that it is easier to *feel* the Palestinians' tragedy than it is to find a solution for it that would not only be acceptable to them but would also prevent an even greater tragedy for Jews. At least in Israel—and, let us hope, in Arab countries too—a younger generation of writers and thinkers is preparing the ground for the emotional détente that is a precondition for any peace settlement.

related themes

All or Nothing   Israel has tried repeatedly to solve the Arab refugee problem. In the Declaration of Independence issued May 14, 1948, the government stated: "We appeal—in the very midst of the onslaught launched against us for months—to the Arab inhabitants of the State of Israel to preserve peace and participate in the upbuilding of the state on the basis of full and equal citizenship and due representation. . . ." At the end of the War of Independence, Israel offered to make the refugee problem the first item on the agenda of the peace negotiations that led up to the armistice agreements of 1949; the Arab governments refused. At the same time, Israel declared its willingness to take back 100,000 refugees as citizens, no questions asked; this offer too was ignored. In 1963, Israel proclaimed to the United Nations a desire to negotiate a solution to the refugee problem; the Arab governments never responded. And ever since 1948, Israel has offered compensation for the landed property abandoned by the Arabs, and has even had a UN body appraise the value of those properties; to no avail. The Arab leaders have consistently demanded all or nothing. At least until after the Six Day War, this could only mean the destruction of the State of Israel.

The Open-Bridges Policy   In 1967, Israel instituted an Open-Bridges policy on its frontier with Jordan. This allowed Arabs living in the areas captured by Israel during the Six Day War to travel freely to Jordan (and through Jordan to other neighboring Arab countries) for family, trade, and educational reasons. Since 1971, Arabs from the occupied territories have been allowed to visit Israel without permit. And for about four months each summer, citizens from various Arab states are allowed to visit relatives in the territories and in Israel proper —and are permitted to move freely throughout the country. In addi-

The Open-Bridges policy seeks to promote trust and understanding between Arabs and Jews.

tion, family reunion programs have made it possible for more than 40,000 Arabs from outside to rejoin their families living in the captured territories. The open-bridges policy has been maintained without interruption, even during the Yom Kippur War. Despite the obvious security risks and the opportunity for terrorists to enter, this policy is supported by most Israelis, both for humane reasons and because they hope that such contact may spark the beginning of the understanding and trust that are necessary for peace between the two peoples.

issues and values

Two Groups of Refugees In his book *The Case for Israel*, the journalist Frank Gervasi makes the following observation:

> Arab aggression has created not one but two groups of refugees in the Middle East. The world has not been allowed to forget the first, but has remained

largely unaware of the second. The first group comprises those Arabs who abandoned their homes in Palestine during the 1947–1949 fighting. They numbered 587,000 and are now the charges of the U.N., which houses, feeds, cares for, and educates them. Because nothing has been done to resettle or rehabilitate them, they constitute a "problem." The second group encompasses the Jews who, between 1947 and 1963, were uprooted from Middle Eastern countries where their ancestors had lived for generations . . . until they suddenly became anathema. They numbered about 650,000 and are now productive citizens in Israel. The overwhelming majority were poor people, but they collectively left behind property valued in the hundreds of millions of dollars. All arrived in Israel penniless, many with only the rags on their backs, but they are no longer a "problem."

What do you think would be a just and fair solution to the refugee problem? What should be the role of Arab countries? Of Israel? Of the international community? Do you think that the Jewish refugees from Arab lands should receive compensation for their losses?

Propaganda   A deep-rooted hatred has been instilled in the Arab refugees, particularly in the younger generation born outside of Israel. They have been told again and again that they are victims of Israeli aggression and that their ultimate goal should be the destruction of the Jewish state and the creation of an Arab Palestine in its place. To reinforce this hatred, the Arab countries have continually issued propaganda. Abba Eban explains the situation in his book *My People: The Story of the Jews:*

> In writing and caricature, Israel was portrayed as a hook-nosed monster, worthy only of physical extermination. There is not a single image, phrase or adjective in the Nazi vocabulary which Arab propaganda has not adopted. . . . The murder of 6 million Jews by the Nazis was alternately denied and applauded. . . .

When Israeli soldiers entered the refugee camps in 1967, they found that this propaganda had even penetrated children's textbooks, which were published under United Nations supervision. How do your history textbooks deal with the problem of the Holocaust or the contribution of the Jewish people to world history? Have you been taught in any way to hate or look down upon other people? How would you go about reeducating an Arab who has a gut-hatred of Israel learned from early childhood?

ENVIRON-
MENT AND
PERSONALITY

172

THE YOM KIPPUR WAR

Photo Essay On Yom Kippur, October 6, 1973, shortly before 2 P.M., Egypt and Syria attacked Israel simultaneously. In the south, Egyptian planes bombed Israeli positions on the Sinai, and some 100,000 men in 1000 tanks surged across the Suez Canal on barges and pontoon bridges. In the north, some 50,000 men and 800 tanks advanced into the Golan Heights.

Most Israelis were quietly observing their holiest of holy days. As is usual in Israel on Yom Kippur, radio and television were not broadcasting. The city streets were deserted; there was little or no traffic. Hundreds of thousands of Israelis were attending synagogue services. The attack came as a total surprise.

The nation was alerted by the wail of air raid sirens, followed by coded radio broadcasts of mobilization orders. In the synagogues, men laid down their prayer books and rushed off to rejoin their reserve and active units.

Along the Suez Canal, in the bunkers and forts of the Bar-Lev line, there were at the time fewer than 1000 Israeli soldiers. They put up a heroic fight, holding back forces that outnumbered them 50-to-1. But at last, through the sheer weight of numbers and armor, the Bar-Lev line was overrun. Egyptian advance columns proceeded to a line some 10 kilometers (about 6½ miles) to the east-northeast, where they paused to stabilize their position.

In the Golan Heights, too, the Syrian attack was met by a force of fewer than 100 Israeli tanks. Retreating slowly, suffering heavy casualties, this small force managed to inflict even greater losses

Kibbutz children survey damage after Syrian bombing, 1973.

upon the enemy. Nevertheless, on the second day it seemed, for a few hours, that the Syrian advance column would descend upon Tiberias and the Hula Valley, right into Israel proper.

Meanwhile, Israel was gathering its forces, and reservists were reaching their units. Within 48 hours the mobilization of reserves was almost complete. Many of the units had reached the front and were striking back at the invaders. By October 9 the enemy advance had been halted at most points—at the cost, however, of hundreds of Israeli lives and thousands of wounded.

During the next two weeks the strength and resilience, the perseverance and tenacity of Israel were put to a test even more awful, more bitter, and more severe than any since Israel's birth in 1948. The cost in human life was terrible: more than 2500 dead, almost 6000 wounded. Hardly a family in Israel was not directly or indirectly struck. (A similar casualty rate in America would mean over 500,000 soldiers wounded or killed within three weeks.)

The Israeli counterattack began along the Syrian front, because it was so much closer than Sinai to Israel's civilian population centers. While holding off the Egyptians in the south, Israel's forces in the north drove back the invaders across the 1967 cease-fire line and advanced into Syria some 30 miles south of Damascus. Next, while holding the Syrians in the north, the Israelis repulsed a massive Egyptian offensive in the south. On October 16, President Sadat of Egypt proclaimed that the war would continue until the Arabs had reconquered all of the territory they had lost in 1967. But even as he spoke, an Israeli task force under General Ariel Sharon crossed the Suez Canal into Egypt proper; as it spread out on the other side of the canal, it threatened the Egyptian capital of Cairo only 60 miles to the north. It also cut off the Egyptian second and third armies, which had crossed the canal, from the rest of the Egyptian forces. This was the turning point of the war. Egypt made desperate but futile attempts to break the Israeli bridgehead on the west bank of the canal,

Israeli tank battalion advances in Sinai.

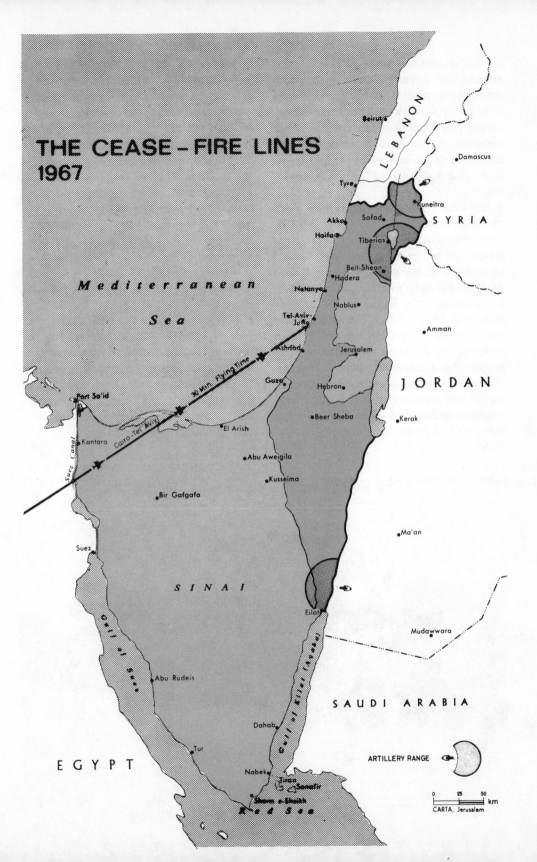

THE CEASE–FIRE LINES
1967

Beirut

LEBANON

Damascus

Tyre

Kuneitra

Akko
Haifa

Safad

SYRIA

Tiberias

Beit-Shean

Hadera

Netanya

Nablus

Mediterranean Sea

Tel-Aviv-Jaffa

Ashdod

Jerusalem

Amman

Gaza

Hebron

JORDAN

Port Sa'id

20 Min. Flying Time

Cairo-Tel Aviv

Beer Sheba

Kerak

Kantara

El Arish

Suez Canal

Abu Aweigila

Kusseima

Bir Gafgafa

Ma'an

Suez

S I N A I

Eilat

Mudawwara

SAUDI ARABIA

Abu Rudeis

ARTILLERY RANGE

Dahab

Tur

EGYPT

0   25   50
km

Nabek

Tiran

Sanafir

CARTA, Jerusalem

Sharm e-Sheikh

Red Sea

Gulf of Suez

Gulf of Eilat (Aqaba)

but the bridgehead grew wider with each attack. The Egyptian position on both sides of the canal became more perilous with each passing day. The Soviet Union, which had begun a massive airlift of weapons to the Arab attackers on the fourth day of the war, began to fear for its allies and suddenly called for a cease-fire.

The United States began its own airlift to Israel on October 14, about a week after the war began. When the Soviet Union realized that the war was turning against the Arabs, they joined the United States in the effort to arrange a cease-fire. On October 24 a cease-fire finally took effect. An eerie silence descended upon the battlefields. Wearily, men on both sides of the trenches eyed one another across the smoldering debris. The demarcation lines were arbitrarily stretched across the desert where the battle had suddenly ended. The biggest bloodletting since 1948 had ended once again in stalemate.

The war had a profound effect on Israel's political life. It shattered many reputations and brought some meteoric careers to an abrupt end. An inquiry commission headed by the chief judge of the Supreme Court thoroughly examined the events that had led up to the war and to the unexpected initial success of the Arab attack. Prime Minister Golda Meir and Defense Minister Moshe Dayan were personally exonerated from responsibility by the commission. Nevertheless, the pressure of public opinion forced both to resign in the spring of 1974.

The new government was headed by a newcomer to Israeli politics, the 52-year-old Yitzḩak Rabin; it included many other new faces. The Israelis sensed the beginning of a new era. The younger generation had been waiting for this moment for at least a decade. They had yet to prove that they could do a better job than their elders had in the first quarter century of Israel's perilous existence.

Captured Russian pontoon bridge tanks.

The tent at Kilometer 101 where talks were held between Israeli
and Egyptian officers.

Russian missiles captured west of the Suez Canal.

Israeli soldiers raise the flag over Mount Hermon on the Syrian front, October 1973.

perspective

Israelis have made archaeology their "national sport" with good reason. The ancient past is, simply, there for the taking, before their eyes and beneath their feet. The land and the history of the Jewish people are bound up together, and the Israelis are eager to establish clear lines of continuity. Finally, because their claim to the land of Israel has been challenged so bitterly, the Israeli participation in archaeology is, in a very real sense, a search for the roots of the Jewish national state.

Because Israel is such a new country, Israelis are constantly seeking to define themselves and looking for their roots. Nowhere is a people more concerned with such questions as "Who are we?" and "Why are we here?" Perhaps it is because the homeland, the land of Israel itself, is so ancient that this raw, new nation has latched onto archaeology as both science and popular hobby. In Israel archaeology might almost be called the national sport!

Israeli archaeologists, professionals as well as amateurs, are not merely digging for objects but for *roots,* which they find in the remains of ancient Israel scattered throughout the country. Not surprisingly, archaeological finds have inspired nearly all Israeli national symbols, including the state seal, emblems, coins, medals, and postage stamps. The country is a treasure house of antiquities.

THE BELIEF IN HISTORY

The best-known amateur archaeologist in Israel is General Moshe Dayan. His home holds one of the country's major archaeological collections. Dayan once told an interviewer that in his diggings he was searching for

the ancient Land of Israel. Everything that ancient Eretz Israel was; those who lived there then, their way of life. You sometimes feel that you

ARCHAE-
OLOGY AND
THE
NATIONAL
CONSCIOUS-
NESS

179

can literally enter their presence. They are dead, to be sure. But you can enter the homes of silenced people and sometimes feel more than when you enter the homes of the living. *I like to stick my head into a hole in which the people of Bnei Brack lived 6,000 years ago* * . . . to have a look at their kitchen, to *finger* the ashes left there from long ago, to *feel* the fingerprints which that ancient potter left on the vessel.

Israel's outstanding professional archaeologist, Professor Yigael Yadin, is a former general and chief of staff. Professor Yadin has said that for young Israelis, a "belief in history" has come to be a substitute for religious faith. "Through archaeology they discover their 'religious values.' In archaeology they find their religion. They learn that their forefathers were in this country 3000 years ago. This is a value. By this they fight and by this they live. . . ."

In modern Hebrew it is customary to speak of an Israeli *bulmus* for archaeology. *Bulmus* is an old talmudic term. It denotes a ravenous hunger, a faintness resulting from prolonged fasting, an exaggerated eagerness, a fit, a rage, a mania.

ARCHAEOLOGY AND THE EARLY ZIONISTS

The present mania for archaeology is of relatively recent origin. The early Zionists had no more than a passing interest in it. Theodor Herzl noted in his diary (September 3, 1889) that his attention was once briefly drawn to a plan by Colonel Henning Melander, a Swedish army officer and world traveler, who proposed to dig up the Temple Mount in Jerusalem. Herzl wrote that he discussed this romantic project with the grand duke of Baden, his powerful friend and supporter at the imperial court of Germany. The duke told Herzl that the kaiser was "greatly interested" in the project. Herzl apparently was not, for he never mentioned the subject again.

In his written plans for the New Jerusalem, there is nothing on archaeology. Rather, his aim was to thoroughly "clean up" Jerusalem, to "remove everything that is not sacred" to one of the three religions, "empty the dirty hovels, burn down the non-sacred ruins," transplant the ancient bazaars and construct a "modern, clean, well-ventilated" town around the holy places.

The many writings of the early pioneers contain remarkably few references to archaeology. Perhaps their hard struggles in the present left them little leisure in which to investigate the past. Even more important was their strong orientation toward the future. Whatever

* Italics added.

free time they had was devoted to their plans for a brilliant tomorrow.

One of the few founding fathers who did turn a backward glance to the past was Yitzḥak Ben-Zvi, the future president of Israel. Ben-Zvi was fascinated not by archaeology but by ethnology, the study of the origins and cultures of differing races. He searched the deserts for lost tribes of Jewish bedouin. He was excited by the discovery of a few authentic Hebrew-Arab peasants who lived in the Galilean village of Pekiin. This was living—not stone-dead—proof of a continued Jewish presence in the country.

AN ISRAELI BULMUS

The present bulmus for archaeology has grown with the second and third generation of settlers. In 1920, men of the famous Labor Brigade were employed as earth diggers at the excavation of Hammat-Tiberias. But the brigade seems to have approached the task with much less respect than they did the building of roads and the draining of swamps. Digging up the past was not building the future.

The first real upsurge of appreciation for archaeology occurred in December 1928. It was a time of low morale and distress. The Jewish community in Palestine was having difficulties with the British mandatory government. There was an economic depression and mounting Arab opposition to Zionist settlement. A much-needed morale booster was the accidental discovery of a sixth-century synagogue on the grounds of kibbutz Bet Alpha. The kibbutzniks hit the mosaic floor of the synagogue while digging an irrigation ditch. The discovery was considered to be of "national importance," so it was at first kept secret from the British regional inspector of archaeology. A Jewish archaeologist, E. L. Sukeṇik (father of Yigael Yadin), was summoned by the kibbutzniks from Jerusalem, and an excavation was arranged under "Zionist" auspices. For weeks, excited left-wing, nonobservant, antireligious kibbutzniks from the entire region volunteered their labor for the excavation of the ancient synagogue.

THE DEAD SEA SCROLLS

The enthusiasm for archaeology expanded during subsequent decades. By 1947 it was fully developed. In the summer of that year, a bedouin shepherd boy, pursuing a runaway goat along the cliffs that rim the Dead Sea, accidentally came upon a previously unknown cave. He threw a stone into the cave and heard the sound of breaking clay. Thus it was that Israel eventually acquired its most important archaeological

ARCHAE-
OLOGY AND
THE
NATIONAL
CONSCIOUS-
NESS

181

"Thanksgiving Scroll":
One of the Dead Sea
Scrolls.

relic to date—the Dead Sea Scrolls. For Israelis, the scrolls have since assumed an almost sacred quality. In the eyes of some, the scrolls are like titles of real estate, like deeds of possession to a contested country.

The seven Dead Sea Scrolls that were purchased by the government of Israel are now housed, along with many later finds, in Jerusalem in a specially built sanctuary appropriately called the Shrine of the Book. Perhaps it is symbolic of the emotional meaning which the scrolls have acquired that the building which houses them (and which is part of the National Museum) faces the Knesset.

MASADA

Emotional involvement in archaeology reached a high point in 1963, during the excavation and painstaking restoration of the ancient fortress of Masada.

Masada was originally built by Herod as a military citadel and as a pleasure palace for himself. It is dramatically perched on top of a cliff 1000 feet above the Dead Sea in the waterless wilderness of Judea. After the fall of Jerusalem in 70 C.E., Jewish zealots established a religious community at Masada and made a last stand against the conquerors. The story of the siege of Masada by the Roman army and the mass suicide of its defenders—how the men, women, and children drew lots and slew one another rather than fall prisoner to the Romans —is well known.

Masada was excavated by Professor Yadin between 1963 and 1965. He was assisted by thousands of Israeli and foreign volunteers. Yadin's otherwise factual account of the dig is filled with emotional descriptions of the enthusiasm of the Israeli volunteers. His text is marked by enraptured exclamations:

> It was an unforgettable moment. Suddenly a bridge was thrown across two thousand years. . . .
>
> How great was their satisfaction, and ours, when they—the young generation of the independent State of Israel—uncovered with their own hands the remains of the last defenders of Masada. . . .

Yadin's excavations at Masada illustrated an interesting, and probably unique, feature of Israeli life and manners. Aside from dangerous military tasks and service in exposed border settlements, unpaid work at archaeological excavations is the single social project that Israelis voluntarily undertake in large numbers.

A young volunteer at the excavations next to the Western Wall told the story of an encounter in the Arab quarter of the Old City of Jerusalem as he walked home tired and dusty after a long day's work. "One puzzled Arab asked me: 'For what do you work, if not for money?' I answered, 'Inspiration,' and he said, 'Where do I find that? There is none in my life.' I told him I must be lucky."

Masada has since been restored and partly reconstructed by the National Parks Authority. It is now fairly easy to reach and is visited annually by a great many tourists. The patriotic ceremonies that regularly take place at the top of Masada provide an example of the meeting

View of Masada showing Yadin's excavations.

ARCHAE-
OLOGY AND
THE
NATIONAL
CONSCIOUS-
NESS

183

of politics and archaeology in modern Israeli culture. Youth movements of all political affiliations hold emotional pageants at Masada. Select units of the Israeli army are marched up to the fortress to take their oath of induction.

Recruits to the armored corps recite their oaths of allegiance on Masada. The rites take place at nighttime ceremonies lit by hundreds of blazing torches. A remark by Professor Yadin, made during a speech at one such ceremony in the summer of 1963, has often been quoted:

> When Napoleon stood among his troops next to the pyramids of Egypt, he declared: "Four thousand years of history look down upon you." But what would he not have given to be able to say to his men: "Four thousand years of *your own* history look down upon you. . . ." The echo of your oath this night will resound throughout the encampments of our foes! Its significance is not less powerful than all our armaments!

related themes

Israelis and the Bible   At the turn of the century, Theodor Herzl wrote a novel about the Land of Israel which he called *Altneuland* ("The Old-New Land"). This title captures the view that most Israelis have of their country and of themselves. What they do—building, reclaiming land, integrating new immigrants, research in science and technology —is aimed at the future. But their sense of who they are and where they are going is rooted in Israel's ancient past. The Bible is studied extensively from primary school through high school, not only as a religious text but also as a fundamental source of Israeli history and culture. The *Ḥidon HaTanach* (National Bible Quiz) is an event that commands the avid interest of the entire country, young and old alike. Israeli tour guides use the Bible as a constant source of reference. Biblical quotations are an active part of the Israeli vocabulary and serve as the inspiration for many modern songs. Hundreds of locations in Israel—including Ashdod, Ashkelon, Beersheba, Jaffa, and Jerusalem —retain their biblical names. And the two ideals that best reflect Israel's mission as the modern Jewish state come directly from the writings of the prophets: "making the Desert Bloom" (Isaiah 35:1), and the concept of *Kibbutz Galuyot*, the Ingathering of the Exiles. As found in the book of Hosea, God proclaims "Now . . . I shall give back her vineyards and the waste valley will I turn into the door of hope. . . . And the children of Judah and Israel shall be gathered together . . . for great shall be the day of their ingathering."

issues and values

Gloomy Underside The Israeli preoccupation with the past has its gloomy underside. Many outside observers have wondered whether Israelis have a "Masada complex" that causes them to think of their country as a fortress under constant siege, and to contemplate the prospect of a last suicidal stand. There is a Samson-like image as well, of an Israel on the brink of destruction using nuclear weapons (which Israel is rumored to possess) to bring the temple of its enemies crumbling down upon them all. Most Israelis dismiss this doomsday speculation out of hand, pointing out that the history of their state has been one of creativity and rehabilitation. Do you think it would be moral for the State of Israel to use nuclear weapons if it seemed that Israel was about to be destroyed? In what ways does the so-called Masada complex protect the Israelis?

The Need for Roots Archaeology is one of the ways Israelis search for their roots in the past. This need for roots is reflected among other peoples as well. At the height of the black movement in this country, many black Americans began to seek out their African origins. There was a surge of interest in African history, poetry, and music, in Afro hairdos and colorful dashikis (a form of African dress). In a related vein, there is a growing demand today on the part of adopted children to be allowed to know who their biological parents may have been— not out of disloyalty to the parents who raised them, but because they feel a need of, and a right to, a knowledge of their origins. This search for origins has helped the Jewish people survive in places other than Israel. In the 1930's, when the Jews of Germany were becoming ever more isolated and anxious about their situation, there was a dramatic demand for Jewish encyclopedias and books of Jewish history and Hebrew grammar. Aḥad Ha'am once observed, "More than the Jewish people preserved the Sabbath, the Sabbath preserved the Jewish people." Which aspects of your past (being Jewish, American, or a combination of the two) mean the most to you? What do you think you will do to make sure that your children do not lose their heritage?

ARCHAE-
OLOGY AND
THE
NATIONAL
CONSCIOUS-
NESS

The seven-branched menorah, symbol of the State of Israel, stands before the Knesset building, Israel's parliament.

THE ISRAELI
WAY OF LIFE

perspective

Politics in Israel is a noisy, disorderly, confusing, emotional, and very serious business. Sometimes there seem to be as many political parties as there are Israelis. Combined parties, such as *Ma'arech* (Israel's majority party composed of four smaller parties: Mapai, Mapam, Rafi, and Aḥdut Avodah) are common. Somehow, the system works—that is, the moods and attitudes of the public are well expressed, and most Israelis feel a sense of involvement in the affairs of government.

The traditional humor of the Jews, with all its biting self-mockery, is by and large dying out among Israelis. It remains a lively art in one area only—government and politics. The main thrust of Israeli political humor remains the destruction of the heroic ideal. In a classic story, a man telephones the prime minister's office shortly after Ben-Gurion has resigned.

"May I speak to Premier Ben-Gurion?"
The operator tells him that Ben-Gurion is no longer in office.
"Oh," says the man, "thank you." A few minutes later he rings again and again asks to speak with Premier Ben-Gurion. Again, he receives the same answer. The third time, the operator begins to get annoyed.
"We've told you three times that Ben-Gurion is no longer in office. Stop calling."
"I am terribly sorry to bother you," says the man, "but I can't hear the news often enough."

There are innumerable examples of this sort.

Israelis endlessly complain that they are a misgoverned people. They continually call for more effective government. And yet, at the same time, few peoples are so suspicious of authority and so skilled at avoiding it. This dual approach to power is a main characteristic of the Israeli political style.

MANY POLITICAL PARTIES

Israelis seem to prefer their government to reflect not one single party but a group of them. The government has always been a coalition of several parties, which must reach an agreement by compromise.

The various Israeli interest groups have at times been represented by as many as 25 different political parties. The past ten or 15 years have seen a gradual merger of the splinter groups.

The present political organizations represent a cross-section of so-called labor interests (city workers and unions, kibbutzim, cooperatives, technocrats, union-owned industries), the religious establishment, the middle class, the professionals, the shopkeepers, and the private businessmen. Each party gets a slice of public funds; each has a share in the state bureaucracy and in the economy. Each party is tightly organized by well-run political machines.

THE PARTY AS A WAY OF LIFE

The political parties were formed long before Israel became a state; indeed, some were born in the Diaspora before the colonization of Palestine. With the exception of a few small groups, most Israeli parties started in Eastern Europe as Zionist clubs.

Before independence was declared, the parties tended to establish separate agricultural settlements, investment firms, urban housing projects, banks, trade unions, labor exchanges, kindergartens and schools, publishing houses, newspapers, and sick funds. At one time or another, several of the parties even maintained private underground armies. The parties were instrumental in creating the state, not vice-versa.

In the prestate period, an immigrant's first stop upon arrival in Palestine would often be his party's local headquarters. He lived in a party-sponsored block of apartments, on a kibbutz or moshav. He found employment through the party labor exchange and played on the party soccer team. His children were educated in party-controlled schools. He read the party newspaper. When sick, he lay in a party-affiliated hospital and recuperated in a party convalescent home. He even took his vacation with his family in a party-owned resort, surrounded by fellow party vacationers.

Since the establishment of the State of Israel, schools, labor exchanges, immigrant absorption, and the bulk of public housing have become state responsibilities. But the many parties remain. The sick funds are still party dominated, as are some of the housing projects. Agricultural settlements remain "affiliated" to their or that party.

GOVERNMENT AND POWER

From time to time, many Israelis will plead: "What we need is a strong leader." Yet when it comes to casting votes, they display a deep distrust of powerful men with strong personalities, the so-called charismatic type. Ben-Gurion was "father of the state," and as charismatic a leader as there ever was. But he never received more than 38.2 percent of the vote. In 1960 the party headed by Ben-Gurion received only 7.9 percent of the vote.

Israelis are quick to criticize their leaders for indecisiveness, or for giving in to special interest groups. The present political system, which rarely allows any one party to attain a majority of the national vote, means that deals have to be made with smaller parties. Such deals have resulted in laws forbidding public transportation and public entertainment on the Sabbath, prohibiting the raising of hogs and the selling of pork, and restricting marriage and divorce to rabbinic courts. The non-observant majority of Israelis normally resent such deals, which give power to a religious minority which has never polled more than 15.4 percent of the popular vote. Yet the public seems to distrust the alternative even more.

There is remarkably little unanimity in Israel on almost any subject. Only on matters of defense is agreement almost universal. In all other fields, there remains an extreme form of self-reliant, sometimes wildly antisocial individualism.

GOVERNMENT AND THE MILITARY

If, as is often said, a state of constant military preparedness tends to enhance the prestige of the army, Israel has had near-ideal conditions for the development of a military ruling class. But such dominance by the army has been successfully avoided. Israel's military ideal remains the embattled farmer, the armed civilian, the unprofessional soldier, an ideal which harks back to the earliest days of settlement.

The percentage of military personnel within the population is one of the highest in the entire world. But the influence of the army leadership on political decisions is small. There have been bitter personal clashes over military and political decisions between army leaders and their civilian chiefs; invariably, the army leadership bowed to the final verdict of the civilians. It could be said that Israelis guard themselves against militarism more than against any other danger except the Arab threat.

ISRAELIS AND AUTHORITY

The attitude of Jews to authority—all authority, including their own—has traditionally been highly skeptical. It still is, to a considerable degree. Jews rarely took the need for government for granted; society was always seen as superior and more permanent than the state. A basic disrespect of authority marks the Israeli Jew.

The Israelis' distrust of authority is rooted in the philosophy of the early pioneers, whose utopian ideas were based on an absolute freedom from restrictive government. There were times in the early 1920's when some of the most important new settlers seriously hoped that the Jewish national home would develop into a community of free and independent villages. They conceived of the entire country as a network of cooperative or collective agricultural and industrial associations, with a minimum of forceful authority and a maximum of voluntary, mutual alliances by free yet committed individuals.

Although the Golden Age of justice and liberty did not materialize, the cult of individual freedom continues. There remains in Israeli life an emphasis on *hitnadvut* (voluntarism) as opposed to legal compulsion, and on social authority as opposed to state organization.

THE INDIVIDUAL AND HIS RIGHTS

This attitude, of course, leads to a very personal sense of individual rights. The Israeli is often likely to feel that while laws and regulations are very good, his particular case requires special attention.

A word commonly heard in Israel is *le'histader*, which means "to take care of oneself," "to fix oneself up," to steer through life by bending the rules to one's own purpose. This has many applications. One may call on the help of one's political party, or make a phone call to a friend, or a friend of a friend, who occupies a key post in government or business. This kind of help is called *protektzia* (influence).

The average Israeli's first reaction, upon finding himself in conflict with the law, is to negotiate with its representative. Passionate debates between policeman and citizen are a common feature of the Israeli street scene. Few Israelis will accept a traffic ticket for jaywalking, speeding, or driving through a red light without an intense effort to convince the officer not to write out his form. Bribes are rare and are likely to be ineffective; persistent argument, whether reasonable or not, is more often crowned with success. There are occasional cases of police harshness, but the timidity of Israeli policemen, especially toward minor offenses, is well known. Some say it reflects a degree of uneasiness in practicing a traditionally non-Jewish profession.

The resulting legal irregularities and lack of civil discipline must be weighed against the advantages of living in a society which manages to permit a tolerable amount of individual freedom without disintegrating into chaos. In fact, though not in theory, Israel is a permissive society. Notwithstanding the pressures for governmental change in the name of order and efficiency, this permissiveness persists and apparently is one of the Israeli's deepest national traits.

related themes

Parliamentary Democracy   The political system in Israel is a parliamentary democracy. The president is the head of state, but he or she performs ceremonial functions and has little or no political authority. Real power lies with the prime minister, the head of government, who has achieved this position because he or she is the head of the party with the largest number of seats in the Knesset (Israel's parliament) or is able to make a coalition of the largest parties. Israelis do not vote for a particular personality but for a party as a whole. The party allocates the various positions it has won according to the seniority of its members. Thus, a party that has received 25 percent of the popular vote will have 30 seats in a 120-member Knesset and will assign those seats to the first 30 names on its list. To date no party has ever achieved a clear majority (51 percent). And there has been no equivalent of a common phenomenon in the United States—say, a Republican president and a Democratic-controlled Congress. Critics of the Israeli system maintain that the people are given little choice as to the candidates they would like to see in office. Its defenders point out that Israelis are more likely to cast their votes on the basis of issues rather than personalities.

"A Man Without Respect"   Israel's anti-heroic impulse can be traced to Eastern Europe, where there were few heroes, and many victims trying to keep their dignity and sanity intact. The most memorable characters of Eastern European folklore were these anti-heroes: *shlemiels* (if a shlemiel was carrying a cup of soup he invariably dropped it), *shlemazels* (the soup always fell on a shlemazel), *shnorrers* (who begged and panhandled and, in the end, survived through *ḥutzpah*,

Moshe Dayan addresses election rally.

gall). The most famous of these types was a character named Hershel
Ostropolier—a pauper, a storyteller, a wanderer from village to village. In his way, he was a keen social critic and a puncturer of preten-
sions. He was known as a man without respect. Here is a sample story
told of Hershel:

> Some townsmen fell to discussing the question of the rich and the poor. . . .
> "Ah, if men could only live a life of ease; if poverty were abolished from the
> world!" one of them said. And another added, "Life is hard when you haven't
> even a copper coin . . . but I have a plan. If all the townspeople would put
> all their money into one common fund, then each could draw upon it according
> to his needs." Everyone agreed it was a perfect plan. "And what have you to
> say to this, Hershel?" one of the men asked.
>
> "I'll tell you," said Hershel. "It is a masterful plan, but the real question
> is how to carry it out. So let us divide the task: I'll undertake to get the poor
> to agree and you can tackle the rich."

issues and values

A Bitter Issue   Unlike the United States, where religion and the state
are separated by the Constitution, in Israel the religious groups have

organized themselves into political parties. Although they are a minority, these parties have become very influential (in the Israeli parliamentary system, minority parties can often exert tremendous pressure on the larger, ruling parties). Thus, a basic and bitter issue has arisen. The nonorthodox Israeli insists that religious observance should be a personal matter; that the separation of religion and state is a cornerstone of true democracy; that there are many definitions of Judaism (national, cultural, and ethical, to name a few) which do not hinge upon religion; that the orthodox imposition of laws and customs upon people for whom these practices have little or no meaning does not promote the cause of religion and, in fact, violates civil rights; and finally, that the Jews constitute the only group in Israel which does not enjoy complete religious freedom.

The orthodox position is that Israel is not just another state, but a Jewish state. Therefore, it should be based on Jewish law and custom; its activity in the political sphere should be designed to halt the secularism that has infected modern Jewish life; it should strive to maintain the Jewish tradition at a time when so many forces are chipping away at it, even if some people are hurt or inconvenienced in the process; and it should protect those laws and customs which bound the Jewish people together during the 2000 years of dispersion, and which ultimately led to the formation of a Jewish state.

Is the separation of religion and state a fundamentally different problem in Israel than it is in the United States? Which arguments do you personally favor? Why do you think the issue is such a bitter one?

perspective

When a revolution succeeds, those who brought it about usually become the establishment, and their values and ideals become the accepted way of life. Israel is a sovereign state. The Zionist revolution has in most ways succeeded. Many of the dreams and ideals are now realities—the kibbutz, the moshav, the army, the Ingathering of the Exiles, and more. And for a quarter of a century or more, the pioneers of the Second and Third Aliyot have had firm control of the government and its institutions. Only recently has the younger generation, those born and raised in Israel, been loudly demanding a share of the power. Now the ideals of the establishment will be put to their ultimate test in the hands of a younger generation.

Noisy with the clatter of endless disagreement, the Israeli political scene can be marred by tremendous personal rivalries, hatreds, antagonisms, and fanatic loyalties. Yet within it there is often a strongly theatrical quality. For the duration of the show the actors assault each other; at the same time, they are animated by a common desire to make the show succeed and hold the public in its spell.

The several parties that dominate the Israeli public scene share a number of common interests. The veterans of all parties share a common suspicion of ambitious young people who impatiently call for reforms in the social and political structures established during the pioneering age. For a long time, the veteran leaders held tight to their positions of power, and until recently they were rather successful in preventing the young from entering the ranks of the Israeli establishment. The establishment was said to be made up of no more than a few hundred men and perhaps a dozen women, who generally shared long-standing ties of friendship.

In the national economy the main function of an establishment is

THE
ESTABLISH-
MENT

to preside over the distribution of income received from local taxes and from the funds contributed by Jews abroad. In political life the establishment controls the assignment of top jobs within the government and in many other areas as well. Among insiders this occupation is known as "distributing the dumplings."

Typically, the very existence of an establishment was hotly denied by many well-known Israelis of the older generation. The mere mention of the word "establishment" was sometimes considered an unjustified attack on values to which the veterans claimed they had devoted their entire lives. A few weeks before his final resignation in 1963—after an almost uninterrupted tenure of 30 years in the highest public office —Ben-Gurion was asked by an interviewer how long he thought he would still remain "in power." His reaction was characteristically irate. He did not like this term "power"; there was no such thing in Israel. He was not "in power," he said. He was prime minister, all right, but that was not being "in power."

THE AGE OF THE ESTABLISHMENT

Until 1974 the establishment was exclusively made up of leaders who emerged during the pioneering period. These veterans still dominate the public scene, but in the aftermath of the Yom Kippur War, for the first time in Israeli history, a prime minister was appointed who had not been among the founders.

Who qualifies for the establishment? Who belongs to it? Theoretically, everybody qualifies, whether young or old, of European or Afro-Asian origin, native-born or recent immigrant. But in reality, the establishment was long restricted to veteran settlers in their 60's and 70's; it has only slowly opened to others. Although Israel is a young country, its present establishment has often been remarkably suspicious of younger people. A 45- or 50-year-old man aspiring to office was long regarded as a "Young Turk" and classed among the ambitious young. In the first Israeli parliament (1949), the average age of members was 43. The average age in the sixth parliament (1969) was 63. In 20 years the average age of the members had risen by exactly 20 years! However, in the seventh parliament (1974) the average age of the members at last droppd to 54, and this trend is continuing.

LIVING IN THE ESTABLISHMENT

As a group, the establishment was largely made up of Eastern Europeans (and their sons) who arrived in the country well before Independence,

Young members of the Irgun in action, December 1947.

although in a few exceptional cases, veteran Zionist leaders from abroad
qualified for membership immediately upon arrival in the country.

The few younger establishment members were involved in some
kind of dangerous underground operation prior to the establishment of
the state. Some were members of the terrorist "army," the *Irgun Zvai
Leumi;* others worked for the more moderate Haganah, ran arms and
illegal immigrants from Europe into Palestine, or carried out dangerous
missions in the Arab countries.

For the most part, the majority of establishment members came
from Poland or, to a lesser extent, Russia. In fact, a circle drawn on a
map of Russia centered on Minsk and with a radius of 500 miles would
probably include the birthplaces of at least two-thirds of the establishment. Their formal education was usually irregular; they either interrupted high school or dropped out of the university in order to come as
pioneers to Palestine. With the possible exception of the orthodox
religious members, most of the establishment worked, at one time or
another, as manual laborers—draining swamps, building roads, planting vegetables and orange groves, or driving a tractor.

As members of the establishment, they led remarkably similar lives.
If they were cabinet ministers, they occupied relatively modest "official"
apartments in Jerusalem. Their salaries were only slightly higher than
that of the average high school teacher. They did enjoy certain privileges, of course. The government paid for their private telephone bills;
they had the free use of a car, which they usually drove themselves;

they frequently enjoyed a free trip abroad. But wealth and power rarely went hand in hand in Israel.

THE KNESSET—ISRAEL'S PARLIAMENT

Members of the Knesset did not automatically belong to the establishment, just as there were important members of the establishment who never belonged to parliament. Nevertheless, the many Eastern European pioneers and their offspring in the Knesset reflected the establishment even more than it reflected the people who elected them.

Despite vast numbers of immigrants from the West and from Arab (Oriental) countries, Eastern Europeans continued to hold a vast majority in the Knesset as late as 1973.

Out of 33 new members elected in 1965, for example, 22 were of Eastern European origin. Of 35 new members elected in 1969, 19 were immigrants from Eastern Europe, and ten were born in Israel of Eastern European parents. Although the population has more than quadrupled since 1948—largely through immigration—only two Knesset members were immigrants who arrived after that date.

In the 1969–1974 parliament, 80 percent of the Jewish members were still either Eastern European immigrants or sabras of Eastern European parents. Only in 1974 did things begin to change.

The importance of these figures becomes apparent if we remember that in 1970 roughly half the Jewish population of Israel was of Afro-Asian origin. This is not to say that Oriental Jews were not allowed to vote or had no political power. A considerable number of Oriental newcomers have reached important positions in the town halls and local party machines of the Labor Party. But even after 1974, the number of Oriental Jews, immigrant or native born, who have reached positions of real power on the national level remains small.

That Eastern European veteran settlers so long dominated the establishment in not surprising. They maintained a firm hold upon the institutions of power partly because they themselves created those institutions.

AN ATTITUDE OF FATHERLINESS

Members of the establishment often expressed a kind of "fatherly attitude" toward the newer members of Israeli society. Veteran politicians scolded grumbling newcomers, even when their complaints were just, with *"Shema, k'shebati* (Now listen here, when *I* came . . .)". They would tell new settlers in remote and difficult regions, "When I myself came to the country 40 years ago, conditions were worse, very much worse. We really suffered, but we did not complain. Now you mustn't complain either, but work as hard as we did, and don't mind if you suffer a little bit." Some add: "Remember what we have done for you."

This attitude has been diminishing in recent years. A new class of politicians, less committed to ideology, has come into being. But their influence is just beginning to be felt. The introduction of television was delayed until as late as 1968, mainly because the old veterans considered television uncivilized.

The "fatherliness" of the establishment sometimes assumed strange forms. It was not unusual for those in power to tell Israeli mothers the number of babies they ought to have. (The public response to such suggestions was, of course, somewhat disappointing.)

The English rock group, the Beatles, were immensely popular in Israel; their songs were played daily on the radio, heard everywhere, hummed, danced to, and even translated into Hebrew. Yet in 1966 an interministerial committee decided to withhold the foreign currency permit necessary to enable the Beatles to perform in Israel because they lacked a "sufficient artistic and cultural standard." The decision was approved "with great satisfaction" by the permanent parliamentary Committee for Culture and Education.

In the new government, headed by Yitzḥak Rabin, which came into power in 1974, a change was noticeable. For the first time, the young and the native born were coming into their own. At least in its new style, this change was immediately evident.

related themes

Young People in Key Positions   Political power on a national level in Israel has been largely in the hands of the Eastern European pioneering establishment for more than a quarter of a century. But there are areas of Israeli life in which younger people have assumed major responsibility at a far earlier age than their counterparts in other countries. For example, the Israeli chief of staff of the armed forces has usually been in his 40's at the time of his appointment, and the first three men to fill that position after 1948—Yigael Yadin, Mordechai Makleff, and Moshe Dayan—were all in their 30's. Ariel Sharon was made head of the paratroopers when he was in his 20's; Yigal Allon commanded the entire Palmach before he was 30. And in the diplomatic arena, Abba Eban was the ambassador to the United States and permanent delegate to the United Nations at the age of 35. Sadia Gelb and Joseph Criden report in their book *The Kibbutz Experience: Dialogue in Kfar Blum* that "In many an older kibbutz, thirty year olds are directing a community in which most of the members are considerably older, and the older members accept the direction of the younger members without hesitation. . . ." In the younger kibbutzim, all the key positions are filled by men and women in their early 20's. Finally, because Israel is a growing country in an early stage of development, there are a number of areas—such as films, radio, television, industry, and research—in which young people have had the opportunity to get in on the ground floor and rise quickly to influence and power.

Crisis in Authority   In some countries it comes as no surprise when the government lies to its people, but in Israel the government had always been honest and forthright. Until, that is, the Yom Kippur War. Suddenly, at a time when the country was most in need of unity, with the guns of the war barely stilled, Israel's top generals (Ariel Sharon, David Elazar, Chaim Bar-Lev, among others) began hurling accusations and counteraccusations at one another (the press named their dispute the "war of the generals"). This came as the people were recoiling from the shock of an earlier government falsehood. At the beginning of the war the government had announced that Israel was on top of things when, in fact, the Golan Heights and the Bar-Lev line had been overrun. The government claimed that it had lied so as not to panic or demoralize the people, but the people began to lose faith in the word of their leaders. The blame could not truly be fixed on any one person (though Moshe Dayan, as minister of defense, was a prime object of public hostility), but the ensuing crisis of authority led, ultimately, to the resignation of Golda Meir and her entire cabinet —and to a dramatic change in Israeli politics, as Yitzhak Rabin, a sabra, and a generation removed from the founders, became Israel's fifth prime minister.

issues and values

Elderly Leaders   Until 1974, when Yitzhak Rabin became prime minister at the age of 52, Israel had never had a prime minister born in the twentieth century. David Ben-Gurion, Levi Eshkol, and Golda Meir, three of Israel's first four prime ministers, were well into their 70's at the height of their power. Even those waiting to come into power—people like Moshe Dayan, Abba Eban, and Yigal Allon—were all in their late 50's. Israelis would grumble on occasion about the vatikim staying in office forever, but for the most part they accepted this situation as normal. Sometimes they even thought of it as desirable. Having the nation's elders in power ensures a certain amount of stability, continuity, and experience. Of course, it may also result in political stagnation, the hoarding of power by the entrenched few, and the exclusion of new talent. What do you think? In what sense is the age of a political leader important?

Preoccupation with Youth In contrast to Israel, where the elderly have retained power, in the United States the situation is precisely the opposite. It is generally agreed that a candidate for the United States presidency should be below the age of 60. If he is older, then age often becomes an issue in its own right. And this preoccupation with youth extends to every area of American life. Advertising campaigns frequently ask us to "think young." Businessmen are sometimes told that they will do better if there are no signs of "telltale gray" in their hair. Looking for a new job after the age of 40 becomes problematic. Movies and television consciously program for a youthful audience. After retirement, the elderly are often separated from the mainstream of society —put out to pasture in golden-age communities, nursing homes, and the like. Their sense of isolation is increased by the fact that their incomes are drastically reduced after they stop working. So many of the elderly feel that they have no legitimate place and no useful function in American society. Their achievements are forgotten; their skills and insights, the fruits of long experience, are politely ignored. The only way that they can retain their former status is somehow to hide their age, hold onto their jobs, and keep in step with the younger generation. Do you know any elderly people in such a situation? Do you think the Israeli situation is better or worse? Have you any personal feelings about growing old?

THE PRESIDENCY

Photo Essay In the United States, the president holds executive power in the government. But in Israel, as in most European democracies, the executive power is vested in the cabinet, headed by the prime minister.

Israel is a parliamentary democracy. That is, the people elect a parliament (the Knesset), which in turn elects the president of the state for a five-year term, one year longer than the term of the Knesset itself. The president first consults the leaders of the various parties, then invites the leader of the largest parliamentary faction—that is, the leader of the party which has received the largest vote in an election—to form a cabinet of ministers. The prime minister and his cabinet must then receive a vote of confidence from the Knesset.

The president is the chief of state, but mainly in name. His function is to reign, not to govern. The president has the power to award amnesties. He countersigns all laws passed by the Knesset, but has no power to veto them. At the government's recommendation, he also appoints all judges. The president can serve two terms, but no more.

The executive branch—that is, the cabinet and the prime minister—may fall from office in midterm if the Knesset so desires. A simple majority of votes is all that is necessary to depose one cabinet and replace it by another. This has happened occasionally in Israel's history.

The president, however, can be removed from office in midterm only by a three-fourths vote of the Knesset—and even then, only after a special, complicated impeachment proceeding in committee. The reason for this is that the presidency of Israel is largely a ceremonial office, symbolizing the continuity

Presidents Truman and Weizmann meet at the White House.

and stability of the state itself. Perhaps the most important of all the president's symbolic duties is receiving foreign ambassadors to Israel and, upon recommendation of the Knesset, appointing Israel's ambassadors abroad.

Although the president is nominated for election by one or more of the parties in the Knesset, and although he himself is usually a veteran party member, he is expected after his elevation to the presidency to remain out of day-to-day politics and party affairs. He is expected to exercise a moderating and conciliatory role between the parties.

Chaim Weizmann was Israel's first president, from 1948 until 1952. A statesman of international renown, the intimate of many of the world leaders of his time, he was instrumental in 1917 in securing the Balfour Declaration and in 1948 in acquiring U.S. support for the newborn State of Israel. Between these two dates he headed the world Zionist movement.

Chaim Weizmann: 1874–1952.

Opening day ceremonies at the Weizmann Research Institute.

Following Weizmann's death in November 1952, the presidency was offered to Albert Einstein, who refused it. Yitzḥak Ben-Zvi was then elected as Israel's second president. Ben-Zvi was one of the early pioneers who had arrived in the country in 1905 with the Second Aliyah. Before that, he had been a socialist activist in Russia. His Zionist leanings were at first overshadowed by his Russian revolutionary sympathies. But his moment of truth came during the abortive Russian revolution of 1905. He recalled standing on a platform in Poltova preaching revolution to a mass of Ukrainians: "As I spoke there appeared in my mind's eye the image of Jerusalem [which he had seen during a short trip on his 1904 school vacation]. I asked myself, 'Why am I here and not there?' I decided that my place is in the land of Israel and that I must go there to build it up, and as soon as possible."

Yitzḥak Ben-Zvi: 1884–1963.

Ben-Zvi meets with Jerusalem's Christian leaders.

Zalman Shazar sworn in as
president, 1963.

Ephraim Katzir: b. 1913.

Zalman Shazar, the third president, was
a prolific writer and poet in Hebrew, Russian, and Yiddish, as well as a minister of
education. A man of great culture and
charm, he lent the weight of his office to
efforts to encourage the arts and
sciences.

Shazar was succeeded by Professor
Ephraim Katzir in 1972. Katzir, the first
president who did not come from one of
the party establishments, interrupted a
brilliant career as a scientist at the Weizmann Institute of Science to become
Israel's fourth chief of state.

Installation ceremony of Katzir, 1972.

205

perspective

The proportion of Israel's population on the kibbutz today is under 4 percent and has never been higher than 8 percent. Yet the impact of the kibbutz on Israeli life and culture has been immeasurable. It has served the country well and has nurtured values and ideals that have become a vital part of the national tradition.

For almost half a century, kibbutzniks have been a powerful group within the Israeli establishment. They still are. Until at least the early 1950's, merely to be a member of a kibbutz almost amounted to membership in the governing establishment.

At the peak of kibbutz power, in the early 1950's, the number of kibbutzniks in positions of power was estimated to be at least seven times their proportion of the population as a whole. Their representation in the establishment has declined in recent years, but it is still four or five times their share of the population. In 1975 the kibbutz population was approximately 100,000, or 3 percent of the total population. Roughly 15 percent of the top political positions in the country were held by kibbutzniks. Kibbutzniks and former kibbutzniks held some 35 percent of all seats in parliament.

The political role of kibbutzniks stems from a deeply developed interest in public affairs. The kibbutzim were created by politically conscious individuals, and their members have long been trained in the practical aspects of decision making and self-government.

The importance of kibbutzniks in the country's public life also stems from Israel's self-image as a nation of pioneers. More than any other group, kibbutzniks were accepted by a majority of the settlers as examples of the highest Zionist ideals. In their personal life-style the kibbutzniks lived the ideals of social justice with which even non-members of kibbutzim liked to identify. In the days of pioneering, kibbutz life was often held up as an ideal even by those who were

THE ISRAELI
WAY OF LIFE

personally unprepared to live by it. The ideal has dimmed somewhat in recent years, but it is still powerful enough to afford the kibbutzim a special role.

ISRAEL'S NOBLES

As a group, kibbutzniks came to accept their share of power as the most natural thing in the world. They accepted their supremacy as easily as did the Virginia aristocracy in the early years of the American republic. And their leadership in the governing bodies before and after the establishment of the state was rarely challenged by others.

The relative weight of kibbutzniks within the establishment is now steadily declining, although this is not always obvious at first glance. However, they still remain a kind of rural nobility, maintaining the spirit and values of a former era within a carefully protected society. The kibbutz is not exactly a closed society; it remains open to outsiders who wish to join. But, in fact, it remains exclusive, since so few outsiders actually join nowadays.

The kibbutz is not integrated into its immediate rural or semirural environment. Kibbutzim do not market their produce through non-kibbutz channels in the area, nor do they buy their personal necessities in the shops of neighboring villages and towns. The share of kibbutzniks in such units is between five and ten times their share in the population as a whole. The number of casualties among kibbutzniks is also disproportionately high.

Kibbutz children commonly are in touch only with the children of other kibbutzim. Their contacts with children of the immediate non-kibbutz environment are rare. (Local, nonkibbutz, children are often of Oriental background and live on a considerably lower cultural and economic standard.) Kibbutz boys usually marry kibbutz girls and vice versa, though usually their partners come from a different kibbutz. "Intermarriage" with nonkibbutzniks often brings the kibbutz member to leave kibbutz entirely.

BEING "ON MISSION"

Kibbutzniks are still seriously trying to remain a nobility of service. Although nowadays they show a growing hesitancy to exchange their agricultural life for other occupations, they are still deeply committed to the kibbutz tradition of public service. In kibbutz jargon this is called being on *shlihut* ("on mission"). Choice "missions" are the army, the foreign service, and government positions. Sometimes a kibbutz member will work outside the kibbutz for many years. His family will remain in the kibbutz, and he will visit them at intervals. Young kibbutzniks often volunteer for crack units, such as the tank corps, air force, paratroopers, and frogmen. These offer a measure of excitement and adventure, but they also call for a great deal of personal effort, unusual dedication, and frequent sacrifice.

After a few years on mission, kibbutzniks usually retire to their old lives. The modern kibbutz is highly diversified. To it come former jet pilots, navy captains, ambassadors, generals, ministers, directors of technical aid programs, administrators of gigantic national enterprises. Nowadays at least 70 percent of these older kibbutzniks have come home to the kibbutz after various missions and outside jobs. They return to their old lives, although not to the old physical labor. They will advance to managerial jobs within the kibbutz—as heads of tractor stations or kibbutz factories, as coordinators of interkibbutz committees, as teachers or research analysts. A number of prominent kibbutzniks have remained on mission for ten, 15, and even 20 years while retaining their kibbutz membership.

LIFE ON A KIBBUTZ

The development of science-based industries and the growth of Israeli cities have changed the image of the kibbutzniks. The general public no longer regards them as glamorous supermen upholding the highest national ideals. The public is now more impressed by technologists, scientists, management consultants, and war heroes.

The modern kibbutzniks lead healthy lives in clean, modern, and frequently beautiful surroundings, surrounded by what are probably the largest, greenest, best-tended lawns and flower gardens in the country. Kibbutzniks breathe clean air while the average Israeli lives in a polluted, overcrowded city. Most of the older kibbutzim now provide recreational facilities comparable to those of an average American country club. Gymnasiums, swimming pools, and tennis courts are available exclusively for residents and guests of kibbutz communities that usually number no more than 1200. These are luxuries that most city-dwelling Israelis could not possibly afford.

The average middle-class apartment in Tel Aviv, Haifa, or Jerusalem is certainly more spacious than individual living quarters in the kibbutz, which are still modest by any standard. Yet, as in the cities, living conditions in the kibbutzim are now improving. Many kibbutzim now offer each married couple an attractive two-room apartment with private bath and often with a tiny kitchen, should they wish to skip a meal in the communal dining room.

Kibbutz pharmaceutical factory.

The kibbutz of today is often referred to as an island of culture. Many kibbutzim have their own museums and art collections. Nearly all boast sizable libraries, drama groups, choirs, orchestras, and art studios. Movies, visiting orchestras, and soloists are regularly scheduled. Kibbutzniks still have the time to read serious books, and Israeli writers often discover their most interested and most critical readers within the kibbutzim. Research has shown that kibbutzniks read more books and newspaper and magazine articles than any other population group. The kibbutz community of some 100,000 individuals publishes nearly 200 magazines, journals, and newspapers on a regular basis, apart from the weekly account of local events and commentary on national affairs that every kibbutz publishes separately. These periodicals range in subject matter from cattle breeding to economics, sociology, education, politics, religion, literature, and music.

EDUCATION ON THE KIBBUTZ

The investment and current expenditure on education is higher in the kibbutzim than anywhere in the country. Even the richest areas and fanciest suburbs do not spend so much on education. Nonkibbutz schools are overcrowded and usually understaffed. Classes of 50 pupils are not unusual in the larger towns. By contrast, in the kibbutzim there are rarely more than 18 pupils to a class; in many there are fewer.

The Israeli public school system is plagued by a shortage of qualified and experienced teachers. Whereas many public school teachers are young girls who consider teaching a temporary job before marriage, the average kibbutz teacher is more mature, has been better trained, and considers teaching a full-time profession. Kibbutz children benefit from having better teachers.

Despite the small percentage of kibbutzniks within the general population, they remain living examples of the grandest, most beautiful dream of the early founders.

related themes

Service to the Nation   There are many ways in which the kibbutz has been more tied to the life of the nation than to the desire to build an ideal community. During the early years of Israel's settlement, the kibbutz served as a framework for rehabilitating the land and creating a community. It was also instrumental in making idealism a way of life throughout Israel—a value deeply ingrained in Israeli society and culture, rather than a departure from the "real world." The kibbutz has always played an important role in the area of defense; especially before the creation of the state and the national army, its role was crucial. When Hitler came to power in the early 1930's, the kibbutz gave shelter, first to those who escaped from Europe, before the war, then to those who managed to survive the Holocaust. Similarly, kibbutzim provided the space for most of the children's villages set up by Youth Aliyah, which was organized in 1934 to rescue Jewish children from Europe and which now helps children who are recently arrived immigrants or whose families are poor and unstable. Finally, since 1948, kibbutzim have served as the first line of frontier settlements in underdeveloped areas and along Israel's borders.

Why Kibbutzniks Leave   The kibbutz is not the answer to every individual's social or personal needs; indeed, many people have found the kibbutz an unsatisfactory way of life. Many have left for family reasons: women wanted a more active role in raising their own children; men and women expressed a longing for more family privacy. Some settlers were disappointed because their dreams for an ideal community seemed so distant. They understood that wishes must be grounded in reality to come true, but they could not wait or make the necessary personal adjustments to the workaday realities. Some found that they were dissatisfied with the work they were assigned to do in the kitchens, the laundries, or the barnyards; others simply did not want to be farmers for the rest of their lives. Some left because they could not get along with fellow kibbutzniks. Some craved personal lives, away from the kibbutz community with its ever-watchful eyes. Then, too, a number of individuals came to the kibbutz hoping that their personal problems would fade away; and while they found some support and comfort in the kibbutz family, their problems remained problems. Some left for professional reasons: physicians, dentists, geologists, engineers, who, perhaps, found that the kibbutz had no present need of their specialties. At first, they sought work on the outside, maintaining their ties to the kibbutz (with their salaries going to the kibbutz as well); but the result was that many became kibbutz members in name only, and eventually cut their ties to the kibbutz altogether. It seems that whether an individual will remain on a kibbutz depends largely on whether his personal needs can be met by the kind of life that the kibbutz has to offer.

issues and values

A Way of Life Joseph Criden and thousands like him who chose to settle on a kibbutz were not just seeking a means of earning a living or achieving security. Nor were they pursuing a career, or success, as we understand it. As he wrote in *The Kibbutz Experience: Dialogue in Kfar Blum:*

> I still believe in the things in which I believed when I first came here, and I think that basically the kibbutz has remained within the framework in which it began 30 years ago. . . . To sum it all up, I came here, and I stayed here, because I had a dream, and this is about as close as I have been able to get to translating that dream into reality. Whatever the future may bring, whatever else I may do in my life, I have the satisfaction of knowing that I have been able to work and to live for ideals in which I believe.

Perhaps this is as close as we can get to an understanding of what the word "success" means to a kibbutznik. What does the word "success" mean to you? How will you be able to judge when you are a "success"?

Social and Economic Security The kibbutz way of life offers its members a degree of social and economic security that would be difficult to match in the outside world. A kibbutznik is assured of full employment, most often in a job of his or her choosing. Food, clothing, housing, child care and education, medical facilities, spending money, and the opportunity to pursue individual interests are guaranteed as a right of membership. If a kibbutznik wishes to study in a university, he will at some point most likely be sent, all expenses paid. A kibbutznik who is ill will receive the best medical care available, and whatever else is needed (a special diet, a stay in a therapeutic resort, and so forth) to restore him to full health. In a kibbutz where the majority of members are already married, single persons are usually given work assignments or sent on special courses that will bring them into social contact with people outside the kibbutz. If a kibbutz child is particularly gifted, provisions will be made for that child to develop its special talent further. And the elderly—whether they be kibbutz members or parents of kibbutz members—are given choice housing, the opportunity to work as much as they are able, whatever conditions will make them most comfortable, and the assurance that they will not be cut off from their children and grandchildren and will always be considered an important and respected part of the kibbutz community. How does your community serve the social and economic needs of its members? How does your local Jewish community help to meet local needs? In what ways might a kibbutz life suit you? What would you not like about living on the kibbutz?

perspective

Change has become a way of life in Israel, but the feeling of being a part of something larger has never disappeared. Israelis have been deeply involved in the tasks of the future—building towns and cities, reclaiming the land, developing industry, science and technology, absorbing large numbers of new immigrants. But they have remained keenly aware of the past, both as a source of illumination and as a framework of identity and commitment.

We now have some clues as to what makes up the Israeli character. We have examined some of the main ideas, the hopes and the dreams that went into its making.

We have also noted the heavy weight of the past upon this modern, still young nation. The early Zionists rebelled against the old Jewish world of Eastern Europe, and yet Israel has become the main heir of that unique world of culture, learning, and feeling which was destroyed in the Holocaust.

Memory, a main source of inspiration for Zionism, remains one of Israel's major emotional resources today. At the same time, Israel is more future oriented than most other countries.

MANUFACTURED IMAGES

This is why both Israelis and non-Israelis have such contradictory attitudes about the country and its people. The conflicting views of past and future are further confused by images that seem unusually powerful. Israelis are probably the only largely Western people whose birth as a nation has been accompanied by a near-total exposure to radio, television, newspaper, and magazine commentary. Its brief years of existence have been so entangled with images manufactured by its friends and enemies that it is often difficult, for foreigners and Israelis alike, to disentangle fact from fiction.

Jews have often inspired such images, and the Israelis have not escaped this peculiarly Jewish fate. The new adjective "fearless" as applied to the Israelis is as trite and often as misleading as the old Diaspora stereotype of the "cowardly Jew." Israelis are viewed by too many as people who do nothing but dance the *horah* when they are not planting trees in the desert; or who busy themselves asking for money when they are not off fighting the Arabs. The girl soldier with a submachine gun in one hand and a volume of philosophy in the other is as false an image as the "crooked-nosed businessman" of old—although it is certainly less harmful. Conflicting images of the Israeli as the underdog or, on the other hand, as the ruthless oppressor of peace-loving Arabs exist side by side in the public mind. In the end, all stereotypes are wrong and dangerous.

This is why you may feel you have read in this text a catalogue of contradictory qualities. You have been exposed to the contradictory ideas and passions that influence the behavior of Israelis as individuals, and to the habits that govern them as a group. Together they add up to what we loosely call the character of a people.

THE CHARACTER OF THE ISRAELIS

The combination of the logical and the illogical in Israeli affairs frequently appears confusing, sometimes tragic, always human. The various findings often cancel out one another, as in the debit and credit columns of a balance sheet.

We saw how men fired by a messianic idea of redemption ended up by "playing the game of the world." We observed the change in the order of priorities which occurred in the early 1930's: the emergence of a new nationalism, more self-centered, considerably less lofty, than that dreamed of by the early Zionist idealists.

We saw how the change came about as a result of the rise of Nazism, the Holocaust, and the desperate need to gather in the survivors, and how the Arabs felt this was being done at their expense. The Arabs bore no responsibility for the breakdown of civilization in Europe. Yet their opposition to Zionism grew so ferocious, their insensitivity to Jewish sentiments so great, their refusal of all compromise so absolute, their violence so indiscriminate, and their policies, finally, so destructive that the original imbalance between right and wrong was lost.

The Arab-Israeli collision profoundly affected the evolution of

Israel as a nation. Today it colors the attitude of Israel toward the outside world and the attitude of the outside world toward Israel.

There is among Israelis today an emotional, almost tribal sense of sticking together which sometimes puzzles outsiders. The memories of the Holocaust, the fierce loyalties aroused by living in a state of permanent siege—these are not easily understood by many young Europeans and Americans. The outsider can learn to understand Israel only when he remembers the unique history which has formed the state and its people.

KEYS TO ISRAEL'S FUTURE

The future of Israel—its political system, its laws, its economy, its arts, the makeup of its society, the quality of its life—depends on how the Arab-Israeli conflict is resolved. Yet, when a solution is achieved—and whatever the future territorial arrangements may be—Israel will always remain a very small country. The Israeli nation will always be a very small one.

The smallness of Israel as a country and as a nation is another key to the future. The narrow strip of land can be crossed by car from Tel Aviv to Jerusalem in less than an hour. It takes 45 minutes by plane to travel the entire length of Israel, from the Red Sea port of Eilat to the Lebanese border in the north. From a low-flying helicopter, in a brief afternoon, after lunch and before dinner, one can crisscross almost the whole of it. There remains a certain sense of spaciousness, caused by the dramatic contrast of desert and fertile areas, but this is only relative. The country remains small, and its confinement increases the isolation of Israeli life, an isolation which is likely to remain even in the event of peace.

Israel's size poses great challenges, promising and dangerous. The very smallness of Israel could well enhance the pleasure of living in it, especially at a time when the sheer size of other nations threatens the individual. A person can more completely participate in a democratic community of 3, 4, or 5 million than in the lonely crowds of 50, 80, or 200 million. A free, relatively small political community enhances pride of collective citizenship, yet it leaves room for individualism.

But if a country is to be a pleasant place, more than liberty is needed. In this respect, Israel has had considerable luck. The institutions and social patterns of a state providing equality and welfare services for all its citizens were set up by the generations of founders. Many of their hopes and predictions never came to pass; but Herzl was right, generally speaking, when he predicted that in the future Jewish state, the individual would neither be crushed between the millstones of capitalism nor cut down by the leveling pressure of socialism. The ideal of university-educated men plowing fields and workers discussing philosophy was defeated by the requirements of a modern economy. Yet much of the freedom of the earlier days has successfully withstood the test of time, and even the restrictions arising from a permanent state of war.

The look of gray shabbiness which marked the society of pioneers —and which was sometimes wrongly taken as the hallmark of equality —has disappeared. New urban wealth now contrasts sharply with pockets of poverty on the edges of the cities and in the countryside. But if we take as our standard of comparison the year 1952—a time when over 100,000 new immigrants were living in canvas tents or shacks of corrugated iron—the conclusion must be that class contrasts in 1970 were considerably less than those of 18 years before. And again, in 1975, the gap between the poor and the rich was less than in 1970; it was, in fact, the smallest in all the world's industrialized countries.

related themes

The U.S.S.R. in the Middle East   The course of Israel's future development depends in large measure on Israeli-Arab peace. Will the violence, tension, suspicion, and hatred persist, or will there be a movement toward peace? When asked if he thought there would be peace, David Ben-Gurion answered that peace would come whenever the U.S. and the U.S.S.R. decided that *they* wanted peace, and not before. Unfortunately, at least until 1973, Soviet policy in the Middle East was geared to keeping the pot boiling—that is, to keeping a certain amount of controlled tension in the area, enough to force the Arabs to turn to the Eastern bloc for weaponry and training. This policy reinforced Arab dependence and Soviet influence. Most observers agree that the problems of the Middle East might have been resolved long ago if the Russians had kept out and allowed the Israelis and Arabs to settle their dispute by themselves. As the political columnist Clayton Fritchey pointed out, "there is little doubt that Egypt would have had to come to terms with Israel long since, had it not been for Moscow's willingness to prop up and rearm the Cairo government after every Israeli victory."

The Importance of Jewish History   The chapter says that memory remains one of Israel's major emotional resources. This is equally true of

Israel helped many developing African nations by sending advisors
to work in cities, in industry, and on farms as shown above.

Jewish life in the Diaspora. A vivid awareness of history and a sense
of connection with the past have helped to sustain the Jewish people
during the 2000 years of dispersion. As Abba Eban points out in his
book *My People: The Story of the Jews,*

> I have also come up against the impossibility of understanding, and therefore
> explaining, the current Jewish reality without a constant probing of ancient
> roots. There is no other modern nation whose motive of existence and action
> requires such frequent reference to distant days. This is as true of Israel in
> the Diaspora as it is of Israel in the community of nations.

In another sense, the Jewish memory was a crucial factor in the
national rebirth of Israel. In the words of Joseph Ernest Renan,
"A nation is a soul, a spiritual principle. To have a common glory in
the past, a common will in the present. To have done great things
together, to want to do them again—these are the conditions for the
existence of a nation."

issues and values

The Truth Behind the Propaganda The way we see things is often
influenced by what we are told to believe about them. For example, the

Arabs have repeated over and over in their propaganda that Israel is an aggressor nation. Barely a day after the Six Day War began, the Arabs and Soviets were calling the Israelis aggressors in United Nations debates, despite the fact that the whole world had witnessed the Arab troop buildup along Israel's borders and heard the Arabs claim that they would destroy the Jewish state in a holy war. While the charge could easily be disproved, it has managed to have a telling impact on world opinion. From your study of Israel and the Israelis, would you call them warlike aggressors? Is the country which strikes first always the aggressor? Why do you think propaganda has such a telling effect on world opinion?

A Sense of Isolation The Israelis' tribal sense of sticking together comes, in part, from a feeling of being isolated in an increasingly hostile world. This feeling has been growing stronger ever since 1967. France, a loyal friend of Israel for more than ten years (at one time the Israelis spoke seriously of replacing English as the second language in their schools with French), suddenly turned pro-Arab after the Six Day War. Seven years later, French Foreign Minister Michel Jobert publicly defended the Egyptian-Syrian surprise attack on Israel. The majority of African nations, to whom Israel had rendered so much assistance in the past, broke off relations with Israel during and after the Yom Kippur War. At the height of that conflict, the NATO countries, with the exception of Portugal, refused to grant landing rights on their territory to the United States military resupply airlift for Israel, because they feared the power of the oil-rich Arab nations. And in November 1974, Israelis and Jews everywhere watched with growing dismay as the UN General Assembly gave a rousing welcome to the head of the Palestine Liberation Organization, Yasir Arafat, who shared with the delegates his dream of creating a "secular democratic" state in Palestine (which is a polite way of saying that Israel would have to be destroyed). Do you think the Israelis should feel isolated? In what ways does your study of Israel help to combat that isolation?

UNDERSTANDING
THE JEWISH
STATE

perspective

One of the major aims of Zionism has been to "normalize" the Jew by making him a citizen in a land of his own. But Israel will never be normal. For one thing, Israel has a continuing responsibility to the Jewish people at large. And for another, Israel must express itself in the light of Judaism's history, traditions, and values.

The next installment in the history of Israel may well be even more revolutionary than the last. In Israel, as elsewhere, the scientific revolutions of the second half of the twentieth century are likely to bring about radical changes that only science fiction writers might prophesy. With the second-highest proportion of university students in the world, with more doctors per capita than any other country on earth, with research centers and advanced agricultural techniques to develop the full potential of climate and soil, and with a rapidly growing economy that is increasingly based on scientific industrial techniques, Israel could well become an example for the development of small nations in the modern world. But Israel will always be a mere speck on the map, and many Israelis realize that to be noticed at all, it will have to sparkle.

Will it? The dangers of smallness and the sense of isolation emerging from the continuous state of siege lead to greater self-involvement and may breed provincialism or even narrow-mindedness.

WHO IS A JEW?

UNDER-
STANDING
THE
JEWISH
STATE

Since Israel is officially defined as a Jewish state, a crucial question is "Who is a Jew?" This is one of the most controversial issues dividing Israelis, and the question is still far from resolved.

What makes someone a Jew? Nationality? Race? Birthright? Religion? Free choice? Labeling by others? Memory? A certain psy-

Israel's role as the Jewish State is evident as scribes copy the Torah.

chology? A combination of all or some of these factors? If being Jewish is a nationality, like being French or Spanish, can there be a Muslim or Christian Jew? If religion determines the Jew, which of the factions within Judaism makes that determination? There is no central authority in Judaism, nor is there a real hierarchy among rabbis, even though Israel boasts two chief rabbis, one for the Ashkenazic community and one for the Sephardic community.

The early Zionist thinkers, most of whom were socialists or liberals, clearly planned to build a thoroughly secular state without any formal religious ties. But with the passing of time, new political arrangements with the orthodox rabbis have brought about an unofficial marriage between orthodox Judaism and the Jewish state. Orthodox Judaism is not the established religion of Israel. Yet, in an important sense, Israeli law distinguishes between "Jewish" and other nationals (Arab, Druze, and sometimes *nochri,* or alien). Since March 1970, the question of who is a Jew is determined to a very large extent by orthodox rabbinical rule.

The power of organized religion has grown in recent years because of the revival among secular politicians, socialists, and liberals of a new piety. A kind of sentimental regard for religion has seized the former rebels against orthodox religion and talmudic observance. They do not necessarily return to the orthodox fold. On the contrary, they often remain totally nonobservant; most Israeli politicians never, or rarely, go to synagogue, nor do they keep a kosher home. They will often violate the Sabbath, and give their children a secular (though Jewish) education. Yet the resurgence of orthodox piety among secular politicians and the direct political power of the religious parties has reached the Knesset, resulting in a sharp clash between religionists and secularists.

THE SEARCH FOR IDENTITY

The religious conflict is, of course, another aspect of the identity problem which disturbs modern Israelis. The problem is a new one for Jews. It was unknown in previous ages. It never bothered Flavius Josephus, although he became first a Jewish rebel leader and then a Roman nobleman. Maimonides worried only about Jews forced to convert who returned to Judaism. Spinoza never considered the matter. The question of Jewish identity first arose with Jewish emancipation from the European ghetto early in the nineteenth century. The early Zionists never dreamed that it would plague the Israelis long after their national independence, which was meant to take care of Jewish identity problems.

The clash between secularists and religionists is likely to grow worse in the foreseeable future. It would be foolish to make any predictions as to its outcome.

related themes

Aliyah Bet   Five aliyot were carried out with the official consent of the governing powers who ruled Palestine—first Turkey and then, after World War I, Great Britain. These came to an abrupt end in 1939 when the British announced their policy of restricting Jewish immigration to Palestine.

The Jews of Palestine responded by setting into motion a far-reaching rescue operation which they called Aliyah Bet (considering the first five aliyot, Aliyah Aleph). Through Aliyah Bet, as many Holocaust survivors as could be smuggled out of Europe were brought to Palestine by illegal means.

After World War II, with the evidence of the destruction of European Jewry laid before the world, the British government refused to change its restrictive policy—and Aliyah Bet went into high gear. Aged and leaking vessels, loaded with human cargo, secretly embarked from

UNDER-
STANDING
THE
JEWISH
STATE

222

unnamed European ports, hovered off the coastline of Israel at night waiting for rafts and rowboats—anything that could float—to transport the refugees into Palestine. Sometimes these operations succeeded; often they were stopped by the British authorities, and the European Jews were herded into makeshift internment camps in Cyprus, where they remained until the end of the British Mandate and the creation of the State of Israel.

With the land of Israel in sight, refugees gained a new hope for freedom.

Zionism or Racism   In November 1975, a clear majority of the member states of the United Nations General Assembly voted in favor of a resolution condemning Zionism as a form of racism. With a few exceptions, the supporters of the resolution included the world's totalitarian countries; its opponents were mainly democracies.

Daniel Patrick Moynihan, then the United States Ambassador to the United Nations, called this vote an "obscenity," declaring that the United States would never be bound by such a ruling. He went on to call the enemies of Zionism "enemies of democracy." The American people seemed to agree. Public opinion polls taken shortly after the UN vote revealed that most Americans dismissed the UN decision as merely political maneuvering. But the vote still stands on the General Assembly's official records; Zionism was branded as a form of racism.

It is hard to find any evidence to support the UN position. Indeed, almost all the facts point in the opposite direction. For example, there is no racist bias in any Zionist writing. Israel has never drafted a law permitting any form of racial discrimination (such as the policy of apartheid in South Africa). There have been no restrictive rulings on local levels (no segregation of the Arab or Christian minorities of Israel, either educational or residential).

Even the Law of Return—Israel's law especially directed to allow any Jew who so desires to immediately claim Israeli citizenship—is not a statement of racial superiority or of exclusiveness, but an affirmation of national identity and of the responsibility Israel feels to serve as a Jewish homeland. Marie Syrkin pointed out in her essay "The Attack on Zionism" (*Midstream*, December 1975)

> . . . The Law of Return was promulgated immediately upon the establishment of Israel to demonstrate to a world that had barred its gates to Jews fleeing from the gas chambers that finally there was one spot on the globe which victims of anti-Semitic persecution could claim as a home . . . at the same time, though Jews were granted automatic citizenship, non-Jews could acquire citizenship after a period of residence.

UNDER-
STANDING
THE
JEWISH
STATE

224

issues and values

Judaism's Key Elements   How necessary is the land of Israel and the State of Israel to Judaism as a whole? How would Judaism fare without the Jewish state? Judah P. Magnes, an American-born Reform rabbi who became president of the Hebrew University, tried to answer the question in his essay "Like all the Nations":

> To me it seems that there are three chief elements of Jewish life, in the following order of importance: the living Jewish People . . . ; the Torah, in the broadest sense of this term . . . all our literature and documents and history, and also the great religious and ethical social ideas the Torah contains . . . ; the Land of Israel. My view is that the people and the Torah can exist and be creative without the Land; that, however, the Land is one of the chief means, if not the chief means, of revitalizing the people and the Torah.

If you had to list the three most important things about being Jewish, what would be on your list? Do you agree with Magnes that the State of Israel "revitalized" the Jewish people? In what ways?

A Basis of Jewish Identity In a sense, the State of Israel provides a mirror in which Jews in the Diaspora may see their Jewish identity reflected. Solomon Schechter, the early twentieth-century Jewish scholar, once wrote an essay called "Zionism: A Statement." In it he explained this process:

> To me personally, Zionism recommended itself as the great bulwark against assimilation. . . . What I understand by assimilation is loss of identity; or that process of disintegration which [is the] defiance of all Jewish thought [and] disloyalty to Israel's history and its mission. . . . It is this kind of assimilation . . . that I dread most, even more than pogroms. . . . Zionism declares boldly to the world that Judaism means to preserve its life. . . . It shall be a true and healthy life, with a policy of its own, a religion wholly its own, invigorated by sacred memories and sacred environments, and proving a tower of strength and a unity not only for those gathered within the borders of the Holy Land but also for those who shall, by choice or necessity, prefer . . . the Galut.

Do you feel that Israel adds to your personal sense of being Jewish? In what ways?

perspective

Israel's future is marked by many uncertainties. Despite the progress toward peace made since the Yom Kippur War, there remains the possibility of another all-out conflict. That conflict would be more destructive than any fought before, thanks to the advanced weaponry pouring into the Middle East. And there are important tasks that cannot be put off: integrating the Russian Jewish immigrants, bridging the cultural gap between Oriental and Western Israelis, forging a creative relationship with world Jewry, and continuing to build a just and compassionate society. In sum, the dream of the early pioneers remains the task of Israel today.

Everything is still fluid. The belief in progress is still very much alive among Israelis; it remains the early settlers' main bequest to the young. Had Israel been established in quieter times, had it been able to develop more slowly in the calm and sunny peace of its green plains and rugged mountains, perhaps its people might sooner have come to share with other, happier nations the traditions of manners and ease. Perhaps it could speak in soothing tones, instead of the tense, taut voice it now strains so often in trying to capture the world's attention.

But this harassed people built its state under troubled circumstances that had not been imagined by anyone. What was planned as an orderly migration became a desperate escape. A people who tried above all to change their historic image and fate—utter dependence on other people's tolerance—were denied their aim. Instead of finding calm and rest, they live in unending and unnerving conflict. Instead of peace, there is war with no end in sight.

Little wonder, then, that issues which might have been more satisfactorily resolved in calmer times continue to fester. In their fight for physical survival, the Israelis remain determined to endure. But as the

UNDER-
STANDING
THE
JEWISH
STATE

226

Israelis come of age as a nation they are torn by conflicting forces, contending for their character as a people.

Let us close by quoting three famous slogans that have inspired the return of the Jews to their ancient homeland:

> If I am not for myself, who then is for me?
> We came to build the land and to be rebuilt by it. . . .
> If you will it, it is no legend.

The first is an ancient rabbinic saying; it requires no further explanation. The second, a song of the early pioneers, reflects their lofty vision of the ability of the Jewish people to create a new life for themselves in a society of freedom and equality. The third was coined by Theodor Herzl; it gives an indication that the story of Israel is not yet done.

related themes

Building Cultural Bridges The dream of Aḥad Ha'am that Israel would become the center and the source of strength for world Jewry has always been one of the goals of the young state. Israel regularly sends shliḥim (emissaries or messengers, usually assigned for purposes of education) to Diaspora communities for periods of two to three years. These shliḥim work with local Jewish and Zionist organizations, and with the Jewish community at large, representing Israel in many ways. Many *ulpanim* (intensive Hebrew language seminars) have been established in the United States and other countries, where adults and teenagers have the opportunity to learn modern, Israeli-style Hebrew.

Going in the opposite direction, there are an increasing number—and a growing variety—of tours to Israel; indeed, tourism has become one of Israel's major industries. Summer courses for high school and college youth feature an educational orientation, contact with Israeli youth, working visits to kibbutzim and moshavim, as well as a full program of *tiyulim* (bus and hiking tours) to various parts of the country. And there are programs, ranging in length from six months to a year, which offer participants opportunities for intensive study, living for extended periods on agricultural settlements, participating in one's profession in an Israeli setting, taking courses at one of Israel's universities, or working with new immigrants in urban neighborhoods, community centers, and development towns.

The future of Israel is in its children and in its land.

Since the Yom Kippur War   There has been a new note of hopefulness since the end of the Yom Kippur War and the beginning of the disengagement agreements with Egypt and Syria in 1974 and the interim Sinai accord of 1975. Although these may prove to be dead ends in the near future, many Israelis, though not without a certain ambivalence, believe that Egypt's President Sadat truly desires an end to the fighting —not because he suddenly sees the State of Israel in a new light, but because he wishes to use the energies and resources wasted in fighting and warmaking to rebuild his own state. As Professor Morton G. Wurtele notes in his personal memoir *You Are Welcome: Notes from a Middle Eastern Journey,* ". . . there exists the obvious and major development since the Yom Kippur War that now in Egypt, Syria, and

UNDER-
STANDING
THE
JEWISH
STATE

228

Jordan officials speak of Israel as an existing state and are prepared to recognize it under certain conditions." There remains the question of what "certain conditions" may mean, but at least there is the beginning of a process, a movement in a more promising direction than was apparent in Israel's first 25 years.

issues and values

Jewish Survival and Jewish Education In an essay entitled "On Nationalism and Religion," Aḥad Ha'am offered this advice for the survival of the Jewish community:

> What we have to do is revert to the system which our ancestors adopted in days gone by and to which we owe our survival: we have to make the synagogue itself the house of study, with Jewish learning as its first concern. . . . Cut the prayers as short as you like, but make your synagogue a haven of Jewish knowledge, alike for children and adults, for the educated and the ordinary folk. . . . "Readings" on Jewish subjects can be arranged every evening for the more and the less educated separately. That is what our ancestors did, with good results. . . . In our day, of course, we must introduce readings better suited to modern requirements. But learning—learning —learning: that is the secret of Jewish survival. . . .

Does your synagogue follow any of the advice of Aḥad Ha'am? In what ways? Do you feel that your study of Israel is crucial to your overall study of Judaism?

A Final Evaluation At the beginning of this book, there was a discussion of the uniqueness of Israel and the Jewish people, and of how this quality has played a major role in the process of national rebirth. Such concepts as "the Chosen People," "a light unto the nations," and "a people unlike other peoples" show that uniqueness has been a part of Jewish and Israeli tradition from the earliest times. It has been constantly reaffirmed; and there has been a constant search for new modes of expression, new ways of retaining its meaning, power, integrity. Now that you have read this book, what do you find unique about Israel? In which ways has Israel proved to be different from other nations? In your opinion, what are Israel's greatest achievements? What failures have you detected? Aside from the Arab-Israeli conflict, what are the most urgent challenges confronting the Jewish state today? In what ways do you see your future as a Jew linked with the future of Israel?

WHAT DOES
THE
FUTURE
HOLD?

A joyous welcome awaits the freed hostages upon their return to Israel.

THE ENTEBBE RESCUE

Photo Essay It was a warm, sunny Sunday afternoon in late June, a workday in Israel, when word began to spread that an Air France jet flying to Paris from Tel Aviv was missing. The first natural fears were that it had crashed; but almost from the moment that the plane lost radio contact after leaving Athens, the greater likelihood was that it had been hijacked by terrorists. When, a few hours later, the airliner landed at Benghazi Airport in Libya, Israeli cabinet ministers were already meeting in emergency session.

By now every Israeli was alert to the fate of the Air France plane. Israel is a small country, a country with a great sense of family. Those few Israelis not within hearing distance of the hourly news broadcast eagerly sought second- or thirdhand reports of each new development. "What's the latest?" "She's come down in Benghazi." "Oh, no. What could be worse?"

It was a well-known fact that Colonel Muammar al-Ghadaffi, Libya's ruler, had boasted of his sympathy and financial support for international terrorist groups which had vowed to destroy Israel. Israelis could think of no more alarming place for the plane to have landed than Benghazi. Thus, when Flight 139 left Libya a few hours later, an audible sigh of relief could be heard throughout Israel. But when word came early Monday that the airliner had reached its destination at Entebbe Airport in Uganda, relief turned to consternation.

Only Uganda's Idi Amin could be more unpredictable, erratic, or cruel than Colonel Ghadaffi. Amin still proudly displayed his Israeli paratrooper wings as a recollection of former close political ties and friendship with the Jewish state; indeed, Israeli technicians and foreign aid had constructed the very airport where the hostages were now being held. But it soon became clear that the Ugandan dictator was in close contact and cooperating with the terrorists who had seized the Air France jetliner.

The five terrorists—two Germans and three Arabs of diverse nationalities—were joined in Uganda by several comrades, as well as additional arms. The Ugandan army was called out to protect the terminal where the hostages were being held. In fact, Ugandan soldiers joined the terrorists in guarding the captives. And during the weeklong ordeal, General Amin himself appeared several times before the hostages to rail against Israel, the "Zionists," and to laud the terrorists' cause.

So began a week of public and private anguish in Israel. The cabinet met in constant session, agonizing and debating the questions on everyone's mind. First and foremost: Can we rescue the hostages? *Must* we, *can* we deal with terrorists? Should we give in and release from Israeli jails convicted terrorists and killers to unleash new terror, new murders upon the people of Israel? Could a military action possibly be mounted? How could the rescue party fly across thousands of miles of hostile territory? What were the risks to the rescuers, and to those they were trying to save?

Throughout the centuries, warmed by memory and faith, Jews have been seeking a return to Zion. For some the reasons were mainly political; for others the return had social meaning, a utopian dream. Zionism rooted in religion was important to others; and many Jews saw a renewed Jewish homeland as a cultural rebirth for the Jewish people.

And yet, of all the justifications and moral reasons and desires for the creation of Israel, none ever was—or is—more overriding, stronger, or more conscious than the *ultimate* urge: to save the Jews from the mercy of others. Beyond all ideology, secular or religious, the idea of rescue was always the prime force that drove Zionism forward: the rescue of a people who for over 2000 years had been badgered, beaten, and murdered simply because they had never been able to control their own fate even to a limited degree. Beyond all other considerations, the desire to save Jews from *total* dependence upon others was the deepest, most fundamental rationale for Zionism. Only after the Holocaust, after 6 million Jews had been slaughtered, had the Gentile world been convinced of what Zionism meant to Jews.

This sense of rescue has remained the overwhelming consideration of Israeli life and public policy, a thread woven through the fabric of society that strengthens it and makes it resilient. Rescue has meant the ransoming and transferral of entire communities of Jews, from Morocco, from Yemen, from Rumania, from Algeria, and most recently from the Soviet Union. It might mean negotiating with the devil himself if Jews somewhere could be saved.

At first the cabinet took no decision; Israel needed to gain time—and intelligence information. But the military possibilities were considered from the beginning. Intelligence agents were soon at work collecting up-to-date information about Entebbe Airport. Working day and night, technicians were able to reconstruct a model for the military experts to study. Specially trained commando units were called up during the course of the week to rehearse their roles in what would later be considered one of the most spectacular air rescues of all time, but which in the planning stage still seemed very difficult and uncertain.

Later people would speak of the Entebbe rescue of 103 Israeli and other hostages in almost mythic terms: daredevil Sabra supermen descending from hostile skies to flex their muscles in a faraway land. In fact, Entebbe was a daring, extraordinarily courageous feat, but the most important factor was the moral thread that binds Israel together, not only the determination to defend the state against its enemies, but also the driving need to rescue even a handful of Jews from certain death. The decision by Israel's political leaders to make the raid on Entebbe was in its human way at least as courageous as the raid's execution. And it underlined once again the most fundamental reasons for the existence of the Jewish state.

The decision, as is proper, was not in the hands of the army but in the hands of the two dozen who comprise the Israeli cabinet. Prime Minister Yitzḥak Rabin, Defense Minister Shimon Peres,

Bird's-eye view of Entebbe Airport, taken in 1966, when Israel was sending technical experts to Uganda.

Shimon Peres, Minister of Defense, reviews the Entebbe operation after its successful conclusion. On the left, Mordecai "Motke" Gur, Chief of Staff; on the right, Dan Shomron, in charge of the operation.

and the other ministers presented arguments for different courses of action; but in the end the entire cabinet had to determine what to do—if possible by a unanimous decision rather than by the normal majority vote, for what was at stake was almost too overwhelming.

It was within the cabinet that the moral issues, the human issues, came into play. It was to these two dozen ministers that tormented relatives made their pleas for Israel to negotiate. It came the turn of every man in the cabinet, as of every adult in Israel, to ask, "If my parent, child, brother, or sister were on that airplane, would I not be prepared to deal with the terrorists, even to release murderers from jail?"

Some argued like this: "After the Yom Kippur War we traded live Egyptian soldiers (prisoners of war) for the bodies of Israeli soldiers left along the banks of the Suez Canal. Surely in this case we have even stronger reason to trade jailed terrorists for living Jews." This argument did not prevail. Israel, of all

countries, could not deal with terrorists, and could not afford to give further license to international murder and piracy, since so much of it was directed at her. True, in prior years the government *had* released terrorists in return for hijack victims seized in foreign lands. But international terror had now reached new heights, and even within the United Nations itself had attained a kind of legitimacy. Dealing with terrorists could only encourage further and further horrors.

And so rescue—a word that is basic to the Israeli temper—became uppermost in the cabinet discussions. Israel had to act. Yet action was not just for action's sake. A military operation was permissible only if it meant a *minimal* risk to the lives of both the hostages and their rescuers. A bloodbath would only serve the cause of terrorism. If the mission failed, Israel would be blamed all over the world, and there would be no rescue. This was the dilemma. It occupied the minds of Prime Minister Rabin and his cabinet as they prepared to open negotiations and try to extend the deadline that the terrorists had set—Thursday afternoon, July 2. If that deadline was not met, the terrorists said, they would begin killing the hostages.

It was only on Wednesday, a day before the deadline, that the prime opening was made. It came, strangely enough, with a grim division among the hostages at Entebbe, when non-Israeli passengers were released and flown to Paris. The selection process (supervised by one of the German terrorists) brought back the most harrowing memories, even among those hostages who had never been in the German death camps—memories of that other "selection" made by Nazi guards among Jews in the camps during World War II, when those Jews destined to be gassed were ordered "right" and those temporarily spared to become slave laborers were ordered "left."

But this time, with information gathered from the released prisoners in Paris, Israel's intelligence and military experts could begin actively to plan an invasion of Entebbe that would still carry risk but could now be seriously considered. Released passengers were able to tell the intelligence officers that there were no major explosives which could instantly be set off; they could also tell them where Ugandan soldiers were placed and how strong the means of defense would be, as well as hundreds of small but important details. Combined with other intelligence reports arriving constantly from African sources and other countries, these details allowed the buildup of a large store of information at the planning center in Tel Aviv. Kenya, a country bordering on Uganda, had been at odds with Amin's government for a long time. Now the Kenyan government

was prepared to offer Israel its help.

On Thursday morning, Israel opened up official negotiations with the hijackers in the hope that the deadline would be extended. The plan worked, and over Uganda's radio station at 1 P.M. came word that the deadline had been moved to Sunday, July 4, at noon.

Now the planning of a military assault went into high gear. Medical staff were assembled for a hospital plane that would accompany the rescue party. Commando units began split-second training in the Negev desert. As more and more intelligence poured in, the military units were able to rehearse the exact particulars of the raid that would take place.

And so it was that on Saturday afternoon, July 3, hours before the terrorists had promised to begin killing the hostages, a flying armada—three giant Hercules transport planes with fighter escorts, a fully staffed emergency airborne hospital, and a command plane above them all—set off down the Red Sea, beginning the 2500-mile trip that would take them over Ethiopia, Kenya, and Lake Victoria, and finally into Entebbe Airport.

They landed as quietly as three enormous six-engine planes can. The young commandos knew their roles perfectly: some assaulted the terminal directly, while others diverted Ugandan troops. Still others blew up several Russian MIG fighter planes that were standing along the runway and might later have been used for possible chase. The commander of the Entebbe operation was American-born, Harvard-educated Yonaton (Yoni) Netanyahu. He had been wounded in the Six Day War, and had talked his way back into the army although he had only partial use of his arm. Entebbe would be his last heroic mission; he was shot

Israeli commandos and a Hercules plane on practice maneuvers.

in the final minutes of the raid and brought back to a hero's burial in Israel.

Once the troop-bearing planes landed at Entebbe (the hospital plane waited at Nairobi Airport in Kenya, where all the planes would stop for refueling for their return trip), it was less than an hour before the first Hercules with its cargo of freed hostages had taken off for the trip home. The other two followed shortly.

In addition to Netanyahu, three hostages died in the crossfire. Another hostage, Dora Bloch, an elderly widow who was left behind in an Ugandan hospital, was later brutally murdered, apparently on General Amin's orders. At least seven and probably ten terrorists were killed, as well as some twenty Ugandan soldiers.

The rescued hostages emerge from the belly of the giant Hercules plane at Ben-Gurion Airport. At left, the captain of the hijacked Air France plane thanks one of the commandos.

But 103 hostages—Israelis and members of the French crew who had chosen to remain with the Israelis—were on their way back to Israel in the first hours of the morning of July 4, 1976.

By 10 A.M. Israeli time the great planes could be seen circling over Jerusalem on their way to Ben Gurion Airport to a tumultuous welcome. An overwhelming pride and joy filled the air at that moment, mostly for the young people who had accomplished the feat that few had even dared to think about. One woman, on her way to Jerusalem from Tel Aviv with a carload of hitchhiking soldiers, looked up proudly at the planes and exclaimed, "My God, could we ever have imagined . . . ?" At which point one of the soldiers grinned broadly at her and said, "You didn't imagine because you're not in the military, ma'am. We never doubted it for a moment."

Often, in the past, when Jews were being murdered, other nations stood idly by. They may have sympathized with the plight of the Jews—yet these nations did little to help them. But this time, when Jews were hijacked and taken to a distant and hostile land, they had Israel to come to their rescue. That is the true meaning of the raid on Entebbe.

THE CURRENT SCENE

Every Arab-Israeli war has kindled great expectations—soon crushed—that peace was finally at hand. In 1949, Israel and the Arab states signed armistice agreements that were to be preludes to formal peace. In 1956, the United States assured Israel that withdrawing the Israeli army from Sinai would certainly be the first step toward formal peace with Egypt. In 1967, after the Six Day War, it was said that after such an Israeli victory the Arabs would surely seek a peace agreement. And so it was in 1973, after the Yom Kippur War.

But there were two big differences after the 1973 war. One was the role of the United States. For the first time it was cast in the role of chief peacemaker. American Secretary of State Henry Kissinger began a series of missions to the Middle East—flying from one capital to another time and again—that came to be known as "shuttle diplomacy."

The other difference was that, for the first time, Arab leaders publicly declared that peace with Israel was a "possibility."

Opinions in Israel were divided on the real meaning of the Arab declarations. The Israel government, in the face of much criticism at home, agreed to a disengagement of forces with Egypt and Syria. As a token of goodwill, Israel withdrew not only from all areas it had occupied during the 1973 war, but also from some areas occupied in 1967.

In 1975, another partial interim agreement was reached with Egypt. It called for further Israeli withdrawals in return for political compromises—some open, others secret—from Egypt. The position of the Israel government was that for a "little peace" it would return a "little territory"; for more peace it would withdraw further.

When Israel's northern neighbor, Lebanon—a half-Christian, half-Moslem country—was shaken by a bloody civil war, the Christian villagers near the border turned to Israel for medical aid and food. Israel's response was to turn the border between the two countries into a "Good Fence" for Lebanese civilians. The Israel government had a clinic and food depot set up, established postal services, and provided employment opportunities.

Against this background, the American initiatives to convene an Arab-Israel peace conference seemed promising, although the question of whether the Palestine Liberation Organization should be a party to the talks remained a serious stumbling block.

Meanwhile, internal problems plagued the Israelis, as inflation soared and corruption was disclosed within the Labor Party. When early elections were held in May 1977 the results shook Israel like a political earthquake. The Labor Party lost its dominance for the first time since the State's creation (actually, for the first time since 1930!). A plurality of votes was won by *Likud,* a right-of-center party.

The Likud platform promised to encourage more free enterprise in Israel's semi-socialist economy, and to retain the West-Bank areas of Judea and Samaria which Israel held since 1967. Likud considered them part of the Jewish biblical homeland. But, like the Labor Party in previous elections, Likud did not win an absolute majority, and had to form a coalition government.

The sudden shift in Israel's political spectrum stunned not only the Israelis, but the nations friendly and unfriendly to the state.

237

GLOSSARY

Al Het Shehatanu *"for the sin that we have sinned"; a Yom Kippur prayer; stresses atonement and communal responsibility*

aliyah, aliyot *ascent; the process of going up; used specifically to describe immigration to Israel since the onset of modern Zionism*

Aliyah Bet *illegal immigration of Jews to Palestine during and after World War II, in response to the British Mandatory Government's White Paper, issued in 1939, which severely limited the number of Jews allowed to enter Palestine each year*

Am Yisrael Hai *"the People of Israel Lives"*

Bilu *acronym for "Beit Ya'akov Lechu Venelchah," "House of Jacob, come and let us go" (to the land of Israel); the name given to the first wave of pioneers, who arrived in Palestine during the 1880's*

bimah *platform; stage*

C'na'anut *a term derived from the ancient name of the land of Israel, Canaan; describes a view of Israel exclusively in national terms, with little relationship to 2,000 years of Jewish dispersion, and no substantive ties to world Jewry*

dugmah hinuchit *"educational example"; belief that one can educate only by personal example*

eddah *"congregation"*

ein brerah *"no choice"; Israel's secret weapon during the 1948 War of Liberation and in the following years ("There is no choice but to win; the alternative is total destruction!")*

Eretz HaKedoshah *"the Holy Land"*

Eretz Israel *the land of Israel*

Haganah *"defense"; the defense arm of the Jewish settlement in Palestine from 1920 (when it succeeded Hashomer) until the creation of the State of Israel in 1948, when the Israel Defense Forces were organized*

hagirah *Hebrew term for migration, either immigration or emigration*

hagshamah *fulfillment; the realization of aims and ideals, particularly those concerning pioneering*

Halukah *"distribution"; donations by Diaspora Jewry to support religious Jews living in Palestine*

halutz, halutzim *pioneer; early Zionist immigrants, particularly those who settled on the land*

Hashomer *"the guard"; first Jewish defense organization, founded in 1907*

Haskalah *Jewish Enlightenment; focus on cultural aspects of Judaism; instrumental in the development of secular Hebrew literature in the nineteenth century; intellectual precursor to modern Zionism*

Hassidism *pietistic movement in Jewish tradition; based on joyous intimacy with God; founded in mid-eighteenth century Poland and the Ukraine; ideological and psychological rebellion against rabbinic scholasticism*

HaTikvah *"the hope"; national anthem of Israel*

horah *Israeli folk dance, popular since early pioneering days*

kehillah *Jewish community; its values are unity, mutual responsibility, and survival of Jewish tradition as an active creative force*

kibbutz *collective settlement, primarily agricultural, in which all property is shared, and goods and services are distributed on an equal basis*

Kibbutz Galuyot *Ingathering of Exiles to Israel*

Knesset *Israeli Parliament*

Leshanah Haba'ah Bi–rushalayim *"Next Year in Jerusalem"; prayer and hope said at the conclusion of the Seder and Yom Kippur services*

leumiut *nationalism*

L'Ḥayyim *"To Life!"; a favorite Jewish expression, often invoked in a toast*

madrich *"leader," ordinarily of an Israeli youth movement*

milla *"word"*

millon *"dictionary"*

moshav *agricultural settlement; land is communally owned, crops are marketed collectively, but farming and profits are on an individual basis*

nochri *foreigner*

olim *those who ascend; Jews who immigrate to Israel*

shikun *housing project*

shliḥim *"emissaries"; those who were sent from Palestine to Diaspora communities to collect Halukah; today, Israelis sent to Diaspora communities as representatives, coordinators, and educators*

siḥah *"discussion"*

tiyul, tiyulim *hike, tour, or trip; often refers to educational trips taken by youth groups to explore Israel*

Torah *the Law; refers specifically to the Five Books of Moses*

vatikim *veterans; old-timers; often used to describe Israel's early pioneers*

Zionism *the movement of Jewish national liberation; from the word "Zion," which refers to Mount Zion in Jerusalem; has become a synonym for Jerusalem and a symbol of the land of Israel itself*

INDEX

Ackerman, Walter, 137
African nations, 218
Aleichem, Sholem, 96
Alexander II (Czar of Russia), 34, 36
Aliens, Jews as, 48–49
Aliyah Bet, purpose of, 222
Allon, Yigal, 199, 200
Aloni, Shulamit, 161
Alterman, Nathan, 123–24
American Jews: as aliens, 48–49; effects of Arab-Israeli conflict on, 31; erosion of Jewish tradition among, 43; Jewish identity of, 137; strength of, 37
Amin, General Idi, 231
Amsalag, Chaim, 61
Angoff, Charles, 43
Anilevicz, Mordechai, 111, 113, 120
Anti-Semitism: in Czarist Russia, 35, 36 (*see also* Pogroms); epidemic nature of, 129–30; as illogical, 22–23; Jewish identity and, 8, 66–67; as law of nature, 61; normalization of Jews to combat, 20, 220; *Sabras* and, 164 (*see also: Sabras*); strength of, 19; in U.S., 49; *See also specific manifestations of anti-Semitism; for example:* Dreyfus Affair; Holocaust; Pogroms
Apartment living in Israel, 151–52
Arab-Israeli conflict, 131–32; basic tenets of, 20–21; effects of, on American Jews, 31; effects of, on Israeli character, 214–15; mistrust at core of, 121; as viewed by *Sabras*, 161–63; *see also* War *and specific wars*
Arab League, 22
Arab Legion, 114
Arab nationalism, 21, 135–36
Arab refugees, 7, 20–27, 29–31, 117–18, 166–72
Arab terrorism, 100, 119, 131–34, 149
Arafat, Yasir, 218
Archaeology, 179–85
Arif, Abdul Rahman, 136
Army, the: age of commanders, 199–200; army life, 156–57; guarding against dangers of militarism, 190–91; Hagannah,

(*Army, continued*)
101, 126, 197; Israelis as soldier citizens, 132–34, 163; *see also* War *and specific wars*
Assimilation: in Czarist Russia, as impossible, 61; first pioneers on verge of, 66–67; of Herzl, 70; to U.S. society, 43
Auschwitz, 35, 129
Authority, 94; distrust of, 191
Azam Pasha, Abdurrahman, 21–22

Balfour, Arthur, 88–89
Balfour Declaration (1917), 3, 89–91, 94–96
Bar-Lev, Chaim, 200
Ben-Gurion, David (David Grien), 17, 25, 76, 80, 195, 204; biographical notes and characteristics, 17–18; as charismatic leader, 190; as elderly leader, 200; feud between Eshkol and, 13, 17; finance minister under, 15; in founding of *Hashomer*, 100; joke on, 188; on peace, 216; as second *Aliyah* pioneer, 51, 71–72, 77, 82, 84; successor to, 14; total commitment of, 93
Ben-Gurion, Geula, 94
Ben-Gurion, Paula, 93–94
Ben Yehudah, Eliezer (Eliezer Perlman), 56, 62–63, 65, 77
Ben-Zvi, Rachel Yanait, 16, 80, 84, 85, 93
Ben-Zvi, Yitzhak, 16, 41, 72, 84, 85; archaeology and, 181; in founding of *Hashomer*, 100; marriage of, 93
Bergen-Belsen, 116
Bet Alpha (kibbutz), 181
Berlin, Isaiah, 35
Bettelheim, Bruno, 145
Bevin, Ernest, 126
Bialik, Chaim Nachman, 44, 46–49, 54, 77
Bible, the, 184; *see also* Torah
Bilu Manifesto, 54
Binationalism, 30, 119
Bittania (kibbutz), 103–8
Bloch, Dora, 236
Brenner, Joseph Chaim, 77
Buber, Martin, 23

241

242

244